PRAYERS

ADAPTED TO

Various Occasions of Social Worship,

FOR WHICH PROVISION IS NOT MADE IN

THE BOOK OF COMMON PRAYER.

BY

ALEXANDER V GRISWOLD, D. D.,
BISHOP OF THE EASTERN DIOCESE.

BOSTON:
E. P. DUTTON AND COMPANY,
106 WASHINGTON STREET.
1860.

RIVERSIDE, CAMBRIDGE:
PRINTED BY H. O. HOUGHTON AND COMPANY.

PREFACE.

Forasmuch as many have taken in hand to set forth forms of prayer to be used on various occasions, it will not, it is hoped, be thought improper, that the author of this little book should offer it to the public. Should it be thought that what renders this attempt warrantable makes it unnecessary, it should be considered, that the Prayers which have been published, though numerous, and many of them excellent, are so limited in regard to the occasions for which they are intended, that none of them with which I am acquainted are adapted to all the purposes for which these are designed. Many of our people, of our clergy especially, have long felt the want of a manual containing prayers suitable for all the occasions on which they are needed, and for which our church has not made particular and full provision. We have in print many excellent forms of prayer for visiting the sick, and for family worship—for the latter especially; and on this subject we have no want of more. But on other important occasions of frequent occurrence we have few; and on some, for which provision is attempted in this publication, we have none. It is from a sense of this need, and of my duty as bishop of this diocese, and from the often repeated request of several of my brethren, and not from a confidence in my ability, that I have thus attempted what I view as a difficult and important work. Should it please God, in his merciful goodness, to make it instrumental of some good, or of inducing some person of more piety and wisdom to give us something better on a like plan, I shall have cause of thankfulness.

To avoid interference with the labors of others, and all unnecessary addition to the price of this manual, the offices of the church are not inserted in it. The Book of Common Prayer is in the hands of the most or all of those who will use this: the price of that is now very low; and can be obtained of any size or convenient form. This is not intended as a substitute for the Prayer Book, nor considered as worthy to be bound in the same volume with any parts of it; but is, at the discretion of our people, permitted to be used when the prayers it contains are judged to be appropriate and fitting. My object being not to *make a book*, but to supply certain prayers that are truly needed, I have been careful not to enlarge the work nor increase its price by the addition of any extraneous matter.

I have endeavored to set forth such as, in my judgment, are most needed for use and edification. That better may be prepared I have no doubt: till such appear these may be used. They are all designed for occasions of social worship. In private devotions forms are less needed; and many of these may be used by one person in his closet, changing the plural of the pronoun into the singular number.

Though we have, in the Prayer Book, an office for visiting the sick, it is generally allowed that something more is wanted in the performance of that important duty; and many prayers for this purpose have been published and used: and it is hoped that what are here published, with some additions for other occasions, will meet with the like indulgence. It will be seen that permission is given to use these forms; but no one is laid under any obligation to do it, who thinks that others are better and more appropriate.

To seek honor for ourselves in praying, or in compiling prayers, would be highly improper and indeed sinful. In preparing these, I seek not the praise of originality; but gladly avail myself of the labors of others. Next after the Holy Scriptures, I have preferred the language of the Book of Common Prayer, and in many instances I have adopted the expressions of other writers. If we have forms of sound words, suitable for those who would unite in God's holy worship, by whom the words were first used is of very little importance, the inspired writings excepted.

With the following prayers, it is understood that the Lord's Prayer, and any others contained in the Prayer Book, may be used, at the discretion of the person who conducts the worship. They are offered to the public as helps to devotion; and any use of all, or a part or parts of them, which will have that effect, will be agreeable to what the author desires.

PREFACE TO THE SECOND EDITION.

WITH diffidence and after long delay, was published a manual of prayers adapted to occasions of social worship, for which provision is not particularly and fully made in the Book of Common Prayer. That such a work was needed appears in the call for another edition; and, as it is not known that any other work on a like plan will be given to the public, the author has endeavored, by corrections throughout, and very considerable additions, to render this more suitable for the purpose intended. It was, and still is his humble hope, that such a publication may, through God's blessing, be instrumental in causing prayer to be offered, at times, and on some occasions, when, without suitable forms prepared, it would be neglected; and also in obviating the necessity of extemporary praying, which, in his opinion, is less suitable for social worship.

The church has set forth forms for some occasions of frequent occurrence and general need; but some even of those contained in the Prayer Book are, as almost all allow, defective. Such are those for families, for the sick, and for funerals. In the service for funerals, we have no prayer appointed to be used at the house of mourning, or in the church. And surely on no occasions do we more sensibly feel the need, and fitness, and comfort of uniting in earnest, appropriate prayer.

The author is aware, that in the opinion of some few of our people, no other forms than those contained in the Book of Common Prayer are, for any occasions, needed. But very many are fully convinced that we should dwell with much earnestness in united prayer for things and on subjects which are but very briefly, if at all, noticed in our Liturgy. That such is the view and intention of our church is evident from her having provided forms for some particular occasions, and given directions for providing others, according as they are needed. The two extremes of wholly rejecting prescript forms, and the using of none but those which the church has already set forth, are departures from that middle course, by which, in this, as in other things, her wisdom is evinced. In the author's belief no one thing has tended more to increase the prejudice against our Liturgy, than the using of it on occasions to which it is not adapted, and for which it was not designed.

It is with the earnest desire that family devotion may be more generally practised by our people, that so great a number of forms for family prayer is added in this edition.

For the accommodation of those who prefer the Collects of the Prayer Book, a few of them are inserted for the use of Sunday schools.

Many of the prayers contained in this book may be with fitness used by individuals, in their private devotion, by changing the first person of the pronoun and the verb from the plural to the singular number. That the Lord will bless this humble effort to the promotion of his honor and worship, and to the salvation of mankind, is the prayer of

THE AUTHOR.

CONTENTS.

PART FIRST.

PRAYERS FOR SUNDAY AND OTHER SCHOOLS.

PART SECOND.

PRAYERS FOR THE USE OF FAMILIES AND FOR OTHER OCCASIONS.

PART THIRD.

PRAYERS WHICH MAY BE USED IN MISSIONARY MEETINGS, AND ON OTHER OCCASIONS.

PART FOURTH.

OFFICES AND PRAYERS THAT MAY BE USED IN CHURCHES, OR IN PUBLIC WORSHIP.

* See last page of Contents.

PART FIRST.

PRAYERS FOR SUNDAY AND OTHER SCHOOLS.

THE prayers used in Sunday schools should be short, not only to give sufficient time for the other exercises, and because such are best adapted to the state and capacities of children and young people; but, chiefly, because the teachers and pupils attend the long services of the church, morning and afternoon, and unite in a great variety of prayers and thanksgivings.

And for this last reason, it seems inexpedient to take them from the Prayer Book: it is supposed that the school have just united, or are about to unite, with the whole congregation in the prayers contained in that book; and to repeat them is less suitable than to have some short forms appropriate to the occasion.

The prayers should also, in my judgment, be designed for all the school—teachers and scholars—to unite in. The minister or superintendent can pray *for the scholars* in his closet. If he does it in the school, it is his prayer rather than theirs: and though *hearing prayer* is no doubt profitable, it is more agreeable to the views of Episcopalians that the prayers should be social; that all present should unite in praying. Yet some of the prayers which follow are accommodated to the views of those who may think differently.

In some of the forms of prayer published for the use of Sunday schools, it would seem, from the directions given, that the *minister* and the *children* are to perform the whole; but surely the *teachers* should always be supposed to bear a part, if not the principal part in the worship. They generally feel most interested; they can pray more understandingly than the children; and none can, more than they, need the grace of God, and the wisdom which is from above, to direct and sustain them in the very important labor of love in which they are charitably engaged. Among the prayers following are some suitable for the teachers, when they desire to unite in praying for those under their care.

When a clergyman visits and prays in a common school, it is not generally expected that the scholars will take a part in the worship; it is his prayer for the school.

Our Father, who art in heaven, hallowed be thy name. Thy kingdom come; thy will be done on earth, as it is in heaven. Give us this day our daily bread. And forgive us our trespasses, as we forgive those who trespass against us. And lead us not into temptation; but deliver us from evil. For thine is the kingdom, and the power, and the glory, for ever and ever. *Amen.*

The grace of our Lord Jesus Christ, and the love of God, and the fellowship of the Holy Ghost be with us all evermore. *Amen.*

A Prayer that we may be thankful for God's blessings, and have grace rightly to use them.

ALMIGHTY and immortal God, the aid of all who need, the Giver of all spiritual grace, and the Author of everlasting life, with humble hearts and sincere devotion, we implore thy favor and blessing upon us, thy sinful creatures. Unable of ourselves to help ourselves, unworthy to appear before thee, and trusting not in our own righteousness, but in thy mercy through Jesus Christ, we beseech thee, for his sake, to pardon our sins, to sanctify our hearts, and to hear our prayers. To thee alone belong mercy and forgiveness; to thee alone it appertains to forgive sins. Blot out, we beseech thee, our manifold transgressions, and renew a right spirit within us.

Great, O Lord, is thy goodness; unnumbered are the benefits which thou art daily bestowing on mankind. We adore thee for thine infinite perfections; we bless thy holy name, for thy unspeakable goodness vouchsafed to our sinful race, and especially for the religious privileges which we enjoy. We give thee thanks for the weekly return of thy holy day, for all the means of grace, and for the hope of life immortal. We desire, O God, with thankful hearts, to acknowledge thy goodness, in causing the Holy Scriptures to be written for our learning, and for giving us various means of knowledge and helps to religious improvement; for the establishment and increase of schools and seminaries of learning throughout our country; and especially of those schools and associations, which have for their object the instruction of children and of others, in the knowledge of thy word, in the doctrines of Christ, and the duties of religion. We bless thee, O God, that many are willing, with patient diligence and pious zeal, to devote a part of the Lord's day to the instructing of the rising generation in the rudiments of gospel truth; beseeching thee, O God, to increase their numbers, to enlarge their hearts, to strengthen their hands, and reward their labor of love. Give us hearts, O Lord, we humbly beseech thee, to be duly thankful for these thy mercies, and give us grace to use them to thy glory, and to the promotion of our own and others' salvation. May we remember the Lord's day, to keep it holy; may it, by all thy people, be religiously devoted to thy holy worship, and to teaching, and learning, and practising the truth and precepts of the blessed gospel. And may thy truth be so grafted inwardly in our hearts, as to establish us in a right faith, and bring forth in us the fruit of good living, to the honor and praise of thy holy name, through Jesus Christ our Lord. *Amen.*

Another, for the use of a Sunday School.

O Lord, our heavenly Father, almighty and everlasting God, who hearest the prayers of those who believe and trust in thee, look down, we beseech thee, with thy favor and blessing, upon us thy servants, here assembled to teach thy truth and to learn thy will. Give us grace to love thy law, and thankfully, and with faithful diligence, to apply our hearts to the teaching, and to the attainment of whatever is most profitable for doctrine, for reproof, for correction, and for instruction in righteousness. Open our understandings, that we may understand the Scriptures; and give us grace, in an honest and good heart, to receive that instruction which will make us wise unto salvation. Preserve us, O merciful Lord, from all sinful vanities! may we love the things which thou commandest, and desire, above all other things, them which thou hast promised to those who love and fear thee. Do thou, who alone canst rule the hearts of sinful men, graft in ours such love of thy truth, that what is our duty may be our chief delight. O, may those of us present who are still in childhood or youth, remember our Creator, and gladly devote our hearts and lives to God who made us, and to him who has redeemed us with his blood: and may we all so number our days, and so truly consider the shortness and the uncertain continuance of this present life, that we may gladly apply our hearts to thy holy, heavenly wisdom: as we advance in age, may we grow in grace, and in the knowledge of Him, who is the way, and the truth, and the life. Give thy blessing, we beseech thee, to this school, and to all and each of us who are present, whose hearts and whose wants thou knowest. O give us thy blessing, according as we need. Preserve us from sin, awaken us to righteousness, and help us daily to proceed in all virtue and godliness of living; so that we may serve thee faithfully in this world, and finally attain to everlasting life: which we ask and hope, only through the merits of our Lord and Savior Jesus Christ. *Amen.*

A Prayer to be used by a Minister, or other suitable person, for a Sunday School.

Almighty and everlasting God, the Father of our spirits, and the Giver of every good thing, mercifully behold and bless this school, here assembled in thy presence to teach and to learn the precepts and truths of thy holy word, and the principles of the doctrine of Christ. Without thee nothing is holy, nothing is good: except the Lord build the house, they labor in vain who build it. May thy blessed Spirit direct and aid them in their humble efforts to know and do thy will: may they receive with meekness the ingrafted word which is able to save their souls. Give thy heavenly benediction to the teachers of this school, who make a free will offering of their labor and care in this pious work. Remember them, O Lord, for good. Give them wisdom and patience and grace to persevere; that they may not be weary in well doing; and may be assured that in due time they shall reap if they faint not. May these hours charitably devoted to the benefit of others, be sanctified to their own temporal good and eternal gain.

And wilt thou, O gracious God, open the tender minds of these children and youth, that they may understand thy word, and love thy law, and delight to do thy will. Preserve them from the sinful vanities which easily beset the youthful mind. Graft in their hearts the love of righteousness and truth: increase in their minds all holy affections, and nourish their souls with the bread of eternal life: and of thy great mercy keep them steadfast in the ways of thy laws and in the works of thy commandments. May they be trained up in the way that they should go, and never depart from it: may they be so sanctified and renewed, that they may be truly members of Christ, children of God, and heirs of his heavenly kingdom.

Direct, O Lord, with thy heavenly wisdom, and bless the care and watchful oversight of all parents, masters, and guardians, in their endeavors to bring up children in the nurture and admonition of the Lord. Grant, if it be consistent with thy unerring wisdom, that the lives of these children and youth may be prolonged upon the earth; that they may fill and discharge, with honor to themselves and usefulness to society, the several stations and duties of life to which thou shalt call them. And when they shall have served thee in their generation, may they be received into heavenly habitations, and enjoy an endless Sabbath of happiness and rest from sorrow, labor, and care. Hear us, O thou God of mercy, hear and bless us all, for the sake of thy Son, our Savior, Jesus Christ. *Amen.*

A Prayer suitable to be used by Sunday School Teachers in the School or in their other Meetings.

ALMIGHTY and everlasting God, unto whom all hearts are open, all desires known, and from whom no secrets are hid, cleanse the thoughts of our hearts, by the inspiration of thy Holy Spirit, and accept our humble supplications and prayers. Trusting in the word and in the merits of our blessed Savior, who has taught us to ask in his name that we may receive; to seek of thee our heavenly Father for wisdom and grace, that we may know and do thy will, we beseech thee to behold, with thy favor and blessing, thy dependent, unworthy creatures, who humbly desire, with penitence and prayer, to bow before thee. Help us to know and to do thy will: direct us in all our doings with thy most gracious favor, and further us with thy continual help, that all our works and all our desires may be to thy glory, and to the good of our fellow-men. Help us especially to be useful in our generation, by imparting to children and youth the knowledge of thy word and will, and directing them in the way in which they should go. If such, O Lord, be thy gracious will, make us instruments of nourishing the tender mind with heavenly wisdom; of instructing the rising generation in the paths of righteousness and truth; of implanting in the minds of those who are or shall be intrusted to our guidance and care, the principles of the doctrine of Christ, and the duties of moral and religious life. Do thou, O God, who alone art sufficient for these things, and whose strength is made perfect in the weakness of thy servants, behold us with compassion, forgive our sins, and uphold us with thy free spirit. Preserve us from every motive and desire which is not according to thy holy will. Defend us from all error; and help us rightly and truly to understand the language of thy word, the doctrines of Christ, and the duties of life. Inspire our hearts with Christian love, and with a holy desire to promote thy glory, and the salvation of ourselves and others. Make us apt to teach. May we not be weary in well doing; but follow the example of him, our blessed Lord, who expressed his love for children, and spent his life in doing good.

And behold, O God, we beseech thee, with thy favor and blessing, the children and youth of our Sunday schools. Open their understandings and dispose their minds to receive instruction, to delight in the paths of wisdom, to love the things which thou commandest, and desire those which thou dost promise. Sanctify to them the instructions of their teachers, and all our humble efforts to enlighten their minds with true wisdom: incline their hearts to virtue and godliness, and raise their affections from the world to thee. Awaken in their minds, we beseech thee, a just and lively sense of the vast importance of early piety and religious knowledge. Give them ears to hear, and hearts to understand, and wills to obey the things of thy law; desiring the sincere milk of thy word, that they may live and grow thereby. Grant that they fall into no sin, neither run into any danger of soul or body; but that all their doings, being ordered by thy governance, may be righteous in thy sight. Grant that they may be useful in their generation, a comfort to their friends, a blessing to their country; and finally, that they may be inheritors of thy everlasting kingdom. These things, and whatever else thou shalt see fitting for us and for all men, we humbly ask, through Jesus Christ. *Amen.*

Another Prayer for the use of a Sunday School.

O God, who art the strength of all who put their trust in thee, and the helper of all who flee to thee for succor, mercifully accept our prayers; and because, through the weakness of our mortal nature, we can do no good thing without thee, grant us the help of thy grace, that in keeping thy commandments we may please thee, both in will and deed. Keep us under the protection of thy good providence, and make us to have a perpetual fear and love of thy name. Increase and multiply upon us thy mercy. Direct us in what we do by the sure guidance of thy Holy Spirit: may all things in this school be done decently, in order, and to edifying. Grant to us, O Lord, the spirit to think and to do always such things as are right; to love the ways of thy laws, and the works of thy commandments, and to be ready to every good work. Grant unto us such a measure of thy grace, that we, running the way of thy commandments, may obtain thy gracious promises, and be made partakers of thy heavenly treasure. Pour down upon us the abundance of thy mercy; forgiving us those things wherein we have displeased thee, and giving us those good things, which we are not worthy to ask, but through the merits and mediation of Jesus Christ, thy Son our Lord.

Thou hast taught us, O heavenly Father, by thy holy apostle, that all our teaching, all our faith, and all our doings, without charity are nothing worth: give us, we beseech thee, that spirit which was in our Savior Christ, that we may follow after that charity which is the bond of peace, and love one another, as thou hast given us commandment. May we love others as we love ourselves, and do unto all men as we would have them do unto us. And wilt thou hear our intercessions, O God, for the whole family of mankind? Let the light of thy gospel shine upon all the nations of the earth, and grant that they who have received it may live as becomes it. Keep thy church and household in thy true religion. Grant that all Christians may be so joined together, in unity of spirit, and in the bond of peace, that they may be a holy temple acceptable unto thee. And especially, O Lord, to the congregation of thy people, with whom we are accustomed to assemble, give the abundance of thy grace; that with one heart they may desire the prosperity of thy holy apostolic church, and with one mouth may profess the faith once delivered to the saints. Give grace, O heavenly Father, to all the ministers of thy gospel, of every grade, that they may, both by their life and doctrine, set forth thy true and lively word, and rightly and duly administer the holy ordinances of Christ's religion.

And to thee, the Father of mercies, we would add our humble and hearty thanks for thy unnumbered mercies bestowed upon thy sinful creatures, who are unworthy of the least of thy favors. Chiefly we adore thy goodness in the gift of thy Son to be our Savior, and that thou hast called us to a knowledge of thy grace and faith in him. We bless thee for all the means and opportunities of religious improvement which we enjoy. Though we are unworthy, through our manifold sins, to offer thee any sacrifice of praise or prayer; trusting in thy promise to give to those who ask in the name of Jesus Christ, we beseech thee to accept our adorations and praise. Behold with thy favor and blessing the occasion of our present meeting before thee. Guide and prosper our feeble efforts to teach and to learn the ways of righteousness and truth. To those who teach, give wisdom and patience and the spirit of love. Open the minds of those who are taught, that they may receive instruction, and know to refuse the evil and choose the good, and, like the child Jesus, grow in wisdom, as they increase in years, and in favor with God and man. Give thy blessing to all those who have the care of educating youth: may they so train them up in the way that they should go, that afterward they may not depart from it. Direct us, O Lord, in all we do, with thy most gracious favor, and prosper us with thy continued help. Dispose our ways towards the attainment of everlasting salvation, that among all the changes and perils of this mortal life, we may ever be defended by thy most gracious and ready help, through Jesus Christ, our blessed Lord and Savior. *Amen.*

Collects suitable for opening a Sunday School.

Almighty and everliving God, who hatest nothing that thou hast made, and dost forgive the sins of all those who are penitent, create and make in us new and contrite hearts, that we, truly lamenting our sins and acknowledging our unworthiness, may obtain of thee, the God of all mercy, perfect remission and forgiveness, through Jesus Christ our Lord. *Amen.*

O almighty God, who alone canst order the unruly wills and affections of men, grant unto us and to all thy people, that we may love the things which thou commandest, and desire that which thou dost promise, that so, among the sundry and manifold changes of the world, our hearts may surely there be fixed, where true joys are to be found, through Jesus Christ our Lord. *Amen.*

Direct us, O Lord, in all we do, with thy most gracious favor, and further us with thy continual help, that in all our works, begun, continued, and ended in thee, we may glorify thy holy name, and finally, by thy mercy, obtain everlasting life, through Jesus Christ our Lord, in whose name and words we humbly pray:—

Our Father, who art, &c.

For closing the School.

Blessed Lord, who hast caused all holy Scriptures to be written for our learning, grant that we may in such wise hear them, and read, mark, learn, and inwardly digest them, that by patience and comfort of thy holy word, we may embrace and ever hold fast the blessed hopes of everlasting life, which thou hast given us in our Lord and Savior, Jesus Christ. *Amen.*

Grant, we beseech thee, almighty God, that what has now been read, and heard, and taught from thy holy word, and according to thy will, may, through thy grace, be so grafted inwardly in our hearts, that it may bring forth in us the fruit of good living, to the honor and praise of thy name, through Christ, our blessed Redeemer. *Amen.*

The grace of our Lord Jesus Christ, and the love of God, and the fellowship of the Holy Ghost, be with us all evermore. *Amen.*

A Prayer that may be used at the Closing of a Sunday School.

ADORABLE and everliving God, through whose merciful goodness we are again permitted to enjoy the comforts and the privileges of thy holy day of rest, give us hearts to be thankful for these and for all thy favors. Grant that the truths of thy holy word may be grafted inwardly in our hearts, and bring forth in us the fruit of pure and undefiled religion. Accept the prayers which have been offered before these, and pardon us wherein they have been defective. May thy blessing be upon all the members of this school, and upon all its exercises. May the doctrines of the gospel be deeply impressed upon our minds, and be made the rule of our conduct. Work in us that repentance for our sins past which is not to be repented of, and that faith in the Lord Jesus Christ which renews the heart, worketh by love, and overcometh the world. Help us to love thee with all our heart, and with all our soul, and with all our mind, and to love our neighbor as we love ourselves. Grant that what is taught us on the Lord's day may be so blessed to the improvement of our hearts, as to influence our life and practice through the week and while we live. Strengthen us by thy Spirit, and guide us in all things by thy heavenly wisdom, that we may do our duty in the state of life to which it shall please thee to call us. Denying ungodliness and worldly lusts, may we live soberly, righteously, and godly in this present world; and when we shall have served thee in our generation, may we be admitted into those mansions of peace and rest which thou hast prepared for those who love the Lord Jesus Christ; in whose name we offer up these our imperfect prayers. And to the King eternal, immortal, invisible, the only wise God, be honor and glory forever and ever. *Amen.*

Directions for a Larger Form of Sunday School Devotions.

The person who conducts the worship may first address the school in the following, or other words suitable to call their attention to the subject of their dependence upon God, and the importance of asking in prayer for his aid and benediction.

Beloved brethren and youthful friends, through the Lord's merciful goodness we are here assembled, on his holy day, and in his presence, to give and to receive instruction and knowledge, especially instruction in God's word, and the knowledge of our salvation in Jesus Christ. But we are not able to know the Holy Scriptures, except God shall open our hearts that we may truly understand them; nor can we keep his commandments, nor do any good thing, without his grace assisting. We ought, therefore, daily and at all times, to ask in prayer for the direction and aid of his Holy Spirit, and humbly and earnestly to call upon him for what we need. Let us now, with humble minds and sincere devotion, unite in beseeching him to behold us with favor on the present occasion, to bestow his blessing upon this school, and that he will direct and aid us in all our endeavors to teach and know and do his will.

A Prayer that may be used in and for any School.

Then may be used any of the preceding Prayers, or a Selection of Collects from the Prayer Book. Afterwards a suitable Psalm, or portion of the Psalter, may be named and used; he who conducts the service reading one verse, and the rest who are present reading alternately; and after the Psalm, the Christian Doxology. The service may end here; or there may be read for a lesson the portion of the Scriptures at that time to be explained: and after the lesson, what follows:—

Blessed Lord, who hast caused all Holy Scriptures to be written for our learning, grant that we may in such wise hear them; read, mark, learn, and inwardly digest them; that, by patience and comfort of thy holy word, we may embrace and ever hold fast the blessed hope of everlasting life, which thou hast given us in our Lord and Savior, Jesus Christ. *Amen.*

Then may be named and sung a Hymn or Psalm in metre; and then:

The grace of our Lord Jesus Christ, and the love of God, and the fellowship of the Holy Ghost, be with us all, evermore. *Amen.*

A Prayer that may be used in and for any School.

ALMIGHTY and everlasting God, unto whom all hearts are open, all desires known, and from whom no secrets are hid, we beseech thee to pardon our sins, to sanctify our hearts, and mercifully to assist us in these our supplications and prayers. We adore thee as a holy and merciful God, whose righteous providence orders all things in heaven and on earth; and from whom all holy desires, all good counsels, and all just works do proceed. Without thee nothing is strong, nothing is holy, nothing good. Except the Lord build the house, they labor in vain who build it; except the Lord keep the city, the watchman waketh in vain. We beseech thee to direct and bless us in what we do. Give us wisdom to choose, and grace to perform, whatever is according to thy holy will. Preserve us from every sin, protect us in every danger, and grant that all our doings, being ordered by thy governance, may be righteous in thy sight. Dispose all our ways towards the attainment of immortal life; that, amidst the manifold perils of our earthly pilgrimage, our conversation may be in heaven. Make us sensible, O blessed Lord, of thy great goodness, and thankful for all thy mercies. We render thee humble and hearty thanks for blessings daily bestowed upon us, and upon all men, temporal and spiritual. We bless thee especially for the means of knowledge and mutual improvement so bountifully bestowed on this our favored country. And we humbly ask for thy blessing upon all our schools and seminaries of learning. Give wisdom and patience to those who teach, and a meek and teachable disposition to all who learn. Defend them from pride and a vain confidence in themselves, and incline their hearts to such things as are truly profitable. May we never forget that the fear of the Lord is the beginning of wisdom, and that the most important knowledge is, to know thee the only true God, and ourselves as unworthy sinners, and Jesus Christ as the only Savior. Give thy blessing, O Lord, to this school and to all who are engaged in its instruction and concerned in its support. May the children and youth who are here present be partakers of thy heavenly benediction; may they be members of Christ and heirs through hope of thy everlasting kingdom. Do thou, their Father who art in heaven, take them under thy holy care and keeping. Incline their hearts and open their minds to the light of truth and the attainment of useful science. Imprint upon their hearts an early and thankful sense of thy goodness in giving them abundant means of intellectual improvement. Preserve them from the snares of sin and all the perils of youth, and conduct them safely through the journey of life. Help them continually to mortify their evil and corrupt affections, and daily to proceed in all virtue and godliness of living. Make them happy and useful as members of society, and an honor and comfort to their relatives and friends, and prepare them for thy heavenly kingdom. Guide and bless the care and patient labor of those who instruct them in what is good and useful; remember them for good, and reward their labor of love. To all who are engaged in the important business of instructing youth, give wisdom and grace, both by precept and example, to teach such things as will best promote the good of their pupils in this world, and in the world to come. Help them to rear the tender thought to ripened wisdom, and to conduct the youthful mind, in all its growth, to manly virtue. To all who are present, give thy heavenly grace; that, denying ungodliness and worldly lusts, we may live soberly, righteously, and godly in this present life; and finally be prepared to dwell with thee in thine everlasting kingdom. For thine is the kingdom and the power, and thine be the glory forever and ever. These things we ask, O heavenly Father, through Jesus Christ, our blessed Lord and Savior. *Amen.*

A Prayer that may be used at the Opening of any School.

Adorable and everliving God, the Author of our being, and the Giver of all good, we beseech thee in mercy to pardon our sins, to hear our prayers, and to give us thy blessing. Without thee nothing is strong, nothing is holy, nothing good. Except the Lord build the house they labor in vain who build. We humbly ask for thy guidance and protection, beseeching thee to direct us in all we design or do with thy most gracious favor, and to prosper us with thy continual help. Look down with thy favor and blessing upon this school now present before thee, and upon all who convene in this place for the acquirement of knowledge. Preserve them from evil and error, and from all things which would be hurtful to them, in body or mind. Incline their hearts to truth and righteousness, and help them, we beseech thee, to receive such instruction as shall fit them to be useful members of society in this world and heirs of thy heavenly kingdom. Inspire them with that fear of the Lord, which is the beginning of true knowledge. May they be duly respectful to their parents, teachers, and others in authority over them, inclining their ears to wisdom, and applying their hearts to understanding. Wisdom is the principal thing; help us, O Lord, to get wisdom, and to walk in thy commandments. We are blind, and weak, and sinful, and need, O heavenly Father, thy mercy and thy care. By thy Spirit and thy providence, be thou, we beseech thee, our Teacher and Guide. May we strive for knowledge, and lift up our voice for understanding. Give thy blessing to parents and masters, and to all who have the care and the tuition of the rising generation. Endue them with wisdom and patience, with kindness and love. May the children under their care be so trained up in the way that they should go, that when they are old they will not depart from it. Behold with thy blessing and favor all our schools and seminaries of learning. May they be instrumental in promoting righteousness and truth; and may knowledge and happiness, and pure and undefiled religion, be spread and increased throughout our land. These things, and whatever else thou shalt see to be good for us, for this school, and for all mankind, we humbly ask in the name of Jesus Christ, our Lord and Savior. *Amen.*

And may the grace of our Lord Jesus Christ be with us now and evermore. *Amen.*

For the Closing of any School.

O LORD, our heavenly Father, in whom we live and move and have our being, we humbly desire to render thee our thanks and praise for all thy daily mercies; and especially for the favors and blessings which have been vouchsafed to us this present day. We thank thee, O God, for the means and opportunities of acquiring useful knowledge, which are bountifully bestowed upon us, and upon the people of this our country, beseeching thee to give us grace rightly to use them, to the promotion of thy honor, and of our own best good. Grant us a right judgment in all things, and guide our steps in the paths of heavenly wisdom. May we love the things which thou commandest, and desire those which thou dost promise to them who love and serve thee. Take us, we beseech thee, and all that appertains to us, under thy holy care and keeping. Preserve us from sin and wickedness, and from every danger of soul and body. Help us in the performance of every duty, and every work which our hand findeth to do. Give us grace to be humble and meek; to be respectful to all to whom respect is due, and just and charitable to all our fellow-men. May we be kindly affectioned one to another with brotherly love; in honor preferring one another; and as much as lieth in us, may we live peaceably with all men. In all the business of our several occupations, direct us, O Lord, and give us thy blessing. Preserve us from an evil heart of unbelief, in departing from thee, the living God. May we set the Lord always before us; be thou on our right hand, that we may not be moved from our steadfastness, nor neglect any duty which we owe to ourselves, to our neighbors, or to thee. Vouchsafe, O Lord, we beseech thee, to sanctify and govern both our hearts and bodies, in the ways of thy laws, and in the works of thy commandments, that through thy most mighty protection, both here and ever, we may be preserved, in body and soul, through our Lord and Savior, Jesus Christ, in whose name and words we offer and conclude our humble supplications:—

Our Father, who art in heaven, hallowed be thy name. Thy kingdom come: thy will be done on earth, as it is in heaven. Give us this day our daily bread; and forgive us our trespasses, as we forgive those who trespass against us. And lead us not into temptation; but deliver us from evil. For thine is the kingdom, and the power, and the glory, forever and ever. *Amen.*

The two following may be used on any occasions of Catechising Children, or in Sunday Schools.

Almighty God, the fountain of all wisdom, the author of all good and the giver of all grace, without whose blessing and aid our designs and labors are fruitless and vain, look down, we beseech thee, with thy favor and heavenly benediction, upon these children and youth who are here before thee, desirous to learn the rudiments of religion—the first principles of the doctrine of Christ. We beseech thee, O God, in thy merciful goodness, to open their tender minds, that they may know thy truth, and understand and receive the doctrines of eternal life in Jesus Christ. Help them to receive with meekness the ingrafted word, which is able to save their souls; and to become in heart and life members of Christ, children of God, and inheritors of the kingdom of heaven. Grant them repentance, whereby they may forsake sin; and faith, whereby they may steadfastly believe the promises of God, made to those who are baptized into Jesus Christ. Direct, sanctify, and govern their hearts and their lives in the ways of thy laws, and in the works of thy commandments; that, through thy most mighty protection, they may ever be preserved from all danger, and that they may live and grow in the nurture and admonition of the Lord. Direct and bless the care and the instruction of their parents, teachers, and others who have, and may have, the oversight of their morals and their education, to their temporal and eternal good. May they all be under thy holy care and keeping; may they live to thy glory here on the earth, and finally, by thy mercy, obtain everlasting life, through the merits of our Lord and Savior, Jesus Christ. *Amen.*

Almighty and immortal God, the aid of all who need, the helper of all who flee to thee for succor, the life of those who believe, and the resurrection of the dead, we humbly call upon thee in behalf of these children and youth now present before thee. Behold them with thy favor and blessing. Open their understandings, that they may receive the instructions of thy word, and be established in the first principles of thy true religion, and that, like young Timothy, they may from childhood know the Holy Scriptures, which are able to make them wise unto salvation, through the faith which is in Christ Jesus. Graft in their hearts the love of thy name; implant in their minds true religion; nourish them with the bread of life; help them to renounce all sinful vanities and all the lusts and pride of life, to believe all the articles of the Christian faith, to keep thy holy will and commandments, and to walk in the ways of thy truth all the days of their life. Help them to love thee, their heavenly Parent, with all their heart and soul and mind, and to do unto all men as they would that others should do unto them; to submit themselves to every ordinance of man for the Lord's sake, and to live soberly, righteously, and godly in this present world. Receive, O Lord, and bless them as thy children; as thou hast promised by our Savior Christ, give now unto us who ask; let us who seek, find; open unto us who knock, that these children may enjoy the benediction of thy heavenly grace. Let thy Holy Spirit lead and guide them through this sinful world in holiness and righteousness all the days of their life; may they be instruments of thy glory, by serving thee in their generation; so that finally, by thy mercy, they may attain to everlasting life, through Jesus Christ, our blessed Lord and Savior. *Amen.*

In Meetings of Bible Classes may be used the following Prayer, or any other in this book that may be thought convenient.

O ETERNAL God, whose wise and unfailing providence orders all things in heaven and on earth; who hast compassion on the sinful sons of men, and hast graciously promised to hear the prayers of those who ask in the name of Jesus Christ, behold us in mercy and hear our prayers. We desire to come before thee, not in our own name nor trusting in our own righteousness, but in the name of Jesus Christ, and trusting in thy mercy through him. May thy Holy Spirit direct and aid our devotion; open thou our lips, that we may show forth thy praise, and ask for such things as shall please thee. Make us deeply sensible of our fallen, sinful state; and work in us that repentance which is not to be repented of; that broken and contrite heart which thou wilt not despise. Make us thankful for thy goodness in preserving our lives from day to day, and from week to week; and in giving us frequent opportunities of social worship, of reading and hearing thy holy word, and talking of thy mercies revealed in Jesus Christ. Thy law is undefiled, converting the soul; thy testimony giveth wisdom unto the simple. May thy righteous statutes rejoice our heart, and thy pure commandment give light unto our eyes. O teach us thy statutes, and help us to talk of thy commandments, and to walk in thy ways. We thank thee, O God, that thou hast caused all Holy Scriptures to be written for our learning: may we in such wise read and hear and understand and receive them, that we may embrace and ever hold fast the blessed hopes of immortal life. While we search those Scriptures which are the word of life, may we never forget that they testify of Christ. May we give such heed to the sure word of prophecy and its fulfilment in him, that we may say, in the fulness of our hearts, Lo! this is our God, we have waited for him, and he will save us: this is the Lord; we have waited for him; we will be glad and rejoice in his salvation. Accept, O Lord, of our humble and hearty thanks for the unspeakable gift of a divine Savior; that while we were yet sinners Christ died for us; and that he has put away sin, by the sacrifice of himself. We thank thee for all the means of grace and for the hope of glory. We bless thee for the weekly return of thy holy day of rest. We adore thy goodness in giving us frequent opportunities of communing as Christian brethren and friends, of meeting in thy presence, of uniting in prayer, of searching the Scriptures, of talking of thy goodness and declaring the wonders that thou dost for the children of men.

Thou art still calling us to the knowledge of thy grace and faith in thee. Increase this knowledge, and confirm this faith in us evermore; help us to receive with meekness the ingrafted word, which is able to save our souls, and to live in all things according to the precepts of thy holy word. Wilt thou, O Lord, reveal thyself to us as thou dost not to the world? Give us that lively faith in Jesus Christ which renews the heart and overcomes the world. May thy word be our study and our delight; and may thy Holy Spirit dwell within us, and so sanctify our thoughts and govern our wills, that we may present ourselves a living sacrifice, holy and acceptable, unto thee, which is our reasonable service. As he who hath called us is holy, so may we be holy in all manner of conversation. Give us grace, O Lord, to make a right improvement from these opportunities of meeting in love, uniting in prayer, and searching for the truths of thy holy word. Grant that what has been or shall be now read or heard, may be duly impressed upon our hearts, and fruitful in our lives. And may we show our thankfulness for these favors not only with our lips but in our lives, by giving up ourselves to thy service, and walking before thee in holiness and righteousness, to thy honor and praise, and to our comfort and salvation in Jesus Christ. And may the grace of our Lord Jesus Christ be with us evermore. *Amen.*

A Prayer that may be used in Meetings of Bible Societies, or Associations.

O HOLY, just, and merciful God, unto whom all hearts are open and all desires known, and who art always more ready to hear than we to pray, grant unto us, thy sinful creatures here before thee, pardon and peace. Forgive those things wherein we have transgressed against thee, and for the sake of thy Son, our Savior, Jesus Christ, give us those good things which we are not worthy to ask, but in his prevailing name. Sanctify our affections, and renew a right spirit within us. We bless thy holy name, that thou didst so love the world as to send thine only begotten Son, not to condemn the world, but that all who believe in him should not perish, but have everlasting life; and that thou hast made that same Jesus who was crucified both Lord and Christ. We bless thee, that after he had made perfect our redemption, by dying for our sins and rising for our justification, he gave commission to his apostles, and commanded them to preach his gospel of salvation to every creature. We bless thee that thou gavest the word, and great was the company of the preachers; and that thou art still calling many to the like ministration and labor of love. Make us duly thankful for these thy inestimable benefits, and work in us a holy and earnest desire to promote the salvation of ourselves and others. Grant that thy name may be known through the earth, thy saving health among all nations.

We humbly beseech thee, O God, to guide and to bless the humble and pious efforts of thy people to extend the knowledge of thy word and the doctrines of Christ to those who are in ignorance and error. Do thou, the giver of all grace, increase their zeal, enlarge their means and strengthen their hands. May all Bible Societies, and all who associate for the distribution of the Holy Scriptures to those who are destitute of thy written word, with all who contribute to their funds and aid this pious work, be under thy paternal care and holy keeping. O stablish thou the work of their hands upon them, and remember them for good. May thy word have free course and run swiftly, and the earth be full of the knowledge of the Lord, as the waters cover the sea. Let thy blessing and the aid of thy Spirit be with those missionaries and evangelists who labor in word and doctrine to spread thy saving truth in foreign lands. Accept, O Lord, of our intercessions for the perishing souls among whom they labor; and also for all sorts and conditions of men, that thou wouldst be pleased to make thy ways known unto them, thy saving health unto all nations. Hear our prayers, we humbly beseech thee, for thy holy church universal, that it may be so guided and governed by thy good Spirit, that all who profess and call themselves Christians may be led into the way of truth, and hold the faith in unity of Spirit, in the bond of peace, and in righteousness of life. Give grace, O heavenly Father, to all Bishops and other ministers of Christ, that they may, both by their life and doctrine, set forth thy true and lively word, and rightly and duly administer the ordinances of the gospel. Open to them an effectual door of usefulness, and bless the word spoken by their mouth, that it may be good to the use of edifying, and minister grace to the hearers. And do thou, the Lord of the harvest, send into it laborers, able ministers of thy word, whose meat and drink it shall be to do thy work. Accept, O Lord, of these our supplications and prayers, and dispose all our ways towards the attainment of everlasting salvation. May we live to thy glory in this world, and in the world to come enjoy life everlasting. These things, and whatever else thou seest to be good and fitting for us, and for any and all for whom we ought to pray, we humbly ask in the name and through the mediation of Jesus Christ, our blessed Lord and Savior. *Amen.*

A Prayer that may be used in a Singing School, or a Meeting to practise Psalmody.

ADORABLE and everliving God, we humbly and devoutly look unto thee, as the Author of our being, and the Giver of every good thing. Let thy merciful ears be open to our humble supplications; and that we may obtain our petitions, help us to ask for such things as shall please thee. Thou knowest, O Lord, our hearts and our wants, and the imperfection of our sincerest prayers. We beseech thee to have compassion upon our infirmities, and to give us those good things, which we are not worthy to ask but in the name of Jesus Christ.

Give us hearts, O Lord, to be thankful for thy manifold goodness to us, and to all mankind. Help us to come before thee with thanksgiving, to show ourselves glad in thee with psalms, and heartily to rejoice in the strength of thy salvation. While we worship and fall down and kneel before thee, may our souls magnify thee, O Lord, and our spirits rejoice in God our Savior. May we praise our God while we have our being. Direct, O Lord, and bless our humble efforts to set forth thy praise and to honor thy holy name. Help us to obtain such knowledge of psalmody and the art of sacred music, that the songs of Zion may be performed devoutly, in due order and to edifying; and that the voice of melody may be heard in thy sanctuary, and in a manner worthy of thy exalted perfections. May we, through thy grace, sing with the spirit and with the understanding; and make melody, not only with our voices, but in our hearts, to the Lord. Fill our hearts with grateful affections, and cause our souls to unite and harmonize in love. May we feel and say with the holy Psalmist, Praise the Lord, O my soul, and all that is within me, praise his holy name; bless the Lord, O my soul, and forget not all his benefits. Defend us, O Lord, from all vain thoughts and worldly affections. May we not desire to honor ourselves, nor seek the praise of men; as thine is the kingdom and the power, may thine forever be all glory and praise. Make our offerings acceptable to thyself. Let our prayer be set forth in thy sight as the incense, and the lifting up of our hands as the evening sacrifice. And give us grace to set forth thy praise, not only with our lips, but in our lives, walking according to thy word, and doing all things to thy glory. And may we at length, through thy mercy and our Savior's merits, join the holy, happy choir of saints above, who sing the song of Moses and the Lamb. Blessing and honor and glory and power be unto him that sitteth upon the throne, and unto the Lamb, forever and ever. *Amen.*

PART SECOND.

PRAYERS FOR THE USE OF FAMILIES AND FOR OTHER OCCASIONS.

INTRODUCTORY REMARKS.

THOUGH we have in print a great variety of Prayers for the use of families, and many of them excellent; that this publication may be complete for the purpose intended, a few are here offered to the public. In compiling them the author, as will be seen, has made much use of the Prayer Book, and some use of the prayers published by others, preferring those which are most common and, by our people, most approved. What is aimed at is to prepare some forms suitable for family worship. They who have better forms, or who can pray better without any, will of course find these of little or no use. If such facilities for the performance of a very essential duty shall be, through God's blessing, the means of introducing prayer into some families in which it is now neglected, we shall have much cause to rejoice and bless his holy name.

Our Father, who art in heaven, hallowed be thy name. Thy kingdom come; thy will be done on earth, as it is in heaven. Give us this day our daily bread. And forgive us our trespasses, as we forgive those who trespass against us. And lead us not into temptation; but deliver us from evil. For thine is the kingdom, and the power and the glory, forever and ever. *Amen.*

The grace of our Lord Jesus Christ, and the love of God, and the fellowship of the Holy Ghost, be with us all evermore. *Amen.*

Morning Prayer.

ALMIGHTY and everlasting God, in whom we live and move and have our being, we, thine unworthy creatures, offer thee our humble thanks and praise for thy manifold goodness to us, and to all mankind. We thank thee, O Lord, especially for the preservation of the past night. To thy watchful providence we owe it, and to thy goodness we thankfully acknowledge it, that we are brought [under circumstances of comfort and peace] to see the light of another day. Give us hearts to be duly thankful for all thy mercies, and give us grace to show forth thy praise, not only with our lips, but in our lives, by a holy and obedient walking before thee. As we advance in age, may we grow in grace, and in the knowledge of our Lord and Savior, Jesus Christ.

Do thou, O Lord, who knowest the frailty of our nature and the temptations which assail us, support us by the aid of thy Holy Spirit; sanctify our hearts, restrain us from sin, and excite us to the performance of every duty to ourselves, to our neighbor and to thee. Imprint upon our hearts such a fear of thy judgments, and such a thankful sense of thy goodness to us, that we may live soberly, righteously, and godly in this present world.

And keep in our minds a lively remembrance of that great day of the Lord, when we must render an account of our conduct in this world, and be judged according to our works.

Grant us, O Lord, we beseech thee, thy grace and protection this day, and whilst we live. Keep us temperate in all things, and diligent in our several callings. Grant us patience under any afflictions which it may seem good to thee to lay upon us, and minds always contented with our present condition, and resigned to thy holy will. Give us grace to be just and upright in all our dealings; quiet and peaceable; full of compassion, and ready to do good unto all men, according to our abilities and opportunities. Direct us in all our ways; prosper us in the lawful business of our several stations. Defend us from all dangers and adversities; and be graciously pleased to take us, our relatives and friends, and all that is near and dear to us, under thy merciful care and protection; that we may be thy people, and that thou mayest be our God.

[This is the day which the Lord hath made; may we rejoice and be glad in it. Let thy Holy Spirit go with us to the place of thy public worship; make us devout and humble, and attentive to the duties of thy sanctuary. May we worship thee, our God and Savior, in spirit and in truth, and receive with meekness the ingrafted word, which is able to save the soul.]

And do thou, O God, the fountain of all wisdom, mercy and grace, who knowest what we need before we ask, and the imperfection of our sincerest prayers, have compassion upon our infirmities; and whatever good things thou shalt see to be fitting for us and for thy church, and for all mankind, we humbly ask, through the merits and mediation of thy Son Jesus Christ, our Lord and Savior.

And may the grace of our Lord Jesus Christ be be with us evermore. *Amen.*

Evening Prayer.

MOST gracious God, who hatest nothing that thou hast made, and hast promised forgiveness to those who confess and forsake their sins, we come before thee, humbly acknowledging our manifold transgressions of thy holy laws. Behold us, O Lord, in mercy; pardon our sins; sanctify our hearts; and give us repentance unto life, for the sake of Jesus Christ, our blessed Lord and Savior.

Without thee, O God, nothing is strong and nothing is holy; grant us, we beseech thee, the aid and direction of thy Holy Spirit. Reform whatever is amiss in the state and disposition of our minds. Preserve us from envy and malice and all uncharitableness. May we never suffer the sun to go down upon our wrath; but go to our rest in peace, charity, and good-will, with a conscience void of offence towards thee and towards men; and be, through thy grace, preserved in thy faith and fear, unto the coming of our Lord and Savior, Jesus Christ.

And accept, O Lord, our intercessions for all mankind. May the light of thy gospel shine upon all nations; and they who have received it, live as becomes it. Be gracious unto thy church, and grant that every member of it, in his vocation and ministry, may serve thee faithfully. Bless those in authority over us, and so rule their hearts and strengthen their hands, that they may not bear the sword in vain. Send down thy blessings, temporal and spiritual, upon our relations, friends and neighbors; may they who are dear to us be dear to thee, and under thy holy care and keeping. Reward those who have done us good, and give us hearts to be duly thankful. If any have done or wished us evil, give to them pardon and better minds, and to us the spirit of mercy and forgiveness. Be merciful, O Lord, to those who are in trouble, sorrow, need, sickness or any other adversity; and do thou, the God of pity, comfort and relieve them, according to their several necessities, for his sake who went about doing good, thy Son, our Savior, Jesus Christ.

And we desire, O gracious God, to render thee our humble and hearty thanks for all thy mercies. We bless thee for the gifts of life and reason; for our health and friends; our food and raiment; and for all the enjoyments of this present life. Above all, we adore thy mercy in sending thy only Son into this world to redeem us from sin and eternal death, and for giving us the knowledge and sense of our duty towards thee. We bless thee, O God, for thy patience with us, thy sinful creatures; for the guidance, aid, and comfort of thy Holy Spirit; for thy continual care and watchful providence over us through the whole course of our lives; and particularly for the mercies and benefits of the past day; beseeching thee to continue these thy blessings to us, and to give us grace to show our thankfulness in a faithful obedience to His laws, through whose merits and intercession we received them all, thy Son, our Savior, Jesus Christ.

Be with us, O Lord, we beseech thee, this night; take us, and all that appertains to us, under thy gracious protection. Watch over us while we rest; defend us from all evil; preserve us from needless fear, and keep us, we beseech thee, both outwardly in our bodies and inwardly in our souls. Prepare us for the labors and for all the duties of another day. May we never forget that a night cometh, we know not how soon, when we can no longer work. When our Lord shall come, whether in the second watch or in the third watch, may we be found faithful, and ready to enter into that rest which remains for the people of God. Grant these things, O merciful Lord, through the merits and satisfaction of thy Son, Christ Jesus, in whose name we offer up these our imperfect prayers. *Amen.*

Morning Prayer.

ALMIGHTY and everlasting God, unto whom all hearts are open, all desires known, and from whom no secrets are hid, cleanse the thoughts of our hearts by the inspiration of thy Holy Spirit, that we, truly lamenting our sins and acknowledging our unworthiness, may obtain of thee, the God of all mercy, perfect remission and forgiveness, through Jesus Christ our Lord.

O Lord, our heavenly Father, almighty and everlasting God, who hast safely brought us to the beginning of this day, defend us, we beseech thee, by thy mighty power: grant that this day we fall into no sin, neither run into any kind of danger, either of soul or body; but that all our doings, being ordered by thy governance, may be righteous in thy sight. Vouchsafe to direct, sanctify and govern both our hearts and lives, in the ways of thy laws, and in the works of thy commandments; that, through thy most mighty protection, we may be preserved in body and soul, through our Lord and Savior, Jesus Christ.

Accept, O Lord, of our prayers for all mankind, and especially for those who are of the household of faith. Do thou, by whose Spirit thy church is governed and sanctified, receive our supplications for all its members; that in their several states, vocations and ministry, they may be free from all adversity, and devoutly given to serve thee faithfully in good works. Inspire them with truth, unity, and concord; grant that all they who do confess thy holy name may agree in the truth of thy holy word, and live in unity and godly love. Send down upon the ministers of thy gospel, and upon the congregations committed to their charge, the healthful spirit of thy grace; and that they may truly please thee, pour upon them the continual dew of thy blessing. Grant that they may, both by their life and doctrine, set forth thy true and lively word, and rightly and duly administer the ordinances of our blessed Redeemer. Grant this, O Lord, for the honor of our Advocate and Mediator, Jesus Christ.

Almighty God, Father of all mercies, we, thine unworthy servants, desire also to render unto thee our humble and hearty thanks, for all thy goodness and loving kindness to us and to all mankind. We bless thee for our creation and preservation; especially that we were kept in safety through the past night, that we are brought to see the light of another day, and for all the blessings of this life: but above all, for thine inestimable love, in the redemption of the world by our Lord Jesus Christ, for the means of grace, and for the hope of glory. And, we beseech thee, give us that due sense of all thy mercies, that our hearts may be unfeignedly thankful; and that we may show forth thy praise, not only with our lips, but in our lives; by giving up ourselves to thy service, and by walking before thee in holiness and righteousness all our days. Dispose our ways towards the attainment of everlasting salvation: and among all the changes, temptations and other trials of this mortal life, may we ever be defended by thy most gracious and ready help, through Jesus Christ our Lord, in whose name and words we humbly pray:—Our Father who art in heaven, hallowed be thy name. Thy kingdom come; thy will be done on earth, as it is in heaven. Give us this day our daily bread. And forgive us our trespasses, as we forgive those who trespass against us. And lead us not into temptation; but deliver us from evil. For thine is the kingdom, and the power and the glory, forever and ever. *Amen.*

Evening Prayer.

O MERCIFUL God, the Giver of all good, who hatest nothing that thou hast made; who wouldst not the death of a sinner, but rather that he should turn with penitence to thee, and be saved through faith in Jesus Christ; mercifully forgive our trespasses; receive and comfort us, thy unworthy creatures, with the light of thy reconciled countenance. There is mercy, O Lord, with thee that thou mayest be feared. To thee only it appertains to blot out offences, and renew the soul with holy affections. Spare us, O Lord, we beseech thee, spare the people whom thou hast redeemed. Shouldst thou be extreme to mark iniquities, no man living could be justified. For the glory of thy name, turn from us all the evils which we too justly have deserved, and grant us perfect remission and forgiveness, through Jesus Christ our Lord.

O God, the Protector of all who trust in thee, without whom nothing is strong, nothing holy, nothing good, increase and multiply upon us thy mercy; be thou in all things our ruler and guide: direct us in what we do, with thy most gracious favor: prosper us with thy continual help; that in all our works, begun, continued, and ended in thee, we may advance thy glory. Graft in our hearts the love of thy name; increase in us true religion; nourish us with all goodness, and of thy great mercy keep us steadfast in thy fear and service, through Jesus Christ our Lord.

O God, who art the Creator and Preserver of all mankind, we humbly beseech thee for all sorts and conditions of men, that thou wouldst be pleased to make thy ways known unto them, thy saving health unto all nations. More especially we pray for thy holy church universal; that it may be so guided and governed by thy good Spirit, that all who profess and call themselves Christians may be led into the way of truth, and hold the faith, once delivered to the saints, in unity of spirit, in the bond of peace, and in righteousness of life. We ask thy blessing upon our benefactors, relatives, and friends. And we commend to thy fatherly goodness all those who are any way afflicted in mind, body, or estate; that it may please thee to comfort and relieve them according to their several necessities, giving them patience under their sufferings, and a happy issue out of their afflictions. Accept, O Lord, of our intercessions for all who desire our prayers, and all for whom we ought to pray. Let thy fatherly hand be over them for good; let thy Spirit be ever with them, and lead them in the way of everlasting life. This we also ask in the name and through the mediation of our Lord and Savior, Jesus Christ.

O Lord, our heavenly Father, by whose power and goodness we have been preserved through the cares and perils of the past day, watch over us, we beseech thee, while we sleep: under the shadow of thy wings may we safely rest through the silent watches of the night, and rise refreshed, prepared in heart and strength to do thy will, with a thankful sense of thy goodness. And whilst we live may we live to thee, through Jesus Christ our Lord.

And may the grace of our Lord Jesus Christ, and the love of God, and the fellowship of the Holy Ghost, be with us evermore. *Amen.*

A Prayer for Sunday Morning.

Almighty and everliving God, who art always more willing to hear than we to pray, and art wont to give more than either we desire or deserve, look down upon us, we beseech thee, in mercy; forgive us the things wherein we have sinned against thee; and give us hearts to be thankful for those good things which we daily receive. We thank thee, O God, that we are brought to see the light of another day, and the commencement of another week. This is the day that the Lord hath made; may we be glad and rejoice in it, with holy joy and thankful hearts.

Give us grace, O Lord, to sanctify thy holy day of rest, according to thy appointment, and to be thankful that the Sabbath was made for man, to be a season for laying aside our temporal cares, and presenting before thee our humble adorations. We look unto thee for thy blessing on our observance of this day which thou hast set apart for thyself. May we spend this holy time to the honor of thy name. May it be to us a season of refreshing from thy presence, and of mercy to our souls. May thy spirit accompany us to thy sanctuary, and make us joyful in thy house of prayer. Give us grace so to join and engage in the service of thy church, that the words of our mouth and the meditations of our heart may be acceptable in thy sight.

May we love the habitation of thy house, and the place where thine honor dwelleth. Help us to pray with the spirit and with the understanding, and to receive with meekness the words of eternal life.

May thy Spirit be with the ministers of thy gospel; and so bless thy word spoken by their mouth, that it may minister grace to the hearers. May it fall upon those who have ears to hear, and in an honest and good heart be received. May the doctrines of life be ingrafted in their hearts, and bring forth in them the fruits of good living.

Dispose, O Lord, and prepare our souls to perform faithfully all the duties suited to this holy time; to receive the full benefit of the ordinances which thou hast prepared for our edification and spiritual good, and to walk before thee in holiness and righteousness all our days.

Grant O Lord, we beseech thee, that all who draw nigh to thee this day, to give thee thanks for benefits received; to set forth thy praise; to confess their sins before thee, and to pray for what they need; may do it according to thy will, and obtain thy heavenly benediction. May all thy people be in the spirit on the Lord's day, and devote themselves to him who is Lord of the Sabbath, and worship the Father in spirit and in truth. Let that light which is above the brightness of the sun shine in our hearts, to give us the knowledge of the glory of God in the face of Jesus Christ. May we this day experience the power of Christ's resurrection; that, as he was raised up from the dead by the glory of the Father, so we may walk in newness of life.

And extend, O Lord, thy heavenly benediction to the whole of thy church universal. Pour out thy spirit upon its members, and in thine own good time bring into its bosom those on whom the light of the gospel has not yet shined; and may all who have received it, live as becomes it.

Hear, O Lord, we beseech thee, these our humble supplications and prayers. Preserve us this day from all evil; give us those good things which thou shalt see to be needful and convenient; and give us grace that we may rightly use them. This we ask in the name of him who died for our sins, and rose again for our justification.

And may the blessing of God Almighty, the Father, the Son, and the Holy Ghost, be with us now and evermore. *Amen.*

Sunday Evening.

Adorable and everliving God, the author and giver of all good, by whose merciful protection we have been conducted through the perils of the day now past, we desire, this evening, humbly to bow before thee with a thankful sense of thy goodness. We bless thee, O God, for all the means of grace, and for every opportunity afforded to us of becoming wise unto salvation. We bless thee for casting our lot in a Christian land, where the gospel of salvation is preached, and thy blessed word is a lantern to our feet and a light to our paths. We bless thee for the privilege of being nurtured in a church which is built upon the foundation of apostles and prophets, Jesus Christ himself being the chief cornerstone. We desire to be duly thankful that thou hast so loved the world as to send into it thy only begotten Son, not to condemn, but to save it; and for his gracious invitations to the weary and heavy-laden to come unto him that they may have everlasting life.

We thank thee, O God, that we are made reasonable creatures, capable of knowing and loving and serving thee: that our lives are still preserved; and especially for the mercies of the day past; that we have enjoyed the privilege of another of the days of the Son of man; that we have had another opportunity of uniting with the congregation of thy people in thy holy worship; and for all the blessings of thy sanctuary. Wherein we have neglected to use and to profit by them, grant us forgiveness, and give us true repentance for all our sins. Help us hereafter to serve thee better and to love thee more, and daily to increase in all viitue and godliness of living. Impress upon our hearts, we humbly beseech thee, a lively and lasting sense of what thou hast done to save our souls from sin and death: that whilst we were yet sinners, Christ died for us, and put away sin by the sacrifice of himself. Grant, O merciful God, that we may not neglect this great salvation, offered us in Jesus Christ. Help us to profit by all the instructions of thy word, and to be a holy people unto thee, zealous of good works.

Accept, O Lord, the adorations, and graciously answer the prayers, which have during the past day been offered before thee; and grant to us and to all thy people, that what of thy truth we have heard with our ears, may be implanted in our hearts, impressed upon our memories, and fruitful in our lives. May we be doers of thy word, and not hearers only, deceiving ourselves. May we contend earnestly for the faith which was once delivered to the saints; and to our faith add virtue, knowledge, temperance, patience, godliness, brotherly kindness and charity, and give diligence to make our calling and election sure. What we are taught on the Lord's day, may we practise through the week; and while we advance in age may we grow in grace and in the knowledge of our Lord and Savior, Jesus Christ.

May we be duly thankful that the Son of man is Lord of the Sabbath, and that the ordinances of his religion are accommodated to our wants, and are profitable to those who rightly use them. May they be profitable to us: may what we have heard read from thy word, and spoken according to thy will, be to us a savor of life. Extend the light of thy truth to those who are in the darkness of unbelief, and thy saving health unto all nations.

We commend ourselves, and all for whom we ought to pray, to the protection of thy good providence. Defend us from the perils of this night: watch over us during the hours of sleep: and if it be thy good pleasure to bring us to the light of another day, give us hearts to be thankful for thy goodness, and grace to live to thee, through Jesus Christ our Lord; to whom, with thee and the Holy Ghost, be all honor and glory, world without end. *Amen.*

Monday Morning.

ALMIGHTY and everlasting God, unto whom all hearts are open, all desires known, and from whom no secrets are hid, behold with favor thy unworthy creatures who desire, under a sense of thy providential care, to offer unto thee our morning sacrifice of prayer and praise.

We are here assembled, O Lord, in thy name and presence, waiting upon thee at the footstool of thy grace. Cleanse the thoughts of our hearts by the inspiration of thy Holy Spirit: blot out our offences and wash away our sins. Who can tell how oft he offendeth? O cleanse thou us from our secret faults. Keep us back, also, from presumptuous sins: let them not have dominion over us. Let a just sense of thy forbearance and long-suffering lead us to repentance not to be repented of, and keep us at the foot of the Savior's cross. Inspire us, O Lord, with true devotion, that while we draw nigh to thee with our lips, our hearts may not be far from thee. Keep us ever mindful of our dependence upon thee, and quicken us in the pursuit of things eternal. Dispose us rightly to discharge the duties of this day. Watch over our paths; preserve us in our going out and coming in, and direct all our steps in the way of thy commandments. In all our dealings, may we be honest and conscientious; make us diligent in the works of our calling; harmless in our conversation; meek in our deportment; charitable and forgiving towards others; watchful over ourselves, and never forgetful of thee. May we love thee, the Lord our God, with all our heart and mind and soul, which is the first and great commandment. And may we love our neighbor as ourselves, and do unto all men as we would that they should do unto us. O help us, as our Savior Christ has commanded, to love our enemies, and to bless them who despitefully use and persecute us. May we never be overcome of evil, but endeavor to overcome evil with good. If it be possible, and as much as lieth in us, may we live peaceably with all men.

We thank thee, O God, for the preservation of our lives, and for all the blessings which make life comfortable; and we humbly ask for the continuance of thy goodness; that thou wilt preserve us from danger and from sin, and give us such things as are needful and convenient for our present comfort, and for our eternal good. Help us to keep in continual remembrance the doctrines of Christ, the precepts of the gospel, and the duties of life, which were taught us on thy holy day of rest. May we live as they should live who are taught of God.

We bless thy name, O God, for the seasons and opportunities of learning our duty and doing thy will which thou art weekly and daily bestowing upon us. Make us duly sensible how much and how wickedly we have neglected the right use of thy blessings, and how little we have profited in seasons of grace. Remember not, Lord, our offences past, nor take thou vengeance of our sins. Withdraw not thou thy help; grant us the comfort of thy salvation, and uphold us with thy free spirit; that our souls may bless thee, and all that is within us may praise thy holy name. Vouchsafe, O Lord, to keep us this day without sin, and to dispose all our ways towards the attainment of everlasting salvation: and among all the perils and changes of this mortal life, may we ever be defended by thy most gracious and ready help. May we continue steadfast in thy faith, and daily increase in thy holy spirit more and more until we come to thine everlasting kingdom. For thine is the kingdom and the power, and thine be the glory, forever and ever. Hear us, O Lord, we beseech thee, for the sake of thy Son, our Savior, Jesus Christ. *Amen.*

Monday Evening.

ALMIGHTY and immortal God, the only Potentate, King of kings and Lord of lords, who hast thy throne in the highest heavens, and yet deignest to behold the things that are on earth, worthy art thou of the praise and adoration of all intelligent beings. What is man that thou art mindful of him, and the children of men, that thou dost vouchsafe to them thy care! Thy glory transcends our utmost thoughts, and goodness shines in all thy works. We, thy sinful and unworthy creatures, humbly desire to approach thee in supplication and prayer, not in our own name, nor trusting in our own righteousness, but in the name and through the merits of Jesus Christ. For his sake we beseech thee to pardon our offences, to sanctify our hearts, and create us again unto good works. We are not sufficient of ourselves to think, and still less to do, any thing good: our sufficiency is of thee. Without thy grace we incline to evil, and to err and to stray from thy ways like lost sheep. Enter not into judgment with thy servants, O Lord; for in thy sight shall no man living be justified. We have an advocate with thee, O our heavenly Father, and may he be the propitiation for our sins. To thee, through his merits, belong mercy and forgiveness, though we have rebelled against thee. Grant us, we beseech thee, redemption through his blood, even the forgiveness of sins, according to the riches of thy grace. O give us the comfort of thy help, and stablish us with thy free spirit. Without thee, nothing is pure, nothing is holy: increase and multiply upon us thy mercy, that, thou being our guide and strength, we may so pass through things temporal, that we finally lose not the things eternal. Work in us that repentance which is not to be repented of, and that faith in the Lord Jesus Christ which renews the heart and overcomes the world.

We bless thee, O God, for thy patience and long-suffering with those who are forgetful of thy goodness, and that time and opportunity for repentance and amendment of life are still vouchsafed to us. We bless thee, O God, that thou hast laid help on one who is mighty, and that Jesus Christ is the end of the law for righteousness to those who believe. May the life we live be by faith in the Son of God. Stablish us in thy love; strengthen us to do good, and guide our steps in the way of righteousness and peace. Help us daily to examine our hearts and lives, and to be conformed in all things to thy holy will.

Thou hast taught us, O God, that all our doings, without charity, are nothing worth; inspire our hearts with true Christian love. May that spirit be in us, which was in our Savior Christ; a spirit of benevolence; and a delight in doing good to all men, and especially unto them who are of the household of faith. May we owe no man any thing, but to love one another with that love which is the fulfilling of the whole law.

Make us thankful, O Lord, that we are called to a knowledge of thy grace and faith in Jesus Christ; increase this knowledge and confirm this faith in our hearts, and make it fruitful in our lives. Grant that we may be also of thy chosen people; and give us grace to make our calling and election sure.

We beseech thee, O God, to behold with thy compassionate goodness those who are visited with sorrow, and all who, in this transitory life, are in need or sickness, or any other adversity. Grant them patience under their sufferings, and a happy issue out of their afflictions.

Extend, we beseech thee, the knowledge of thy truth; bless thy word wherever it is spoken, and send it where it is not heard; and may the borders of Zion be more and still more enlarged, till all the ends of the earth shall see the salvation of our God. We ask these things in the name of Jesus Christ, our blessed Lord and Savior. *Amen.*

Tuesday Morning.

Adorable and everliving God, the fountain of all wisdom, mercy and grace, who hast formed the spirit of man within him, and fitted him to serve and worship thee, we desire, as thy children and the work of thy hands, to lift once more our heart and voice in prayer and praise to thee. Once more have we laid us down in peace and taken rest, and through thy goodness are risen again in safety. May the lives which thy goodness renews every morning, and thy providence every moment sustains, be devoted to thee. As a father spareth his son that serveth him, wilt thou, O Lord, have mercy upon us!

We desire, O God, to adore thy name, which is excellent in all the earth, and whose glory is above the heavens. We bless thee for the rest and preservation of the night past. O cause us to hear thy loving kindness in the morning, for in thee do we trust. Make us to know the way wherein we should go, for which we would continue daily to lift up our soul unto thee. Cast us not away from thy presence, nor take thy Holy Spirit from us; but direct our hearts into thy love, and our feet into the way of thy testimonies. May we be ever found in the way of duty, fearing God and working righteousness; walking in the steps of thy blessed Son; making it evident to all that we are influenced by his spirit, guided by his example, and pressing forward to his kingdom. Day by day would we magnify thee, O Lord, and worship thy name forever and ever.

But we are unworthy, through our manifold sins, to offer unto thee any worship. Enter not into judgment with thy servants, O Lord, but spare those whom thou hast redeemed. Have mercy upon us after thy great goodness; according to the multitude of thy mercies do away our offences.

We beseech thee to take us this day under thy holy care and keeping. Grant us such measures of thy grace as may fit us for the duties of our respective stations. Make us respectful to our superiors; friendly to our equals; kind to the poor, and charitable and forgiving to those who do us wrong. Cause us to delight in thy holy worship and in the performance of all religious duties. Grant that we may be doers of thy word, and let our light so shine before men, that they may see our good works, and glorify thee, our heavenly Father. Help us to honor thee in our lives, and give us understanding that we may keep the law with our whole heart. Preserve us from all idolatrous affection for the things of this world; may we never be lovers of pleasure more than lovers of God.

And accept, O Lord, of our intercessions for all mankind. May the light of thy glorious gospel shine throughout this sinful world; and to all those who are sitting in darkness and the shadow of death, may the Sun of Righteousness arise with healing in his wings. May thy word have free course, and, through thy blessing, be a savor of life to those who hear it, producing repentance towards God and faith towards the Lord Jesus Christ. Give thy blessing to thy church; and especially to the congregation of thy people with whom we are more particularly connected. Endue the ministers of thy gospel with heavenly wisdom and holy zeal; and grant that, by their preaching and living, they may show the truth of thy word and the power of thy grace. Do thou, O God, who knowest our necessities before we ask, and the infirmity of our nature, forgive the imperfection of these our prayers, and answer them in thy wisdom and mercy, for the sake of thy Son, our Savior, Jesus Christ. *Amen.*

Tuesday Evening.

O ETERNAL God, mighty in power, and of majesty incomprehensible, who art exalted above the heavens, while we, thy sinful creatures, are here upon the earth, we desire, from this our humble state, to laud and magnify thy glorious name. It is a good thing to give thanks unto the Lord, and to sing praises unto thy name, O most Highest; to tell of thy loving kindness early in the morning, and of thy truth in the night season.

We present ourselves, O Lord, before thee, in humble adoration, as creatures unworthy the least of thy mercies. Blessed are they who dwell in thy house, and blessed is the house where thou dwellest; blessed is the man whose strength is in thee, and in whose heart are thy ways. Grant, we beseech thee, that this blessing may be ours; visit us with thy gracious presence, and rejoice us with the tokens of thy love. Let our prayers be set forth in thy sight as incense, and may the lifting up of our hands in supplication be an evening sacrifice holy and acceptable unto thee.

We acknowledge, O heavenly Father, that we have sinned against heaven and before thee, and are not worthy to be called thy children, nor to ask for thy grace. May thy Holy Spirit convince us of sin, of righteousness and of judgment; and so quicken our repentance and strengthen our faith, that we may obtain of thee, the God of all mercy, perfect remission and forgiveness, and enjoy that peace which the world cannot give. As the heavens are higher than the earth, so great let thy mercy be towards us; as far as the east is from the west, do thou, the God of mercy, set our sins from us. May our Savior Christ be to us wisdom and righteousness and sanctification and redemption, and all our glorying be in him. O may thy grace be sufficient for us, and thy strength be so made perfect in weakness, that we may be strong in the Lord and in the power of his might, and strive successfully to enter in at the strait gate.

And help us, O Lord, to offer, and graciously accept our evening sacrifice of praise and thanksgiving. Every day would we give thanks unto thee, and praise thy name forever and ever. Great art thou, O Lord, and marvellous; worthy to be praised; there is no end of thy greatness. One generation shall praise thy works unto another, and declare thy power. Thou art gracious and merciful, long-suffering and of great goodness; thou art loving unto every man, and thy mercy is over all thy works. All thy works praise thee, O Lord, and thy saints give thanks unto thee. Make us truly thankful that our voices may be heard among them.

We bless thee, O God, for thy daily goodness to us and to all men; for our life and health, our food and raiment, our mental endowments, and for all our social enjoyments. We bless thee that we live in a land where the gospel is preached and thy word is known; and that we have the offer and the means of salvation in Jesus Christ. Make us, we beseech thee, duly thankful for these thy mercies; and give us grace that we may rightly use them to thy glory, and to our own and others' salvation.

And we pray that these privileges which we enjoy may be extended to all who need them. Let thy Spirit be with thy ministers who labor to evangelize the nations of the earth. May thy word be truly spoken, and in an honest and good heart received. And grant that all Christians may be so joined together in unity of spirit and in the bond of peace, that thy church may be a holy temple, acceptable unto thee.

And wilt thou, O merciful Lord, grant to this family the abundance of thy grace! Defend us from evil; watch over us for good, and take us, and all that appertains to us, under thy holy care and keeping. These things, and whatever else thou seest fitting for us, for our neighbors, relatives and friends, and for thy whole church, we humbly ask, through the mediation of Jesus Christ, to whom, with thee and the Holy Ghost, be all honor and glory, world without end. *Amen.*

Wednesday Morning.

Almighty and everlasting God, the Maker of all things, the Father of our spirits, the Life of them who believe, and the Resurrection of the dead, thou alone art worthy of all adoration and praise. To thee all angels cry aloud; the heavens and all the powers therein. The holy church throughout all the world doth worship thee; and with angels and archangels, and with all the company of heaven, we laud and magnify thy glorious name. We bless thee for thy adorable perfections, and for all the wonders thou doest for the children of men. We thank thee for thy unnumbered mercies vouchsafed to us thy unworthy creatures; and especially that our lives are still preserved, and that we are permitted this morning to open our lips that we may show forth thy praise. May these our thankful offerings flow from lips unfeigned, and from hearts sincere.

We are unworthy, through our manifold sins, to offer unto thee any sacrifice, and our humblest supplications will need thy pardon; yet we beseech thee to accept this our bounden duty and service, not weighing our merits, but pardoning our offences. Give us, O Lord, the spirit of humble supplication: help our infirmities, and teach us how to pray.

Help us, O Lord, each one to do his duty in that state of life to which respectively we are called, with diligence and fidelity. May we abound in love; abhor that which is evil, cleave to that which is good; not be slothful in business, but fervent in spirit, serving the Lord. Give us grace to rejoice with them that do rejoice, and to weep with them that weep. May we recompense to no man evil for evil; but endeavor to overcome evil with good, and to provide things honest in the sight of all men. Help us to resist temptation and escape the snares of sin. Make us ever mindful of thy presence and desirous of thy grace. Open thou our eyes that we may see the excellence of thy law: give us understanding that we may know thy testimonies and write the words of thy gospel in our hearts. Direct and bless us in our endeavors to know and to do thy will: make us contented with what thou shalt provide for us; industrious in some honest calling, and temperate in all things. Make us thankful for all the good that we receive, and kind to those who need the blessings which we enjoy. May all bitterness and anger and evil speaking be put away from us, with all malice: and may we be kind one to another, tender-hearted, forgiving one another, even as thou hast, we hope and pray, for Christ's sake, forgiven us.

Have mercy, O Lord, upon all those who are still in the gall of bitterness and in the bond of iniquity, living in sin, and without God in the world. Convert their souls and bring them home, blessed Lord, to thy flock, that they may be saved among the remnant of the true Israelites, and become one fold under one Shepherd.

We beseech thee, O God, to bless our country

with prosperity and peace. May this nation be a people serving thee, having thee for their God, and thy word for their guide. Bless our civil rulers, and all who are in authority over us, with wisdom, justice and truth. And wilt thou extend the blessings of light and liberty, and pure and undefiled religion, to all the nations of the earth. May thy kingdom come: may the time arrive when the mountain of the Lord's house shall be established in the top of the mountains, and shall be exalted above the hills, and all nations shall flow unto it.

Let thy spirit, O Lord, be with us this day and while we live. Give us grace to love and fear thee, and diligently to live after thy commandments. In all our doings and desires; in our going out and coming in; in the business of our callings, and in the work which our hands find to do, wilt thou rule our hearts, strengthen our hands, and give us thy blessing. May we love the things which thou commandest, and desire those which thou dost promise; and among all the manifold changes and perils of this world, may our hearts be surely fixed where true joys are to be found, through Jesus Christ.

And may the grace of our Lord Jesus Christ, and the love of God, and the fellowship of the Holy Ghost, be with us evermore. *Amen.*

Wednesday Evening.

Adorable Creator, who art exalted above all thrones and dominions, dwelling between the cherubim, in the holy place of the highest heavens, and yet humblest thyself to behold the things that are in heaven and on earth, and to hear the prayers of thy unworthy creatures, be pleased now, we beseech thee, to hear the petitions which we would offer in the name of Jesus Christ.

Another day is taken from our scanty span of life, and may it awaken in us a lively sense of the importance of time, and that the period is swiftly approaching when time with us will be no more. Teach us, we beseech thee, so to number our days that we may apply our hearts to true wisdom. Grant that the time and opportunities which thy patient goodness may yet vouchsafe to us, may be rightly used to the purposes of our Christian calling. As we advance in age, may we grow in grace.

We beseech thee, O God, to turn thy face from our sins, and to blot out all our iniquities. Make us a clean heart, and renew a right spirit within us. The sacrifice in which thou delightest is a meek and humble spirit: a broken and a contrite heart, O God, wilt thou not despise. Remember not, Lord, our offences, nor the offences of our forefathers; neither take thou vengeance of our sins. Spare us, good Lord, spare thy people whom thou hast redeemed with thy precious blood, and be not angry with us forever. Cleanse the thoughts of our hearts by the inspiration of thy Holy Spirit, that we may perfectly love thee, and worthily magnify thy holy name.

Though we have wickedly transgressed, to whom can we go for pardon and acceptance but unto thee, O thou Savior of men, who alone hast the words of eternal life? If thou speak the word, we shall be healed. Cast us not away from thy presence, nor take thy Holy Spirit from us. Direct, sanctify and govern both our hearts and our bodies in the ways of thy laws, and in the works of thy commandments. May we seek first, and above all things, the kingdom of God and his righteousness. Increase and multiply upon us thy mercy, that, thou being our ruler and guide, we may so pass through the perils and trials of this life, that we may arrive at the glorified state of thy heavenly kingdom. Create us again unto good works. Inspire in our hearts that charity which is the bond of perfectness; which suffereth long and is kind; which envieth not; which seeketh not her own, and thinketh no evil: inspire us with that Christian love which worketh no ill to our neighbor, and is the fulfilling of the whole law.

Grant, O Lord, that the course of this world may be so peaceably ordered by thy governance, that thy church may serve thee in all godly quietness; and that all those who confess thy name may agree in the truth of thy holy word, and live in unity and godly love. May it please thee to bring into the way of truth all such as have erred, and are deceived; to strengthen such as do stand; to comfort and help the weak-hearted; to raise up those who fall, and subdue our spiritual foes.

We beseech thee, O Lord, to bless the people of this our country; defend them from every evil, and from every foe. Surely trusting in thy defence, may we not fear the power of any adversary;—may the Lord be our God, and his word our guide. Bless the people and the government of this state in which we live. Give thy blessing to the inhabitants of this town, and inspire thy church and people here with godly zeal and Christian love. Send down upon the ministers of thy gospel, and upon the congregations committed to their charge, the healthful spirit of thy grace and the continual dew of thy heavenly benediction.

Do thou, who hast graciously promised to hear the petitions of those who ask in thy Son's name, mercifully incline thine ears to us who have now made our prayers and supplications unto thee, and grant our petitions for the sake of our Savior, Jesus Christ.

And may the peace of God, which passeth understanding, keep our hearts and minds in the knowledge and love of God; and the blessing of the Father, Son, and Holy Ghost be ever with us. *Amen.*

Thursday Morning.

O Lord God, who art the hope of all the ends of the earth; who alone givest life and health and peace; thou art our God, and early will we seek thee. Thou art nigh unto them who call upon thee faithfully. Thy eyes, O Lord, are over the righteous, and thy ears are open to their prayers. Thou art nigh unto them who are of a contrite heart, and wilt save such as are of an humble spirit. Create and make in us new and contrite hearts: hear the prayers and accept the praise which we desire this morning to offer before thee. Have respect, we beseech thee, to us and to our offering, and meet with thy blessing those who desire to seek thee in prayer, and make thy throne to us a throne of grace.

We would look unto thee, O God, as our Father who art in heaven, and the Creator and Preserver of all mankind. Thou hast made us, and not we ourselves: we are thy people, and the sheep of thy pasture; we worship and fall down and kneel before thee as the Lord our Maker, and the Giver of all good. If any man sin, we have an Advocate with thee, O heavenly Father, and may he be the propitiation for our sins. We are unworthy to offer unto thee any sacrifice; through Him alone, our meritorious High Priest, we approach thee, O God, that we may find mercy and grace to help us in the time of need. O Lord, increase our faith, and let thy Spirit help our infirmities, and teach us to ask for such things, and with such devotion, as shall please thee, and that our prayers may ascend as grateful incense.

We give thee thanks for the preservation of the night past, and for the comforts vouchsafed to us this morning; beseeching thee to take us, this day, and all that is ours, under thy guidance and protection. Grant that all our doings may be ordered by thy governance, and righteous in thy sight. Teach us the worth of our immortal souls, and the great salvation wrought for us in Jesus Christ. May we never be ashamed to confess him before men; but glory in bearing his cross, and being his disciples. May our conversation be such as becometh his gospel; and may the whole conduct of our lives, the words of our mouth, and the meditation of our heart, be always acceptable in thy sight, through Jesus Christ, our strength and our Redeemer.

We thank thee, O heavenly Father, for all the blessings we receive, both of providence and grace. But above all we adore thee for thy inestimable love in the redemption of the world by our Lord Jesus Christ. Give us, we pray thee, that due sense of thy goodness, that our hearts may be duly thankful, and our lives be devoted unto thee. May thy Spirit lead us into all truth, and make us fruitful in every good word and work. Let not the cares of this world cause us to neglect the one thing needful; but help us rather to lay up our treasures where moth and rust cannot destroy them. According as we have opportunity, may we do good unto all men. May we love those that love the Lord Jesus, and may the spirit which was in him be also in us. May we abhor that which is evil, and in all things cleave to that which is good: be kind and affectionate; rejoicing in hope; patient in tribulation; given to hospitality.

Hear us, O Lord, in mercy: in all we think and

do, may thy Holy Spirit aid and guide us; that in this world we may live to thy glory, and finally, by thy mercy, obtain everlasting life, through Jesus Christ, our Lord, to whom, with thee and the Holy Ghost, be all honor and glory, world without end. *Amen.*

The Lord bless us and keep us; the Lord lift up the light of his countenance upon us and give us peace, now and evermore. *Amen.*

Thursday Evening.

O ETERNAL God, thou Shepherd of Israel, whose all-seeing eye surveys the inhabitants of this lower world, behold us thy dependent creatures with thy favor and blessing. Thou, Lord, hast been our refuge from one generation to another. Before the mountains were brought forth, or ever the earth and the world were made, thou art God from everlasting, and world without end. All thy works praise thee, and thy saints give thanks unto thee. Thou art righteous in all thy ways, and holy in all thy works. Thou art about our bed, and about our paths, and spiest out all our ways. There is not a word of our mouth, nor a thought or intent of our heart, but thou, O Lord, knowest it altogether. The darkness is no darkness to thee: with thee the night is as clear as the day. Wherewith shall we, thy sinful creatures, come before thee, and bow ourselves before the high God? What sacrifice shall atone for our multiplied transgressions? Will the Lord be pleased with thousands of rams, or with rivers of oil? Thou hast shown us what is good; thou hast laid help on one who is mighty. Thou hast given thy only Son to be our Savior, who has put away sin by the sacrifice of himself. O give us that faith in him which worketh by love, that we may do justly, love mercy, and walk humbly with thee.

We beseech thee, O heavenly Father, mercifully to look upon our infirmities, and through the merits of our Savior, and for the glory of thy great name, turn from us all those evils that we most justly have deserved; and in all the afflictions that we may suffer, may we confide in thy mercy and submit to thy will. May we ever look unto thee as the greatest good, and to thy loving kindness as better than life itself. May we never neglect thy great salvation: being justified by faith, may we have peace with thee. Make us wise and faithful in all the duties of life and of religion. Let not sin reign in our mortal bodies, nor any vain desire possess our hearts. Help us so to number our days, and to view the uncertainty of their continuance, that we may ever be watchful and prepared, as they who wait for the coming of their Lord. Restrain us from all immoderate desire of temporal things, that we may use the world as not abusing it. Help us rightly to value the true riches, and to have our conversation in heaven. Cause us to love thy word, and to delight in thy laws; and so enlighten our minds and purify our affections, that we may embrace and ever hold fast the blessed hope of everlasting life, which thou hast given us in our Lord and Savior, Jesus Christ.

Accept, O Lord, of our prayers for all of our fellow-men; that thy ways may be known unto them, and thy saving health be extended to all the nations of the earth. Have mercy upon all who are now living in sin, and in the darkness of unbelief. Take from them all ignorance, hardness of heart, and dislike of thy holy word; and bring them, blessed Lord, into thy flock, that they may be all of one fold, and under the one true Shepherd, Jesus Christ.

Be pleased, O God, to continue thy gracious protection to us this night. Keep us both outwardly in our bodies and inwardly in our souls. O thou Keeper of Israel, who never slumberest nor sleepest, take charge of us and ours, and watch over us for good. Preserve us from sin and from peril: may we lie down in peace and take our rest in the comforting belief that it is thou, O God, who makest us to dwell in safety. Fit and prepare us for that heavenly rest which remaineth for the people of God. We offer these, our evening devotions, in the name of Jesus Christ: and may his grace be ever with us. *Amen.*

Friday Morning.

O God, the King of kings and Lord of lords, who art eternal, immortal, invisible, the Maker of the world and of all that is therein, worthy art thou to receive glory and honor and power; for thou hast created all things, and for thy pleasure they are and were created. Our life is thine: our hearts are in thy hand, and our secret thoughts are known to thee. We adore thee as the giver of all good. The eyes of all wait upon thee; thou openest thy hand and fillest all things living with plenteousness. Thy mercies fail not, but are new every morning; of the least of them we are unworthy. What shall we render unto thee, O Lord, for all thy benefits! Awaken in our souls an earnest, thankful desire to take the cup of salvation offered us in Jesus Christ, and through him to call upon thy holy name, as the only hope of all the ends of the earth. Accept, we beseech thee, this our morning sacrifice of praise and thanksgiving, and hear the supplications and prayers which we desire, with humble adoration, to offer before thee.

We bless thee, O God, for thy preservation of us from the commencement of our lives to this present time, and especially for the rest and refreshment of the past night; that we were permitted once more to lie down in peace and take our rest, and that thou, O Lord, hast made us to dwell in safety. We thank thee for this and for all thy daily goodness to us and to all men; but chiefly do we bless thy holy name for the redemption of mankind in Jesus Christ; that in him mercy and truth are met together, righteousness and peace have kissed each other; that through his offering himself for our sins thou canst be just in justifying those who believe in him. We rejoice with thankfulness that he is the resurrection and the life; that, by rising from the dead, he became the first fruits of those who sleep in death; that when he ascended on high he led captivity captive, and gave gifts unto men—even the unspeakable gift of the Holy Ghost to be our comforter.

Grant, O merciful God, that we may not neglect this great salvation. For his sake who came to call, not the righteous, but sinners to repentance, behold us with pity and forgive us our sins. Though we have erred and strayed from thy righteous ways, have left undone what thy word requires, and often transgressed thy holy laws, cast us not away in thy displeasure; but sanctify our hearts, and work in us repentance towards thee, and faith towards the Lord Jesus Christ.

May we engage, O Lord, in the business and active duties of this day with a just sense of thy overruling providence, knowing that except the Lord build the house they labor in vain who build it: except the Lord keep the city, the watchman waketh in vain. It is but lost labor that we haste to rise up early, and late take rest, and eat the bread of carefulness: without thy blessing our labor will not prosper. Though we plant and water, thou only canst give increase. Wilt thou, O gracious Lord, direct and bless us in all we do. Take us, we beseech thee, and all that appertains to us, under thy guidance and protection. Keep us ever mindful of thy presence, and of the one thing needful. Prosper us in the business of our several stations, and give us grace to be diligent in every duty.

Give thy blessing to those who are set in authority over us; direct their counsels and strengthen their hands. May we remember that the powers which be are ordained of God, and that they bear not the sword in vain. Bless the people of our country with union, prosperity and peace. Send down thy blessings upon our neighbors, relatives, and friends. May they who are dear to us be dear to thee.

These things, and whatever thou seest to be fitting for us and for all men, we humbly ask in the name of Jesus Christ. *Amen.*

Friday Evening.

Almighty and everliving God, who art always more ready to hear than we to pray, and art wont to give more than we desire or deserve, pour down upon us the abundance of thy mercy, forgiving our manifold transgressions, and assisting us in our supplications and prayers. O thou God of mercy, absolve us from our offences and cleanse us from our sins. May it please thee to give us true repentance; to forgive us all our sins, negligences, and ignorances, and to endue us with the grace of thy Holy Spirit to amend our lives according to thy holy word, that we may obtain of thee, the God of all mercy, perfect remission and forgiveness.

To thee, O Lord, belong mercy and forgiveness, though we have rebelled against thee, and have not obeyed thy voice, to walk in the laws which thou hast set before us. Thou art glorious in holiness, fearful in praises, doing wonders; great in majesty, and great in mercy. Give us grace, in deep contrition, each one for himself, to say, God be merciful to me, a sinner.

Gracious is thy word, declaring that there is no condemnation to those who are in Christ Jesus; and that he is the end of the law for righteousness to those who believe. Grant unto us that righteousness which is by faith in the Son of God; and may thy Spirit bear witness with our spirit that we are thy children, accepted in the Beloved.

We thankfully acknowledge thy goodness in the blessings vouchsafed to us during the day past; in preserving our lives, continuing to us many blessings, and giving us time and means for knowing and doing thy will. Give us, we beseech thee, a more lively sense of thy benefits; awaken us to righteousness; turn thou us, and we shall be turned. Work in us to will and to do that which is pleasing in thy sight. May we put on the whole armor of God; fight the good fight of faith, and be conquerors, and more than conquerors, through him who loved us and gave himself for us. While thou art pleased, in thy patient goodness, to hold our soul in life, give us grace to serve thee better and love thee more. Do for us, we beseech thee, and work in us whatever shall be necessary and convenient for our present comfort and our eternal good. Take from us all sinful ignorance and hardness of heart, and preserve us from the deceitfulness of worldly things: may we pass the time of our sojourning here in thy faith and fear; and live so soberly, righteously, and godly in this present world, as becometh those who expect shortly to give an account to thee, who wilt judge all men according to their works. Make us a household fearing thee and working righteousness.

Hear our prayers and supplications for all mankind. Inspire, continually, the universal church with the spirit of truth, unity, and concord; and grant that all they who do confess thy holy name, may agree in the truth of thy word, and live in unity and godly love. May those in authority truly and impartially administer justice; and the people perform their respective duties, in all godly quietness. Give grace, O heavenly Father, to all bishops and other ministers, that they may, both by their life and doctrine, set forth thy true and lively word, and rightly and duly administer thy holy sacraments. And grant that all thy people, with meek heart and due reverence, may hear and receive thy word, and truly serve thee in holiness of life. Hear us, O Lord, for the sake of Jesus Christ. And to thee, our only God and Savior, be glory and majesty, dominion and power, both now and ever. *Amen.*

Saturday Morning.

O BLESSED Lord, who hast caused all Holy Scriptures to be written for our learning, grant that we may in such wise hear them, read, mark, learn, and inwardly digest them, that by patience and comfort of thy holy word, we may embrace and ever hold fast the blessed hope of everlasting life. Bless to our edification all that we read and hear from the

Holy Scriptures; may it be so grafted in our hearts as to bring forth in us the fruit of good living.

Thy statutes, O Lord, are right, and should rejoice the heart; thy judgments are true and righteous altogether. By them are thy servants taught, and in keeping of them there is great reward. Give us understanding, that we may keep thy law with our whole heart. Make us to go in the path of thy commandments, and to have a delight therein. Enlighten our minds with the truths of thy gospel and the doctrines of life, and help us to receive with meekness the ingrafted word, which is able to save our souls.

We are here assembled, O Lord, in thy name and presence, waiting upon thee at the footstool of thy grace. Cleanse the thoughts of our hearts by the inspiration of thy Holy Spirit: blot out our offences, and wash away our sins. Who can tell how oft he offendeth? O cleanse thou us from our secret faults. Keep us back, also, from presumptuous sins; let them not have dominion over us. May we never so presume upon thy mercy as lightly to esteem the riches of thy goodness, or neglect the work of our salvation. Knowing that the righteous are scarcely saved, may we give all diligence to make our calling and election sure. Cause us to be humble, and devoutly given to serve thee by good works.

Keep alive in us a true spirit of devotion, that while we draw nigh to thee with our lips, our heart may not be far from thee. Quicken us in the pursuit of spiritual things. May we never be so cumbered with worldly serving, as to neglect those things which are truly needful to our eternal good.

Dispose us, O Lord, we beseech thee, rightly to discharge the duties of this day. Watch over our paths; compass us about with thy favor; preserve us in our going out and coming in; and direct all our steps in the way of thy commandments. In all our dealings may we be honest and conscientious; diligent in the works of our calling; godly in our conversation; meek in our deportment; charitable and forgiving towards others; watchful over ourselves, and never forgetful of thee. Sanctify to us such pains and sorrows, and other afflictions, as thou mayest see it fitting to lay upon us; make us patient in suffering, and in all things resigned to thy holy will.

Make us diligent in using all the means of grace. Give us ears to hear the truth as it is in Jesus Christ, and hearts to be doers of the word, and not hearers only. May we be faithful in searching the Scriptures; and never go beyond the word of the Lord our God to do less or more.

May we abound in that love which is not in word and tongue, but in deed and truth; and show forth thy praise, not only with our lips, but in our lives, by letting our light so shine before men, that they may see our good works, and glorify thee, our heavenly Father. And when we shall have served thee in our generation, may we be gathered unto our fathers, having the testimony of a good conscience; in communion with thy church; in the confidence of a certain faith; in the comfort of a reasonable, religious, and holy hope, and in perfect charity with all mankind. We ask it, O heavenly Father, through the merits of Jesus Christ, our blessed Lord and Savior. *Amen.*

Saturday Evening.

O God, our Father who art in heaven; who dost from thy throne behold all that dwell upon the earth, and hast the hearts and the wants of all thy creatures before thee, we, the most unworthy of them, desire, this evening, to come before thee in prayer and supplication. But wherewith shall we come before thee, O Lord, or bow ourselves in thy presence, O thou Most High? We would come in the only prevailing name of thy blessed Son, in whom thou hast declared thyself well pleased. In the plenitude of thy mercy, thou hast sent him into the world, not to condemn the world, but to save it, and hast made him unto us wisdom and righteousness, and sanctification and redemption. In his name, O thou Father of our spirits, and trusting in his merits, do we present ourselves before thee, beseeching thee to have respect unto the prayer of thy servants. Hear thou in heaven, thy dwelling-place, and when thou hearest, for Christ's sake, forgive.

Assist us mercifully, O Lord, in these our supplications and prayers, that we may approach thee with reverence, and obtain our requests. Dispose our hearts and direct our ways towards the attainment of everlasting salvation. In all the changes, temptations, and other trials of this mortal state, may we ever be defended by thy most gracious and ready help. May we be of the number of thy peculiar people, zealous of good works, doing justly, loving mercy, walking humbly with thee, and adorning the doctrine of God our Savior in all things.

Make us thankful, O God, for all the blessings which we enjoy, both temporal and spiritual. Help us to discern the hand of thy providence in all that befalls us. In prosperity and adversity; whether we abound or suffer need; may we never forget that the Lord rules; that thou art righteous in all thy ways, and good to all thy creatures.

We desire of thee, O Lord God, our heavenly Father, who art the Giver of all goodness, to send thy grace unto us and to all people, that we may worship thee, serve thee, and obey thee as we ought to do. And we beseech thee to send us all things that are needful, both for our souls and bodies: and that thou wilt be merciful unto us, and forgive us our sins; and be pleased to save and defend us in all dangers, both of soul and body: and that thou wilt keep us from all sin and wickedness, from our spiritual enemies, and from everlasting death.

During the week which is now near its close, many of our fellow-men have departed this life, and entered into their eternal state: we yet survive, monuments of thy forbearing mercy. While our life is continued, may we live to thee. Prepare us for the duties, and for the right observance of the Lord's day which is approaching, that we may sanctify it as holy unto thee, and a season sacred to thy worship. Be with the assemblies of thy worshipping people; meet them in mercy, and visit them with thy salvation. May all who seek thee be joyful and glad in thee, and find by happy experience, that one day in thy courts is better than a thousand spent in vanity and sin.

May the close of each day remind us of that night near at hand, in which no man can work; and stimulate us to do, with all our might, what thou hast appointed our hand to do. Protect us, O Lord, this night, that no evil may befall us, nor plague come nigh our dwelling; watch over us for good, and keep us in safety. May we go to our rest in charity with all men; and may we rise refreshed, disposed and strengthened, to do thy will. We ask this for Christ's sake. And unto thee, O God, who art able to do for us abundantly more than we can ask or think, be glory in the church, by Jesus Christ, throughout all ages, world without end. *Amen.*

Second Week. Sunday Morning.

O Lord God, who art glorious in holiness and power, and whose goodness is infinite, thou art worthy of all adoration and praise. The heavens and the earth are full of the majesty of thy glory. The holy church throughout all the world doth acknowledge thee as the Father of our spirits, the Redeemer of the world, and the Sanctifier of the faithful. And with thy saints on earth, and with all the company of heaven, we would laud and magnify thy glorious name.

Wonderful art thou, O God, in thy adorable perfections. When we consider the heavens, the works of thy fingers,—the moon and the stars, which thou hast ordained, what is man, that thou art mindful of him! or the sons of men, that thou visitest them with unnumbered mercies! We are vile and sinful; it is of thy mercy that we are not consumed; that our lives, unprofitable to thee, are continued from day to day, and from one week to another.

We thank thee, O God, for the comforts continually bestowed upon us, thy unworthy creatures: and chiefly for thy mercy in Jesus Christ. We bless thy holy name that thou didst so love the world as to give thine only begotten Son, that whosoever believeth in him should not perish, but have everlasting life. We bless thee for the means and ordinances which are mercifully appointed for our benefit, as the channels of thy grace, and for building us up in a holy religious faith.

Make us duly thankful that the Son of man is Lord of the Sabbath, and that we are brought to see again its weekly return. This is the day which the Lord hath made, which he hath sanctified to himself, by rising from the dead: may we rejoice and be glad in it. Save us now, O Lord, we beseech thee; send us now prosperity.

We beseech thee, O God, mercifully to direct and aid us in all the duties suitable to this day, according to thy gracious purpose in its appointment. May thy Spirit be with all who unite in thy holy worship. Sanctify their affections and help them to withdraw their thoughts from worldly cares, to hold their conversation in heaven, and to worship thee in spirit and in truth. May the power of godliness possess their hearts. Make us sensible, O Lord, how great are the privileges of thy sanctuary: how blessed it is to enter into thy gates with thanksgiving, and into thy courts with praise; to fall down and kneel before the Lord our Maker.

We beseech thee of thy compassionate goodness to pity those who, by sickness or other causes, are deprived of the privilege of uniting with thy people in thy house of prayer. May they consider that thy gracious presence is not confined to temples made with hands: that the hearts and the wants of thy creatures are all before thee, and that thy mercy is over all thy works. Help them, in faith and hope, to raise their souls in prayer and praise to thee. Comfort them with a sense of thy goodness, and give them peace.

Let thy Spirit, O Lord, be with those of us who shall be permitted this day to meet with thy people in the place of thy public worship. Fill our hearts with seriousness and devout affections, and make us attentive to the duties of thy house. Give us, we entreat thee, repentance unto life, and make us joyful in thy house of prayer. Dispose us, in an honest and good heart, to hear the gospel of our Savior Christ, and to receive the words of eternal life.

Wilt thou, O gracious Lord, accompany thy word with power, and adapt it to the wants of all who hear it. May sinners be awakened to righteousness and flee from the wrath to come. May they seek thee while thou mayst be found and call upon thee while thou art near. May the wicked forsake his way, and the unrighteous man his thoughts. Alarm the careless; comfort and help the weak-hearted, and reclaim those who have erred from the paths of truth. May we never be forgetful hearers, but doers of thy work, manifesting in our lives that we are the disciples of Jesus Christ. May we know him and the power of his resurrection: as he was raised up by the glory of the Father, may we also walk in newness of life.

Make us duly thankful for the Holy Scriptures written for our learning, and for the religious privileges, and all the means of knowledge and grace which we enjoy. Help us, O Lord, so to estimate and to use these blessings, that we may become wise unto salvation. May we remember the Lord's day to keep it holy, and have grace to profit in the religion of our Savior, Christ.

Look, we beseech thee, with thy favor and blessing upon all Sunday schools, and upon that especially with which we are more particularly connected. Give thy blessing to the teachers who are occupied in this labor of love, and remember them for good. Bless the children and youth who attend upon their instruction. Help them to receive in their hearts and to evince in their lives the precepts of thy word, and the principles of the doctrines of Christ. Open their understandings, and incline their ear unto thy testimonies. Graft in their tender minds a religious faith and a godly fear, and nourish them with the doctrines of life. Help them so to proceed in all virtue and godliness of living, that finally they may be inheritors of thine everlasting kingdom.

Assist us, O Lord, with thy heavenly grace; direct our hearts and dispose our ways to the attainment of everlasting salvation; and in all the pains and perils of this mortal life, may we ever be defended by thy most gracious and ready help, through Jesus Christ our Lord. *Amen.*

Second Week. Sunday Evening.

ALMIGHTY and most merciful Father, we desire once more to bow before thee, with reverence and humility, and with a thankful sense of thy goodness. It is a good thing to give thanks unto thee, O Lord, and to praise thy name; to show forth thy loving kindness in the morning, and thy faithfulness in the night season. A pleasant thing it is to be thankful for thy mercies; to acknowledge thy goodness, and to adore thy perfections. How manifold are thy works; in wisdom hast thou made them all. The heavens declare thy glory, and the firmament showeth thy handy work. Thou hast appointed the moon for certain seasons, and the sun knoweth his going down. Day unto day uttereth speech, and night unto night showeth knowledge.

But far surpassing all the glory of the starry heavens is the Sun of Righteousness, who hath risen upon this sinful world with healing in his wings. We adore thee for the gift of a divine Savior; that thou, who didst command the light to shine out of darkness, hast shined in the hearts of thy people, to give the light of the knowledge of the glory of God, in the face of Jesus Christ. Grant that we may walk as the children of light, and while it is called to-day, before that night cometh in which no man can work.

Sanctify to us all the means of grace, and especially thy appointment of a holy day of rest. Make us duly thankful that we have been favored again with its weekly return, and sensible that one day in thy courts is better than a thousand spent in vanity and sin. Help us to profit in seasons of grace. May we not be of those who are ever learning, and never able to come to the knowledge of the truth; but receive with meekness and with joy the ingrafted word, which is able to save the soul.

Enter not into judgment with thy servants, O Lord; but in mercy pardon our neglect of thy word, and our having profited so little by Sabbaths and ordinances and other means and blessings. Awaken in our minds a lively sense of thy goodness, and grant that we may ever hereafter serve and please thee in newness of life.

Give us hearts, O Lord, to pity and to pray for those who need the blessings which we possess. Extend the light of the gospel and the saving truths of thy word to all the families of the earth. Be merciful to those who are still sitting in darkness and the shadow of death. Send, we beseech thee, O gracious Lord, send laborers into that great harvest, the heathen world. If thou speak the word great will be the company of the preachers. At thy command let their sound go out into all the earth, and their words unto the ends of the world. O may thy kingdom come with power, and truth and righteousness increase, till thy will shall be done on earth, as it is in heaven.

And grant that the kingdom of God may be within us; that the word of Christ may dwell in us richly, in all wisdom. May thy Spirit convince us of sin, of righteousness, and of judgment, and excite us to diligence, watchfulness, and prayer. May that mind be in us, which was also in Jesus Christ, that it may be our meat and drink to do thy will, and that we may love one another, as he has given us commandment. May the fruits of the Spirit so appear and abound in us, that we may adorn the doctrine of God our Savior in all things. Grant, O Lord, that the prayers which have been, during this day, offered unto thee may be graciously heard. What prayer and supplication soever has been made by any man or by all thy people, hear thou in heaven thy dwelling-place, and forgive, and do and give to every man according to his ways and his need; for thou, O Lord, knowest the hearts and the wants of all the children of men. And grant, O Lord, that thy word, which has been read and preached this day, may be a savor of life to those who have heard it. May they not be forgetful hearers, but look into the perfect law of liberty, and so faithfully continue therein, that they may be blest in their deed. Gracious art thou, O Lord, and long-suffering: all day long dost thou stretch out thy hand unto a disobedient and gainsaying people. O let not the means of knowledge and of grace which we receive rise up in judgment and condemn us. While we call thee Lord, may we do the things which thou commandest, and daily grow in grace and in the knowledge and love of God.

And wilt thou bless to our edification all the religious privileges which we have this day enjoyed. O may thy counsels and thy precepts, and the revelations of thy mercy, take root in our hearts and be fruitful in our lives. May we never neglect the great salvation which thy gospel brings to our ears. While our lives, through thy goodness, shall be prolonged, may we live to thee. Take us and ours, O heavenly Father, under thy care and keeping, and fit and prepare us, we humbly beseech thee, for that eternal Sabbath and heavenly rest which remains for the people of God. May every passing day and week bring us nearer to those everlasting joys which thou hast promised to those who love thee. Keep us this night, both outwardly in our bodies, and inwardly in our souls; preserve us from all adversities and evil thoughts, and grant that we may rise refreshed, and be strengthened and disposed to do thy will, through Jesus Christ, our Lord and Savior. *Amen.*

Second Week. Monday Morning.

ALMIGHTY and everlasting God, who dost govern all things in heaven and on earth, mercifully hear our supplications and prayers. Make us truly sensible of our wants and of thy goodness, and may thy Spirit help our infirmities and make intercession for us. Grant us, we beseech thee, the spirit to think and to do always such things as are right, that we, who cannot do any thing good without thee, may, by thy aid, be enabled to live according to thy will.

We would draw nigh, in full assurance of faith, unto thee, who hast graciously promised that they who ask through faith in Christ shall receive; that they who seek shall find. We approach thy gracious throne, not trusting in our own righteousness, but in thy manifold and great mercies, beseeching thee to behold us in love, not weighing our merits, but pardoning our offences. We approach thee in the name of our High Priest, who gave himself a sacrifice for our sins.

If thou shouldst mark iniquities, O Lord, who should stand? but there is mercy with thee, that thou mayest be feared, and with thee is plenteous redemption. We beseech thee to wash us from our iniquity, and cleanse us from our sin. Enter not into judgment with thy sinful creatures; for in thy sight shall no man living be justified. Being justified by faith, may we have peace with thee our God, through Jesus Christ.

We acknowledge, O Lord, that of ourselves we are not able to walk according to thy will; that from thee all holy desires, good counsels, and just works proceed. Grant us the constant assistance of thy Holy Spirit, that we may please thee both in will and deed. May we ever be found in the way of duty, fearing God and working righteousness. O may thy truth shine in our hearts and give us the light of the knowledge of thy glory, in the face of Jesus Christ. Whatever may be our state or occupation, help us to walk in the way of thy commandments, and preserve us from all sinful affection for worldly things. Strengthen us with might by thy Spirit: raise our hearts and desires to heavenly things, and dispose all our ways towards the attainment of everlasting salvation. In all the changing scenes and the various perils of this mortal life, may we put our whole trust in thy providential care.

We beseech thee, O God, to keep constantly in our minds a lively remembrance of thy mercy to us in Jesus Christ, who came into this world to seek and to save that which was lost; who made himself of no reputation, took upon him the form of a servant, and became obedient unto death, to obtain for us eternal life. Make us humble after the example of his humility. May the spirit of love which was in him be also in us. May we die to sin and rise again unto righteousness, continually mortifying all our evil and corrupt affections, and daily proceeding in all virtue and godliness of living.

And wilt thou, O Lord, receive our supplications and prayers for all for whom we ought to pray. Bless our rulers and magistrates, giving them grace to execute justice and to maintain truth. We pray for those who are visited with sorrows, and all who are afflicted in mind, body, or estate, beseeching thee to comfort and relieve them, according as they have need. May it please thee to preserve all who travel by land or by water: may thy presence be with them to shield them from danger and all manner of evil. Be thou in all things their conductor and guide, making their way prosperous and their business successful.

We ask thy blessing upon our neighbors, relatives, and friends, and for those especially who desire our prayers. Do thou, the God of all mercy and grace, who knowest what they desire and what they need, do for them, and work in them whatever is best for their present comfort and for their final good. Help us, O Lord, to love and to do good unto all men, and especially may we love those who love the Lord Jesus Christ, and for his sake delight in doing them good.

Give us hearts to sympathize in the joys and the sorrows of our brethren,—to weep with them who weep and to rejoice with those who rejoice. May we feel compassion for all who need the blessings which we enjoy. Though silver and gold we have none, such as we have, our prayers, and sympathy, and love, may we gladly give. Wilt thou, O merciful God, succor, bless, and comfort all who are in danger, necessity, and tribulation. May they who are visited with sorrow despise not thy chastening, nor faint under thy rebuke; may their affliction, through thy blessing, work in them a far more exceeding and eternal weight of glory.

Let thy grace, O Lord, and thy blessing be with us through the day on which we have entered. Preserve us from sin and from all manner of danger. Vouchsafe, we beseech thee, to direct, sanctify, and govern, both our hearts and bodies, in the ways of thy laws, and in the works of thy commandments, that, through thy most mighty protection, we may be preserved in body and soul through our Lord and Savior Jesus Christ. *Amen.*

Second Week. Monday Evening.

Almighty and immortal God, the aid of all who need, and the helper of all who flee to thee for succor, let thy merciful ears be open to us, thy unworthy creatures, and hearken to the supplications which we would offer in the name of Jesus Christ. May we come unto thee duly sensible of our unworthiness, relying on his merits for pardon and acceptance. We have erred and strayed from thy righteous ways: we have followed too much the evil devices and desires of our own hearts, and have often offended against thy holy laws. Thou hast taught us, O heavenly Father, that when the wicked man turneth away from his wickedness that he hath committed and doeth that which is lawful and right, he shall save his soul alive. Help us, O Lord, to turn from our evil ways, and to do all those good works which thou hast ordained that thy people should walk in them. Hide thy face from our sins and blot out all our iniquities. The sacrifices acceptable to thee, our God, are a broken spirit; a contrite heart thou wilt not despise. O make us truly contrite, and grant us repentance unto life. Give us grace to resist temptation, and to mortify every evil desire. Cleanse the thoughts of our hearts, by the inspiration of thy Holy Spirit.

Give us hearts, O Lord, to be thankful for thy manifold goodness to us and to all men. Make us thankful that we live in a land where thou art known and worshipped: that the gospel of salvation in Jesus Christ is taught amongst us, and that we have the great privilege of searching the Scriptures, and knowing the certainty of those things wherein we have been instructed. We thank thee, O God, for the ordinances of religion, for the means of grace, and for all the privileges of thy sanctuary. Give us grace, we beseech thee, so to use them, that we may be truly members of Christ, children of God, and inheritors of thy heavenly kingdom. Give us the comforting assurance of thy favor and goodness towards us; that we are members incorporate in the mystical body of thy Son, which is the blessed company of all faithful people, and are also heirs through hope of thy everlasting kingdom, by the merits of the most precious death and passion of thy dear Son. And we humbly beseech thee, O heavenly Father, so to assist us with thy grace, that we may continue in that holy fellowship, and ever live to thy glory and praise.

We beseech thee, O God, to raise our hopes and our desires above the things of time and sense, to the high and holy place where the Lord our Savior reigns. By patient continuance in well doing, may we seek for honor, glory, and immortality in the world to come. Give us that faith which is the substance of things hoped for and the evidence of things not seen. Increase in us faith, and hope, and charity; and that we may obtain what thou dost promise, make us to love that which thou dost command. Grant us the influence of thy Spirit, to convince us of sin, to awaken us to righteousness, and fit us to enjoy thy presence in thy heavenly kingdom. Put away from us all hurtful things, and give us those which are profitable.

Grant that we may be diligent and faithful in searching the Scriptures. Open our understanding, that we may know and receive what they testify of Christ, and dispose us to hear and receive the doctrines of eternal life.

Grant that we may do all in our power to extend the knowledge of Christ and the means of grace, and to promote the practice of pure and undefiled religion. And chiefly may we do it by our own good example, and by living a life of faith in the Son of God. May the truth, and power, and excellency of the gospel be in our life and conduct so displayed, that they who see it may glorify thee, and the ignorance of foolish men be put to silence. Enlighten our minds, increase our faith, elevate our hopes, and so awaken our zeal, that we may run and not be weary. May we never dishonor the religion of Christ, nor put a stumbling-block in the way of others, but be holy in all manner of conversation, and show forth thy truth and thy goodness, both with our lips and in our lives.

Make us continually sensible that we are stewards of the good things committed to our care, and are accountable to thee for the use we make of them. O may we never be unjust stewards, nor bury thy talent in the earth. Preserve us, we beseech thee, from idleness; may we be profitably employed in what is useful to ourselves or others; not slothful in business, but fervent in spirit, serving the Lord and redeeming the time.

And we now, O Lord, would commit ourselves and all that concerns us into thy hands. Defend us, while we sleep, from every evil to which we may be exposed. Shouldst thou call us hence this night, may it be to thyself in a better world. If thou shalt mercifully preserve us till the morning light, may we rise with thankful hearts, and devote to thee the life thou givest. We ask these favors in the name and through the merits of our blessed Savior, Jesus Christ. *Amen.*

Second Week. Tuesday Morning.

O HOLY, just, and merciful God, who art always more ready to hear than men to pray, look down, we beseech thee, with thy favor and blessing upon us, thy dependent creatures, and accept the renewal of our morning sacrifice of praise and prayer. Wonderful art thou, O Lord, in goodness, and patience, and long-suffering. Impress upon our minds a just and lively sense of thy mercies to us and to all the children of men.

We thank thee, O heavenly Father, that our lives are still preserved; that we were kept in safety through the silent watches of the night past; and that we are brought, encompassed with many blessings, to see the light of another day, and are permitted again to lift our hearts and voice to thee, in humble adoration. We thank thee for all thy favors of providence and grace, sensible that all our enjoyments are the fruits of thy bounty. And chiefly, O Lord, do we desire, with thankful adoration, to bless thy name, that thou hast so loved the world, as to send into it thy only Son to be our Savior, and hast graciously promised that they who come unto thee, through faith in him, shall not perish in their sins, but have eternal life. We thank thee that our lot is fallen in a Christian land; that the Holy Scriptures, containing the revelation of thy mercy in Jesus Christ, are in our hands; that the gospel is preached in our ears, and that means, and ordinances, and opportunities are still given, to instruct us in righteousness, and to build us up in thy holy faith.

Give us grace, we beseech thee, to be duly thankful for these and for all thy mercies, and to show forth our thankfulness by making a right use of them. Open our minds that we may understand the doctrines of Christ, and the duty of Christians. Do thou, who alone canst change the hearts and govern the affections of sinful men, create and make in us new and contrite hearts; sanctify our affections and our desires, and direct all our ways towards the attainment of everlasting salvation. Preserve us from self-righteousness, and pride, and from envy, hatred and malice, and all uncharitableness. Purify our hearts by the indwelling of thy Spirit, and work in us to will and to do whatever will promote thy glory, and our own and others' salvation. Give us that repentance which is not to be repented of, and that faith which renews the heart, worketh by love, and overcometh the world; and grant that we may so pass through the changes and perils of this world that we may finally attain to everlasting life.

And we beseech thee to extend thy mercy to all mankind. May they who are now living in sin be awakened to righteousness, and in a time accepted turn to thee, with penitence and prayer. O may they not perish in unbelief, but seek thee while thou mayest be found, and call upon thee while thou art near. Make with them, O blessed Lord, an everlasting covenant, even the sure mercies of David. Hasten the time when the light of the gospel shall shine in the darkest places of the earth; when all nations shall bow down before thee, and the heathen become thine inheritance.

Be merciful, O Lord, to those humble, penitent souls, whom thy Spirit has convinced of sin, and of judgment, and who are inquiring what they must do to be saved. Wilt thou convince them of righteousness, and reveal to their souls the comforts of thy mercy in Jesus Christ, that they may go forward, rejoicing to bear his cross. Direct them by the counsels of thy heavenly wisdom, and encourage them with a just view of thy promises of spiritual aid. Give unto those who ask; let them who seek find; open the door of thy heavenly kingdom to those who knock, giving them pardon and peace.

May it please thee to strengthen such as do stand and to comfort and help the weak-hearted. Continue thy mercy to those whose hearts have been renewed by a living faith. Do thou, who hast begun a good work in them, perform it until the day of Jesus Christ. Stablish, strengthen, and settle them in the faith which was once delivered to the saints, and fix their affections on things above. And while the door of thy mercy is yet open, may every sinner flee from the wrath to come, and lay hold on eternal life.

And wilt thou, O gracious Lord, be merciful to this family and household. Our hearts are in thy hand, and our wants and our sins are all before thee. Cause us to be penitent and submissive to thy will, and give us such knowledge and sense of thy goodness, and our duty, that while we live we may live to thee. Give us also, we pray thee, such temporal comforts and good things of this world as to thy unerring wisdom may seem fitting, and give us grace rightly to use them. Direct and bless us in all we do, by the aid and guidance of thy Holy Spirit. May we go on from strength to strength till we are crowned with victory. Help us to fight the good fight of faith, and to finish our course with joy. O may we at last receive the crown of righteousness, which the Lord, the righteous Judge, shall give unto all them who love his appearing. Grant that our whole spirit, and soul, and body, may be preserved pure and blameless, unto the coming of our Lord Jesus Christ, in whose name we offer these our humble supplications. *Amen.*

Second Week. Tuesday Evening.

RIGHTEOUS, adorable, and eternal God, in whom we live and have our being, and to whose merciful forbearance we owe it that our lives are yet prolonged, we thank thee for thy great goodness. Praised be thy name, that we are permitted once more to assemble around our family altar, and offer thee the incense of thankful hearts. The day is thine and the night is thine. Thou makest the outgoings of the morning and the evening to rejoice. The heavens declare thy glory, and the earth is filled with the riches of thy goodness. It is of thy mercy, and because thy compassions fail not, that we are permitted still to call upon thy holy name.

But wherewith shall we, thy unworthy creatures, come before thee? We beseech thee, O heavenly Father, in the name and through the merits of our blessed Savior Jesus Christ, to forgive our sins, and favorably with mercy to hear our prayers. Thou knowest, O Lord, our necessities before we ask in prayer, and our ignorance of what we ought to pray for. May thy Spirit help our infirmities and teach us how to pray. Let the words of our mouth and the desire of our heart be acceptable in thy sight, through the worthiness of Jesus Christ, who is our strength and our Redeemer. Grant that we, who are the creatures of thy power, may become the subjects of thy grace.

The heart of man is deceitful and desperately wicked. Who can tell how often he offendeth? Cleanse us, we beseech thee, from our secret faults. Search us, O God, and know our hearts; prove us and examine our thoughts. Look if there be any way of wickedness in us, and lead us in the way of eternal life. O deal not with us according to our sins, nor reward us as our transgressions deserve.

To whom can we go for pardon and peace but to thee, O Lord, who alone hast the words of eternal life? but to thee, who hast graciously promised, that if the wicked forsake his way and the unrighteous man his thoughts, and turn to thee, thou wilt have mercy upon him, and abundantly pardon? We beseech thee to pardon our sins and renew a right spirit within us. Grant us that righteousness which is by faith in Jesus Christ. Sanctify and govern our hearts and our bodies, in the ways of thy laws and in the works of thy commandments, and grant that our hopes and our desires may centre in Jesus Christ, our only Savior, and our souls be united with him, in a holy faith, as branches are with the vine. May he be made unto us wisdom, and righteousness, and sanctification, and redemption, and all our glorying be in him. Give us grace to cast away the works of darkness and to put upon us the armor of light, while we sojourn in this state of mortality, in which our Savior once visited us in great humility. And in the last day, when he shall come again, in glorious majesty, to judge the world, grant that we may rise to life immortal, through him, who died for our sins and rose again for our justification.

Hear our prayers, O Lord, for all mankind; may the light of thy truth extend through the world, and increase, until all the nations of the earth shall rejoice in thy salvation. Bless all thy churches and all thy people, and those especially with whom we are connected in the fellowship of the gospel. May Zion be in prosperity; peace be within her walls, and plenteousness within her palaces. And may the kingdoms of the earth become the kingdoms of the Lord and of his Christ.

And we pray thee, O Lord, to remember, and

help us to remember the afflicted and distressed. Hearken to the sighing of the needy; cause the widow's heart to sing for joy, and in thee may the fatherless find mercy. Give to them who mourn in Zion beauty for ashes, and the garment of praise for the spirit of heaviness. Comfort all who are visited with affliction. Sanctify their sorrows, and raise their minds from the world to thee.

Look in mercy upon those who are visited with sickness and bodily distress. May they bow with submission under thy rod, knowing who hath appointed it, and through thy grace make all the improvement which thou requirest. Help them to glorify thee, whether it be by life or by death, knowing that to live is Christ, and to die is gain, to those who die in the Lord.

May we remember them who are in bonds as bound with them, and them who suffer adversity as being ourselves also in the flesh. Let thy goodness, in preserving us from many evils which others suffer, make us humble and compassionate, and thankful to thee, who makest one to differ from another and art equally good to all.

We beseech thee to comfort and to strengthen all such as are fearful of thy terrors and distrustful of thy mercy. The bruised reed thou wilt not break; a broken and contrite heart thou wilt not despise. May all who mourn for their sins be comforted through thy mercy in Jesus Christ. In the light of thy reconciled countenance, may they dwell in peace and rejoice in hope. And grant, O Lord, we may not, for any troubles of life, or allurements of this world, lose our confidence in thee, nor place it in any other.

Make us thankful for the mercies of the day past, and that we are yet spared to speak of thy goodness. Preserve us, we pray thee, through the perils of this night. Let no evil happen unto us, nor plague come nigh our dwelling. May we lie down in peace and take our rest, and through thy mercy rise again in safety. And while we live may we live to thee, through Jesus Christ, our Lord and Savior. *Amen.*

Second Week. Wednesday Morning.

ALMIGHTY and immortal God, the Creator and Preserver of all mankind; the Giver of all spiritual grace and the Author of everlasting life, we desire humbly to look this morning unto thee, as our Father, who art in heaven, and the hope of all the ends of the earth. The eyes of all wait upon thee, and thou givest them their meat in due season; thou openest thy hand and fillest all things living with plenteousness. Through thy goodness are we again permitted to unite in praising thee for thy goodness, and in asking for those things which we daily need. And may thy Spirit help us to ask for such good things as to thy wisdom it may seem fitting to bestow. We acknowledge that we are unworthy to ask or to receive of thee any thing good. Our sins deserve thy displeasure; we have followed the evil devices and desires of our own hearts. Work in us, we beseech thee, a hearty contrition, that we may obtain, through Jesus Christ, perfect remission and forgiveness.

With thankful hearts we would bless thy name, that to thee, O Lord, belong mercy and forgiveness; that through thy love to mankind, and the redemption that is in Jesus Christ, thou canst be just in justifying them who believe in him. We bless thee that life and immortality are brought to light in his gospel, and for all thy goodness and loving kindness to us and to all mankind. We thank thee that our lot has fallen where his gospel is preached and its ordinances administered, and that we may know from childhood those Scriptures, which, if truly received, will make us wise unto salvation. We thank thee for the ministry of those who are ordained to preach thy word; for the means of grace, and for all the privileges of thy sanctuary.

Give us hearts to be duly thankful that we are brought in safety to see the light of another day, and that we again have the opportunity of renewing our humble sacrifice of praise and prayer. We beseech thee to incline our hearts unto thy testimonies, and to guide our steps in the way of thy precepts. May we love the things which thou commandest, and strive for those which thou dost promise. Give us just views of ourselves, what we are and what we need. Do for us and work in us that which thou shalt see fitting for our present comfort and eternal good. Increase our faith, enliven our hope, and shed abroad thy love in our hearts. Give us grace to follow after that charity which is the bond of perfectness; which suffereth long and is kind; which envieth not and vaunteth not itself; is not easily provoked and thinketh no evil. May we never rejoice in iniquity, but rejoice in the truth.

And accept, O Lord, our prayers for all our fellow-men, that they may be subjects of thy mercy and obedient to thy will. Bless thy faithful people, wherever they are dispersed throughout the world; peace be on them, and mercy, and upon the Israel of God. Grant that, by the operation of thy Spirit, all Christians may be so joined together in unity and love, that they may be a holy temple acceptable unto thee. Prosper thy word wherever it is spoken and send it where it is not heard, that thy way be known through all the earth, thy saving health among all nations. Let the people whom thou hast redeemed praise thee, O Lord; let all the people praise thee. May the borders of Zion be enlarged, till all the kingdoms of the earth become the kingdoms of the Lord and of his Christ.

Grant that the ministers of thy word may be faithful stewards of thy mysteries and the instruments of converting men to God, and of saving themselves and others. Open to them an effectual door of usefulness. Give them, we beseech thee, utterance, that they may open their mouth with boldness to make known the mystery of the gospel: may they rightly divide the word, and give to all their portion of meat in due season; and may their own lives bear testimony to the truths which they teach. And grant that all who are desiring or designed for the office of that sacred ministry, may, by thy sanctifying Spirit, be prepared for a faithful and successful discharge of its duties. Prepare them to labor in word and doctrine, in season and out of season, and to spend and be spent in thy work. And give us grace so to account of them as stewards of thy mysteries. To those who are faithful in word and doctrine, may we render double honor.

Behold, O Lord, in thy mercy, Israel after the flesh. Remove the veil of ignorance which blinds the mind of the Jews: may they see and know that Jesus is the Christ, the Son of the living God, and the only Savior of the world; and may they seek with penitence and faith Him whom their fathers rejected. Pity that blindness which has in part happened unto Israel, and hasten on the time when, as the natural branches, they shall be grafted into their own olive tree; when the fulness of the Gentiles shall come in, and all Israel shall be saved.

We pray for thy blessing upon our churches—upon our country—upon our rulers, and upon all who are in authority. Give them wisdom and grace, that they may execute justice and maintain truth; and that thy people, being secured by the ministration of wise and equal laws, may serve thee in all godly quietness.

Pardon, O Lord, our sins and accept our prayers, granting us those good things which we are not worthy to ask, but in the name and through the merits of our Lord and Savior Jesus Christ. *Amen.*

Second Week. Wednesday Evening.

GREAT and eternal God, the infinite Jehovah, who only hast immortality, and dwellest in the light which no man can approach unto, we humbly look unto thee as the Father of our spirits, and the Giver of all good. Whom have we in heaven but thee, and who is there on earth that we can desire in comparison of thee! Thou alone hast the words of eternal life, and art the hope of all the ends of the world. Thou hast laid the foundation of the earth, and the heavens are the work of thy hand. They shall perish, but thou shalt endure, and thy years shall have no end. Though thy dwelling is in the heavens, and thy glory above them, yet thou dost humble thyself to behold the things that are in the earth: thou raisest the poor out of the dust; thou hearest the prayer of the weak and destitute.

Let thine ears, we beseech thee, be attentive to our humble supplication. We would approach thee, O Lord, not trusting in our own righteousness, but in thy manifold and great mercies, and in the merits of our Mediator, Jesus Christ. May thy blessed Spirit aid our devotions, sanctify our hearts, and raise our affections from this world to thee. Open thou our lips, that our mouth may show forth thy praise.

Make us deeply sensible that thou art in heaven and we upon earth; that thou art wise, and just, and good, while we are blind, and frail, and sinful. With humble reverence may we rejoice that thou art a God hearing prayer and forgiving sin; and art more ready to give good gifts than we to ask. Extend to us, O Lord, thy pardoning mercy, forgiving our multiplied offences, and giving us those good things, which of ourselves we are not worthy to pray for. Be merciful unto us and bless us, and cause thy face to shine upon us. Grant that thy way may be known upon earth; thy saving health among all nations. Let the people praise thee, O Lord; let all the people praise thee.

Fill us with hope and joy in believing thy promises in Jesus Christ: may we esteem all things but loss for the excellency of the knowledge of him. May we know him and the power of his resurrection, and be in all things conformed to his image, knowing that he who hath the Son hath life, and shall never come into condemnation. May we be followers of God, as dear children, and be perfect in love, as our Father in heaven is perfect. Give us grace to put on, as the elect of God, bowels of mercy, kindness, humbleness of mind, meekness and long-suffering, forbearing one another, and forgiving one another. Teach us what thou wilt have us to do, and make us ready to every good work.

We beseech thee, O Lord, to preserve us from all self-righteousness, and vain reliance on the merits of what we do. May we never forget that by grace we are saved, through faith, and that not of ourselves it is the gift of God. Give us, we beseech thee, a right view of that living faith in Christ which does not make void, but establishes the law; which renews the heart, and is fruitful in good works. May we ever remember that in Jesus Christ neither circumcision availeth any thing nor uncircumcision, but faith which worketh by love and keepeth the commandments of God. May we not deceive ourselves, by trusting in the Savior, while we neglect his great salvation; by calling him Lord, while we do not the things which he commands. O suffer us not to perish amidst the means designed to save us. May we never be weary in doing well. Though faint may we still be pursuing, pressing towards the mark for the prize of the high calling of God in Christ Jesus. Let our trust and our hope be ever in him. As our Prophet, may we hearken to his word; as our Priest, let our trust be in the merits of his one sacrifice for sins; and as our King, may we faithfully observe his precepts.

Help us, O Lord, to love our neighbor as we love ourselves, and to perform faithfully every duty which we owe to others. Preserve us from envy, selfishness and pride, and from all manner of uncharitableness. Give us grace to bear with patience and a forgiving spirit the faults of men, and the injuries of those who may do us wrong, not rendering evil for evil, but endeavoring to overcome evil with good. Let the spirit which was in our Savior Christ, his love and forbearance and long-suffering, be also in us. As he loved us, may we also love one another. Though pains or sorrows should be our portion, let us always rejoice in the good and prosperity of other people, and be ever ready to praise thee for thy goodness, and for all the benefits bestowed upon our fellow-men. Especially give us grace to rejoice in their hopes of salvation; in their repentance, and faith, and obedience to thy holy word.

We beseech thee, O Lord, mercifully to accept this our evening sacrifice. Give us hearts to be thankful for all thy goodness, and especially for the favors of the day past; and we humbly ask for thy protection through this night. Preserve us, we pray thee, from every evil; refresh our bodies with needful rest; and may we rise in the morning with thankful hearts disposed to do thy will. We ask these things in the name of our only Savior, Jesus Christ. *Amen.*

And to the God of our salvation, the Father, the Son, and the Holy Ghost, be ascribed the kingdom, and the power, and the glory, forever and ever. *Amen.*

Second Week. Thursday Morning.

ADORABLE and everliving God, whose throne is the highest heaven and the earth thy footstool, we desire this morning to raise our heart and our voice to thee, as the Father of mercies; the giver of all good; the God of all comfort. Thou dost according to thy will in the armies of heaven and among the inhabitants of the earth. The day is thine and the night is thine, and as thou art graciously pleased to renew our time, and our strength, and our comforts, help us to renew our purposes to walk in the way of thy commandments. May our souls praise thee, who saveth our life from destruction, and crowneth us with mercy and loving kindness. Do thou, who hast brought us safely to the beginning of this day, defend us from its perils, and grant that all we do may be ordered by thy governance and righteous in thy sight. Whether we eat, or drink, or whatsoever we do, may it be to thy glory in Jesus Christ.

Let our prayer, we beseech thee, come before thee as the morning incense. We trust not in our own righteousness, but in thy manifold and great mercies. We are not worthy to appear before thee, nor to ask or receive the smallest favor. Enter not into judgment with thy sinful creatures; for in thy sight shall no man living be justified. With the light of the morning, may we enjoy the light of thy countenance. Grant that the Sun of Righteousness may enlighten our souls in the ways of heavenly wisdom, and our path be as the shining light, which shineth more and more unto the perfect day. Do thou, who makest the outgoings of the morning to rejoice, help us to walk in the way of thy commandments, and faithfully to discharge the duties of our several stations. Preserve us from all idolatrous affection for worldly things. May we seek first and as the greatest good the kingdom of God and his righteousness; and while we are diligent in our lawful business, may we use the world as not abusing it. Do thou, who art about our bed and about our paths, direct us in the way that we should go, and suffer not our feet to slip.

We pray for thy blessing upon this family; may our youth be trained up in the nurture and admonition of the Lord, and through thy grace never depart from the way in which they should go, nor from the holy commandment given unto them. Pour thy blessing upon our seed, and thy Spirit upon our offspring; that our sons may be as plants growing in thy vineyard, and our daughters be adorned with the ornament of a Christian spirit. Give thy blessing to all the rising generation. May they remember their Creator in the days of their youth; may they seek thee while thou mayst be found and call upon thee while thou art near. Preserve them from the snares and temptations of this evil world. May they remember the Lord's day to keep it holy, rejoicing to view it, not as a burthen, but as being made for man, and knowing that the Son of man is Lord also of the Sabbath.

Help those, O Lord, who are advanced to riper years, to do with diligence what their hands find to do, while the day continues, and before the night cometh in which no man can work. Awaken to righteousness the aged; let the hoary head be a crown of glory. May we all aspire to that honorable age which standeth not in length of time, nor is measured by number of years; to that wisdom which is the gray hair unto man, and an unspotted life, which is old age.

Increase our love and Christian affection for all mankind. May we weep with those who weep, and rejoice with them that rejoice, and pray for all who desire and all who need our prayers. Be merciful, we beseech thee, O be merciful to them who do not pray for themselves. May they be convinced of sin, of righteousness, and of judgment, and call upon thee in a time accepted.

Be merciful to those who are far from the kingdom of God. By the power of thy grace, bring them near to thyself, that they may see the light of thy truth, and rejoice in thy salvation. Hear our prayer for the poor and needy; such as we have, our prayers, at least, may we ever be ready to give, and according to our means and opportunity bestow upon them the things they need. Grant them grace to be contented and resigned to thy will: may they be rich in faith; heirs of thy heavenly kingdom, rejoicing in hope, and knowing that all things work for good to those who love and fear thee.

Preserve them who are rich from being high-minded and trusting too much in worldly things. Let them not forget who it is that giveth men power to get wealth, and maketh them to differ from the poor and wretched. Help them to be faithful stewards of the wealth and other good things committed to their trust. May they be ready to give and glad to distribute, laying up for themselves a good foundation against the time to come, that they may attain eternal life.

We ask thy blessing, O Lord, upon our friends and benefactors. May we ever remember, with grateful affection, all who have done us good, and wilt thou reward them for their kindness and love. Bless, we beseech thee, all who are near and dear to us: may they be dear to thee, and under thy merciful care and protection. Preserve us from ingratitude, and help us to make due returns of kind affection to all who have been kind to us.

Regard with favor the people of this our country, and be gracious to our native land. May that righteousness increase which exalteth a nation; and preserve us, we entreat thee, from sin, which is a reproach to any people, and has been the ruin of thousands.

We beseech thee, O Lord, to incline thine ears to us who have now made our prayers and supplications unto thee, and grant that the things which we have asked may mercifully be obtained, to our comfort, and to thy glory, through Jesus Christ, our blessed Lord and Savior. *Amen.*

Second Week. Thursday Evening.

O Lord God our heavenly Father, who hast promised, by thy Son, that where two or three are gathered together in his name, he will be with them, and that if a few shall agree on earth, as touching any thing that they shall ask, it shall be done for them, behold with thy favor and blessing us few in his name here assembled, who would unite in asking of thee those things which are requisite and necessary for our bodily comfort and for our spiritual good. Make us duly thankful that thou dost vouchsafe to forgive the sins, and to hear the prayers, and to relieve the wants of thy unworthy creatures. For this thy great goodness we bless thy holy name, beseeching thee to give us the spirit of grace and supplication, and help us to ask for such things as we truly need.

We entreat thee, O merciful God, to forgive our sins, to accept our prayers, to sanctify our hearts and renew a right spirit within us; and grant that we may ever hereafter serve and please thee in newness of life. Awaken in our minds such a sense of thy love and of thy goodness, that we, loving thee above all things, may walk in thy ways and attain to thy promises, which exceed all that we can ask or think. Do thou, who hast delivered our soul from death, preserve our feet from falling, and give us grace to walk according to thy holy precepts. According to the riches of thy grace strengthen us with might by thy Spirit in the inner man; that Christ may dwell in our hearts by faith; that we may be rooted and grounded in love; that we may know the love of Christ, which passeth knowledge, and be filled with all the fulness of God.

Prepare us, O Lord, for all the changes of this present world: may we know how to be abased and how to abound, and learn, in whatever state we are, therewith to be contented. Give us grace to cast away the works of darkness and to put upon us the armor of light; to do justly, love mercy and walk humbly with God. O may thy Spirit bear witness with our spirit, that we are thy children and joint heirs with Christ of thy heavenly kingdom.

And the blessings which we supplicate for ourselves, would we ask for our fellow-men. We beseech thee to extend the light of thy truth and the power of thy grace through the darkness of this sinful world, and among all the nations of the earth. May our heart's desire and prayer for Israel be that they may be saved. Call in the Jews, with the fulness of the Gentiles; say to the north, Give up, and to the south, Keep not back. Bring thy sons from far, and thy daughters from the ends of the earth.

We beseech thee to hear our prayer for the unnumbered millions who still remain in heathen darkness. Grant that the Sun of Righteousness may rise upon them with healing in his wings. O wilt thou raise up and send forth laborers into this great harvest. Let thy Spirit and the richest blessings of thy grace be with those ministers of thy word, who, with their life in their hand, and thy love in their hearts, go forth to preach the gospel in foreign lands. Preserve their health and give them aid from above: according to their day may their strength be. Stretch out thine arm with power until thou hast obtained the heathen for thine inheritance, and the utmost parts of the earth for thy possession.

Give thy blessing to those who associate for benevolent and religious objects; who contribute of their substance and by their prayers to the promotion of Christian knowledge and to the propagation of the gospel in foreign parts. Wilt thou enlarge their means and bless their labors.

And we beseech thee to keep thy household, the church, in continual godliness, and preserve it by thy perpetual mercy. Enlarge its borders, and daily add to it such as shall be saved. Defend it from error in faith and practice, and to all its members give the abundance of thy grace, that they may adorn their profession by living soberly, righteously and godly in this present world. We pray especially for that part of thy church to which we belong, and for those of thy people with whom we are more particularly connected in religious privileges. Strengthen, we beseech thee, those who stand; comfort and help the weak and wavering; raise up those who fall, and bring all who err into the way of truth. May grace and mercy and peace be upon all who love the Lord Jesus Christ in sincerity.

And wilt thou grant to all, who profess and call themselves Christians, union, peace and love. May they, with one heart and one mind, hold the true doctrines of eternal life, and strive together for the faith of the gospel. May we never forget that the end of the commandment is charity, without which all our words and faith and works are nothing. May we abound in the fruit of the Spirit, which is in all goodness and righteousness and truth. Preserve us from all heresy and schism: may we do nothing which will cause or perpetuate divisions among the disciples of Jesus Christ. Him that is weak in the faith may we receive in love, rather than to doubtful disputations. Help us to rejoice in the good that is done by all or any Christians of any name: and especially that Christ is preached, and that the doctrines of life are made known to men.

Give us, O Lord, a right judgment in all things, and hearts disposed in all things to do right; and be thou the strength of our heart and our portion forever. We ask these things in the name and through the mediation of Jesus Christ, to whom, with thee and the Holy Ghost, be all glory and praise, both now and ever. *Amen.*

Second Week. Friday Morning.

Adorable and everliving God, to whose patient goodness we owe it that we thy dependent creatures are again permitted to bow our knees and unite in prayer before thee, let, we beseech thee, thine ears be attentive to our humble supplications. Thankful for the preservation of another night, and the renewal of thy mercies this morning, and sensible that our wants are also renewed, we pray thee, O heavenly Father, to accept our thanks and hear our prayers. We praise thee for thy goodness; we acknowledge our transgressions, and we entreat thee, for the worthiness of our Savior Christ, to blot our offences and to wash away our sins. There is not a thought in our heart but thou, O Lord, knowest it altogether. Cleanse the thoughts of our hearts, by the inspiration of thy Holy Spirit, that the worship which we now offer may please thee, and that the rest of our life hereafter may be pure and holy.

We beseech thee, O Lord, to give us that knowledge of thy word and thy will which will make us wise unto salvation. Wilt thou reveal thyself to us as thou dost not to the world, that we may know thee the true God, and Jesus Christ whom thou hast sent. May thy law be our study and our delight, and thy Holy Spirit dwell within us, and so sanctify our thoughts and govern our wills, that we may present our bodies a living sacrifice holy and acceptable unto thee, which is our reasonable service. As thou, O Lord, art holy; so may we be holy in all manner of conversation: and as He, who lived and died for our benefit, spent his life in doing good; so may we never be weary in well-doing.

We are sensible that at best we are imperfect, and that our best deeds merit punishment, rather than reward. Great is thy mercy in accepting unworthy sinners, and justifying those who have transgressed thy laws; unspeakable thy goodness in promising, through faith in Christ, immortal life to those who were dead in trespasses and sins. Make us truly thankful for thy mercies, and in all things obedient to thy will.

Give us hearts, O Lord, to feel and to pray for our fellow-men. May the truths of thy word be grafted in their hearts and fruitful in their lives. Let not those who hear the gospel of their Savior Christ neglect his great salvation. O let not them, who have transgressed thy laws, add to their sins by refusing thy offered mercy. When thou callest, give them ears to hear; when thou stretchest out thy hand to save may all regard it.

We ask for thy blessing upon our neighbors, relatives and friends. Unite them all in friendship, peace and love; give them prosperity, and every blessing of life and religion. May every heart be filled with thankfulness for thy unbounded goodness. May all the habitations of Christians be houses of prayer, and every family offer thee daily the incense of holy, thankful hearts.

Help all thy people to walk with wisdom and prudence towards those who are without the pale of thy church, and to grow in grace and in the knowledge and love of Jesus Christ. Endue them with spiritual gifts. Let love be without dissimulation. Preserve them from bigotry and from all uncharitableness. May they be kindly affectioned one towards another, with brotherly love; in honor preferring one another. May all bitterness and evil-speaking be put away from them, with all malice. May they mind not high things, but condescend to men of low estate, and endeavor, as much as is possible, to live peaceably with all men.

May it please thee, O God, to give to all thy people increase of grace: may they hear meekly thy word, and receive it with pure affection and bring forth the fruits of the Spirit. May it please thee to succor, help and comfort all who are in danger, necessity and tribulation. Wilt thou, O Lord, preserve all who travel, by land or by water. Grant that they who are called to journey, who have occasion to travel to distant countries and to various parts of the earth, may be under the constant care and protection of thy good providence. [And *him* especially who, &c. *Any particular case may here be mentioned.*] Keep *them* in safety to their journey's end. In all dangers of soul or body cover *them* with the shadow of thy wings: give thy angels charge over *them*, to keep *them* in all *their* ways. May thy merciful goodness lead and follow *them* in all *their* pilgrimage, giving success to the business in which *they* may be engaged, and making all *their* affairs prosperous and of happy termination. Be with *them*, we beseech thee, in all the journey of life, and bring *them* at last to thy holy, heavenly rest.

Grant, O Lord, that all they who go down to the sea in ships and do business on the great waters of the deep, may be under thy special care and keeping. They are called to see the wonders of thy hand, and how great is thy power, which the winds and the seas obey. We earnestly commend them to thy providential care, [and *him* especially, for whose preservation on the great deep we particularly desire to offer up our prayers.] Do thou, who alone spreadest out the heavens and rulest the raging of the sea, protect them through the path of the mighty waters. Though the floods lift up their voice and their waves, thou, Lord on high, art mightier than many waters. Guard them in the time of peril; preserve them from sickness, from the violence of enemies, and from every evil to which they may be exposed. Conduct them in safety to the haven where they would be, with a thankful sense of thy mercy. Hear us, O Lord, for the sake of thy Son, our Savior Jesus Christ. *Amen.*

Second Week. Friday Evening.

O Lord God of our salvation, who art the hope of all the ends of the earth; all eyes wait upon thee as the Giver of life and breath, and of all things good. Thy glory is above the heavens: thou hast created all things and upholdest them with thine almighty hand. In the name of Jesus Christ we bow at thy footstool, to thank thee for the mercies of the day past, and humbly to ask for the continuance of thy goodness.

We desire, O heavenly Father, to acknowledge our unworthiness and to bewail the sins which from time to time we have committed, in thought, word and deed, provoking thy just wrath against us. Give us grace, most merciful God, truly to repent, and to be heartily sorry for all our misdoings. The remembrance of them is grievous; the burthen of them is intolerable. For the sake of Jesus Christ forgive us what is past, and grant that we may ever hereafter serve and please thee in newness of life. And because without thee we are unable to please thee, mercifully grant that thy Holy Spirit may, in all things, direct and rule our hearts.

Give us grace to receive the record that thou hast given unto us eternal life, and this life is in thy Son. May we look to him as our Advocate with the Father; on him depend for pardon and life, and may all our glorying be in him. We would desire above all things to be accepted in him, and have redemption through his blood, viewing him as the end of the law for righteousness to those who believe.

Wonderfully hast thou manifested thy love to our fallen race, in that, whilst we were yet sinners, Christ died for us, and that salvation is offered to all through faith in him. Herein is love indeed; not that we loved God, but that thou hast loved us, and hast given him to be the propitiation for our sins. Grant that our souls may be united with him by a divine and living faith. What things have been gain to us may we count but loss for Christ. May we ever know him, and the power of his resurrection, and the fellowship of his sufferings; and may we be made conformable to his death, by dying to sin, and rising again unto righteousness. Deliver us, we entreat thee, from the dominion of sin, and save us, by the washing of regeneration and the renewing of the Holy Ghost.

Grant, O Lord, that the love of Christ may constrain us, and that, as he loved us, we also may love one another. In all our intercourse with our Christian brethren and with the world may we follow after that charity which is the bond of perfectness, and the fulfilling of the whole law.

Preserve us from inordinate affections and desire of worldly things. May we learn, in whatsoever state we are, therewith to be content. Deliver us from covetousness, which is idolatry and the root of all evil. In seasons of prosperity make us humble, and in adversity resigned to thy will. We beseech thee to give us all such good things, temporal and spiritual, as are needful to our present comfort and peace, and give us grace rightly to use them. May all our conversation be such as becometh the gospel of Christ. Knowing that by our words we shall be justified and by our words condemned, may we set a watch at the door of our lips, that we may speak evil of no man; and take heed to our ways, that we offend not with our tongue. Help us ever to speak the truth in love, having our conversation in the world in simplicity and godly sincerity.

And we desire, O God, in our prayer, to remember the wants of our neighbors, beseeching thee, who knowest the hearts and the wants of all men, to give them what they need. So far as thou shalt see it to be fitting, and that it will promote their best good, give them, we pray thee, health and prosperity and peace. Chiefly we pray that they may be brought to know and to love thy truth, and to be partakers of thy grace and of thy salvation in Jesus Christ.

Have mercy upon all who are erring and straying from thy righteous ways, having no sure hope and without God in the world. May thy Spirit convince them of their evil ways, and fetch them home to thy flock, and to the fold of the one Shepherd, Jesus Christ.

Extend, we entreat thee, the blessings of useful knowledge, rational freedom and true religion to all the people of the earth. May harmony and friendly intercourse unite all nations. Preserve them from injustice, contention and pride, and so rule their hearts and direct their ways, that they may walk in love and dwell in peace. O hasten the time when wars shall cease in all the world; when nation shall no more lift up sword against nation, nor kingdom against kingdom; when all shall submit to thy righteousness, and learn war no more.

Let thy blessing attend thy word, wherever it is preached throughout the world. From the rising of the sun unto the going down of the same may thy name be great among the Gentiles, and in every place incense be offered unto thy name and a pure offering. Send thy word and the means of grace to all who are yet destitute, and make thy truth to them a savor of life. Arrest the progress of ungodliness and wrong, till the wickedness of the wicked shall come to an end.

Bless all our institutions designed for the spread of the gospel in foreign lands and for the promotion of truth and righteousness and peace among ourselves.

And now we desire, O thou Keeper of Israel, who never slumberest nor sleepest, to commend ourselves and all that appertains to us to thy merciful care and keeping. Thy power has preserved us through the day past; by thy great mercy defend us, we beseech thee, from all perils and dangers of this night, for the love of thy only Son, our Savior Jesus Christ. *Amen.*

Second Week. Saturday Morning.

O ETERNAL God, mighty in power, and of majesty incomprehensible, whom the heaven of heavens cannot contain, and who yet, in thy wonderful mercy, dost vouchsafe to hear the prayers of those whom Christ has redeemed from sin and death, look in mercy upon us the chief of sinners. Grant us the aid of thy Spirit, that we may approach thee with humility,—with lips unfeigned and with hearts sincere, and in the name of Him who died for our sins and rose again for our justification. May our reliance be on his merits, and on thy promise of pardon and peace through faith in him. Help us to pray according to thy will, that we may obtain mercy, and find grace to help us in every time of need. Let the words of our mouth and the desires of our heart be acceptable in thy sight.

And wilt thou impress upon our minds a deep and permanent sense of thy goodness. Abundant are the mercies, temporal and spiritual, which are our happy portion. Through many dangers and deaths, seen and unseen, hast thou conducted us from the commencement of our lives to this present time. Many blessings do we enjoy, of which others are deprived. What shall we render unto thee, O Lord, for all thy benefits! Help us to take the cup of salvation, and to call upon thy name, as the Giver of all good, and our only refuge in time of need. May thy goodness which sustained us through the silent watches of the night, be our guide and protection during the active labors of the present day. Defend us from sin, and from every danger. May all our conduct be ordered by thy governance and righteous in thy sight.

Thou hast taught us to make prayers and supplications, and to give thanks for all mankind, and we humbly beseech thee for all sorts and conditions of men, that thou would be pleased to make thy ways known unto them, thy saving health unto all nations. They are the work of thy hand and the creatures of thy care: may they know that thou hast so loved them, as to give thy Son to die for their sins, and may they rejoice in thy salvation.

We ask for the continuance of thy blessings upon this our favored country. Thou hast distinguished us by unnumbered mercies, and given us a great name among the nations of the earth. We would call to remembrance thy mercies, which have ever been of old. We have heard with our ears, and our fathers have declared unto us the noble works which thou didst in their days, and in the old time before them. Be with us, O God, and make us a nation fearing thee. Be thou our safeguard and defence. May salvation be to us for walls; our officers be peace, and our exactors righteousness: surely trusting in thy defence, may we not fear the power of any adversaries. Bless the government and all the people of the United States, and of this State especially in which we live, with wisdom, righteousness and peace. Give counsel to our counsellors, and teach our senators wisdom. Bless all who are set in authority over us, and so guide their counsels and strengthen their hands, that the hearts of the disobedient may be turned to the wisdom of the just, and our people serve thee in quietness and peace.

And grant, O Lord, that a sense of the many and great blessings which, as a people and a nation, we enjoy, may engage our hearts and lives in the ways of thy laws, and in the works of thy commandments. May we not forget that it is thou who makest us to differ from others. May we not be high-minded, but fear. Preserve us from a vain confidence of boasting; from self-dependence, and from party dissensions. May we not use our liberty for a cloak of maliciousness, but follow after charity, and the things which make for peace. Help us to enjoy the bounty which thy hand bestows, with temperance, sobriety and thankfulness to thee. Defend us from pride, selfishness, and love of the world. Dispose us in all things to give that measure to others which we exact from them, and to live soberly, righteously and godly in this present world.

We ask too for thy blessing upon all our churches and religious institutions, that they may be conformed to thy will and instruments of promoting thy truth. Give them grace to look with a single eye to thy glory, and to the best interests of mankind. May they follow after the things wherewith one may edify another. Let nothing be done through strife or vainglory; and let there be no divisions among us, but help us rather to stand fast in one spirit, with one mind, striving together for the faith of the gospel. May thy truth spread and godliness increase throughout the earth, and all who profess the faith of Christ walk worthy of their vocation. Enlarge the borders of the Redeemer's kingdom, till to the name of Jesus every knee shall bow, and all the ends of the earth shall rejoice to call him Lord.

Hear our prayers, O Lord, and behold us [of this family] with thy love and favor. Enlighten our minds with the truths of the blessed gospel; graft in our hearts the love of thy name; increase in us true religion; nourish us with all goodness, and of thy great mercy guide and bless us in all we do, that in this world we may live to thy glory, and in the world to come enjoy eternal life, through Jesus Christ, our Lord and Savior. *Amen.*

Second Week. Saturday Evening.

ALMIGHTY and everliving God, unto whom all hearts are open and all desires known, let our prayers, we beseech thee, be as incense and as an evening sacrifice. Cleanse our hearts and sanctify our affections, and let thy ears be attentive to our supplications. May thy Spirit help us to ask for such things as are fit for us to receive, and which we truly need.

We are unworthy, through our manifold sins, to offer unto thee any sacrifice, or to ask for any blessing, and our humblest prayers and sincerest supplications will need thy pardon. Daily and often have we offended against thee, who art holy, good and merciful. Trusting not in our own righteousness, but in thy great mercy through Jesus Christ, we would bow this evening in humble supplication before thy throne. Create and make in us new and contrite hearts; grant us, through thy grace, repentance not to be repented of, and pardon and remission of our sins.

Make us truly sensible of our wants and of thy goodness, and help us to cry earnestly unto thee, to whom belong mercy and forgiveness. Grant unto us a hearty desire to pray, and let thy Spirit direct and aid our devotions, that we may worship thee in spirit and in truth. Dispose us to be penitent and humble, and to serve thee in all godliness of living. May we be careful to maintain good works, while we trust only in the merits of our Savior.

Give us grace to walk before thee in all lowliness, meekness and long-suffering, forbearing one another in love. Give us piety and wisdom that we may accommodate our desires and our whole conduct to the state of life in which it shall please thee to place us, ever praying that thy will may be done. In seasons of affliction may we neither despise thy chastening nor faint under thy rebukes, but in our patience possess our souls. Under bereavements, may we never murmur, nor charge God foolishly; but call to mind the days that are past, and remember thy mercies which have ever been of old, and how little we deserve the blessings which are continued to us. May we not forget that we must through much tribulation enter the kingdom of God, and that our afflictions in this life, which are light and of short continuance, will, if we trust in thee, work in us a far more exceeding and eternal weight of glory. From the sorrows of life may we, through thy grace, gather the peaceable fruits of righteousness: may tribulation work in us patience, and patience experience, and experience hope.

But thou knowest, Lord, our weakness, and how little it is that we can bear; if it be consistent with thy wisdom, wilt thou mercifully turn from us the sorrows and other evils of life: O lead us not into temptation, but deliver us from evil. And in all our sufferings and distress, may we, like thy holy martyr Stephen, raise our eyes and our hopes to Him who once suffered for us upon the cross, and is now exalted at thy right hand: may we also forgive and pray for those who do us wrong. If thou art for us, none can be effectually against us.

Help us, O Lord, in all things to live according to thy word, and to let our light so shine before men, that they may see our good works; that they may take knowledge that we have been with Jesus, and give glory to thee for the power of thy grace. Make us ready to take the Savior's cross: may the disciples be willing to be as their Master, and the servants as their Lord. Set continually before us his holy example, that we may walk as he walked, and that the Spirit which was in him may also be in us.

And grant, O Lord, that we may grow in grace, and in the knowledge of Christ, and faithfully obey the gospel. Strengthen in us the things which remain and are ready to die. May we, through thy grace, be renewed day by day, and continually increase in all virtue and godliness of living.

Make us thankful for our religious privileges, and for all the ordinances of the gospel; and especially for thy appointment of one day in seven to be a season of holy rest from worldly cares, and to be devoted to the securing of that heavenly rest which remains for the people of God. May the Lord's day which is approaching be our delight: prepare and sanctify us that we may keep it holy. May we be in a right spirit on the Lord's day, and experience the blessedness of those whose strength is in thee, and in whose heart are thy ways. By thy holy inspiration may we think those things that are good, and by thy merciful guidance perform them.

Assist all thy people in their public adorations and praise. May thy Spirit rest upon thy churches, and upon the ministers of thy gospel. Endue them with wisdom, piety and zeal: may they go forth in thy strength to their work, and thy blessing attend their labors. Let utterance be given them, that they may open their mouth boldly and make known the mystery of the gospel. Grant that they may not labor in vain, nor spend their strength for naught. Replenish them with the truth of thy doctrine, and adorn them with innocency of life, that both by word and good example they may faithfully and successfully preach the word. Pour upon them, and upon all thy people, every gift and grace necessary for the work of the ministry; for the perfecting of the saints, and for the edifying of the body of Christ; till we all come, in the unity of the faith and of the knowledge of the Son of God, unto the perfect man;—unto the measure of the stature of the fulness of Christ, through whom be rendered unto thee all might, majesty and dominion, forever and ever. *Amen.*

The most of the Prayers preceding may be used on any day of the week; and if found to be too long, any parts of them may be used, omitting the rest. The following are some shorter Collects or Prayers, which may be used with any parts of the foregoing, on particular days or occasions.

For Christmas Day.

O Lord God, our heavenly Father, the Giver of all spiritual grace, and the Author of everlasting life, we render thee our humble and hearty thanks that thou didst so love the world as to send thy only-begotten Son to take our nature, to be born as an infant, and become the Redeemer of mankind from the power of sin and death. We thank thee, that he who was in the form of God, and might have continued equal with God, in that glory which he had with thee before the world was, for us men and for our salvation made himself of no reputation. We bless thee, O God, that he took not the nature of angels; but that we might have a high priest touched with the feelings of our infirmities, he took the seed of Abraham, and became perfect man without sin. Help us, O God, to be duly thankful for this unspeakable mercy. May glory to God in the highest, and peace on earth and good will towards men, inspire our hearts, and shine forth in our lives. May the example of Christ's humiliation make us penitent and humble. Give us grace that we may cast away the works of darkness, and put upon us the armor of light; now especially, in this season of the year, when to us the Child was born; when to us the Son was given. May we be regenerate, and truly thy children by adoption and grace; that in the last day, when he shall come again to judge the world, we may rise to life immortal, through Him who liveth and reigneth with thee and the Holy Ghost, now and ever. *Amen.*

For Ash Wednesday or other Fast.

ALMIGHTY and everlasting God, who hatest nothing that thou hast made, and dost forgive the sins of those who are truly penitent; who wouldst not the death of a sinner, but rather that he should turn to thee and live, mercifully forgive us our trespasses: create and make in us new and contrite hearts. To thee, O Lord, belong mercies and forgiveness; to thee only it appertaineth to renovate the heart, and renew a right spirit within us. Spare us, we beseech thee: O Lord, spare thy people for whom the Savior shed his precious blood. Have mercy upon us, O God, after thy great goodness; according to the multitude of thy mercies do away our offences. Make us a clean heart, and renew a right spirit within us. Turn thou us, O Lord, and we shall be turned; make us sensible of our vileness, and of the wickedness of our sins. Enter not into judgment with us, O Lord, for in thy sight shall no flesh living be justified. Make thy face to shine upon us, and be gracious unto us; lift upon us the light of thy countenance, and give us peace. Give us grace to set the Lord ever before us, and to use such abstinence, that our flesh may be subdued to the spirit, and that we may ever obey thy godly motions in righteousness and true holiness, and finally obtain everlasting life, through Jesus Christ, our Lord. *Amen.*

For Good Friday.

O Lord God, our heavenly Father, who of thy tender mercy didst give thine only Son, Jesus Christ, to suffer death upon the cross for our redemption; whose love to us was so great, that whilst we were yet sinners he died for us, behold us, we beseech thee, with favor and compassion. Make us deeply sensible of the sins which caused him to bleed and die; the just for the unjust. Raise us, we beseech thee, O heavenly Father, from the death of sin to a life of righteousness. May we never by our transgressions crucify him afresh; but sanctify the Lord God in our hearts, and live soberly, righteously and godly in this present world, through him who loved us and gave himself for us.

O blessed Lord Jesus Christ, who, in love to us unworthy sinners, didst leave the glories of thy heavenly throne, and come into this world to put away sin by the sacrifice of thyself; who didst become a man of sorrows and acquainted with grief; and didst humble thyself and become obedient unto death, even the death of the cross; spare us, good Lord; spare those for whose sins thou didst vouchsafe to bleed and die. O Lord God, Lamb of God, Son of the Father, who takest away the sins of the world, have mercy upon us. Thou that takest away the sins of the world, receive our prayer. By thine agony and bloody sweat; by thy cross and passion; by thy precious death and burial; by thy triumphant resurrection and gift of the Holy Ghost, deliver us, O Lord, from the guilt and the power of sin, and save our souls from eternal death.

O Lord, bless and keep us; make thy face to shine upon us; lift up the light of thy countenance upon us, and give us peace, both now and evermore. *Amen.*

For the Beginning or Close of a Year.

Adorable and ever gracious God, whose days are without end and whose mercies cannot be numbered, thou art from everlasting to everlasting; the same yesterday, to-day and forever. Thou hast laid the foundations of the earth, and the heavens are the work of thy hands. They shall perish but thou remainest: they shall all wax old as doth a garment, and shall be changed; but thou art the same, and thy years shall not fail. Though days, and months, and years do pass away, and time itself shall be no longer, thy kingdom shall endure forever and ever. Behold in mercy thy needy, dependent and perishing creatures, whose life is but a span, and whose age is even as nothing in respect of thee. It is of thy mercy that we are not consumed, and because thy compassions fail not. Thou holdest our souls in life, and to thee we lift our eyes as the only hope of all the ends of the earth. We thank thee, O blessed Lord God, that while another year has [nearly] passed away, and thousands and tens of thousands of precious souls have departed to the eternal world, we yet survive; that we have been, by thy merciful providence, conducted through a thousand perils to this present time. Help us, O heavenly Father, so to number our days, and so duly to consider the shortness and uncertainty of human life, that we may apply our hearts to true wisdom. Shouldst thou, O Lord, in thy goodness, let us alone another year also, give us grace, we beseech thee, to serve thee better than in times past. Create us again unto good works, and renew us day by day. Our life and breath are thine; our times are in thy hand; and may our whole heart and soul be devoted unto thee, and we be ever prepared to say, To live is Christ, and to die is gain. Support us in all dangers, both of soul and body. Lead us not into temptation; but deliver us from evil. We ask it in the name, and through the mediation of our Lord and Savior, Jesus Christ. *Amen.*

For a Family under Afflictive Visitation.

O FATHER of mercies and God of all comfort, who art our only hope in time of need, and who hast taught us in thy holy word that thou dost not, without wise and good intentions, afflict or grieve the children of men, mercifully behold us in this season of sorrow and distress. Lord, hear our supplications and prayers, and let thine ears consider well the voice of our complaint. Righteous art thou, O God, in all thy ways; just in all thy dealings with the sons of men. Sickness and pains and death are the dispensations of thy hand, and are less than our sins deserve. Wherefore should a living man complain!

Do thou, O God, who despisest not the sighing of a contrite heart, nor the desire of such as are sorrowful, mercifully assist us in the prayers which, in this time of trouble and adversity, we would make before thee. Turn from us, we beseech thee, the evils which we most justly have deserved; and grant that in all our troubles we may put our trust in thy mercy, and be submissive in heart and life to thy holy will. Sanctify to our spiritual and eternal good thy fatherly correction. Give us grace, O heavenly Father, to be patient under affliction, and resigned to thy holy will. May we see and know, to our comfort, that if God be for us, nothing can be against us; that neither tribulation or distress can separate us from the love of Christ. May such be our improvement under thy chastening hand, that we may find it good for us to have been afflicted.

And we commend to thy fatherly goodness all of our fellow-creatures who are in any way afflicted or distressed in mind, body or estate: that it may please thee to comfort and relieve them, according to their several necessities, giving them patience under their sufferings, and a happy issue out of all their afflictions. Hear us, O thou God of mercy, for the sake of our Savior, Jesus Christ. *Amen.*

A Prayer for Persons newly Married; which, with very little alteration, may be used by them.

O MERCIFUL Lord and heavenly Father, the Giver of all good things, and the Author of all blessedness, who, of thy bountiful goodness towards mankind, hast instituted the holy estate of matrimony, and by the union of husband and wife hast provided for the peace and order and happiness of society in this world, behold us, we beseech thee, with thy favor and blessing at this time, and on this occasion. Grant that these thy servants, who in thy fear and presence, and according to thy holy ordinance, have mutually pledged their love and fidelity, and have been united together in marriage, may enjoy the perpetual smiles of thy heavenly benediction. Bless them, O God, in their health and their friends; in their family and affections; in their goods, and in all the business of life. Guide and bless them in all that they design, and all they do. Defend and preserve them from sin, and from all the evils and calamities of life. May they ever live in perfect love and peace together, sympathizing in all the pains and all the endearments of life; and find their greatest earthly happiness in making each other happy. In their fidelity, may they find perfect confidence; in temperance, health; in honest industry, riches; and in virtuous, godly living, may they find comfort in this life, and the sure hope of a better.

Wilt thou, O merciful God, enlighten their minds by the doctrines of eternal life, revealed in Jesus Christ, and make them happy subjects of thy saving grace; that, being married in the Lord, they may live to him. May they view the married state as a great mystery, symbolizing the union between Christ and his church. As Christ loved the church, and gave himself for it, may the husband love his wife, even as himself, and the wife see that she reverence her husband.

May they love and cherish each other in all the cares and concerns of life; and counsel and strengthen each other in every duty of religion.

O God the Father, God the Son, God the Holy Ghost, bless, preserve and keep them. Grant that they may so live together in this world, that in the world to come they may enjoy life everlasting; through our Lord and Savior, Jesus Christ. *Amen.*

A Prayer suitable to be used by Parishioners for their Minister.

O MERCIFUL God, Sanctifier of the faithful, the Giver of all good, whose ears are open to the prayers of those who ask in the name of Jesus Christ, cleanse the thoughts of our hearts by the inspiration of thy Holy Spirit. Mercifully assist us in these our supplications and prayers, and help us to ask for such things as shall please thee. Grant us true repentance, that we may obtain of thee, the God of all mercy, perfect remission and forgiveness. Give us hearts, O Lord, to be thankful for thy manifold goodness to us and to all men. Make us duly thankful that we live in a land where the gospel of our blessed Redeemer is faithfully preached, and taught from house to house; that thy holy word, written for our learning, is in our hands; and we have the inestimable privilege of searching for ourselves those Scriptures which will make us wise unto salvation, and help us to know the certainty of those things wherein we have been instructed. We thank thee, O God, for the means of grace, for the ordinances of religion, and for all the privileges of thy sanctuary. We bless thy holy name for the gift of thy only Son to be our Savior, and the author of everlasting life; who, after he had made perfect our redemption, sent his ministers into all the world to preach his gospel to every creature. We bless thee, that thou art still graciously pleased to call others to the same office and ministry, who are continually laboring in word and doctrine. Make us thankful that our teachers are not removed into a corner, but that our eyes see our teachers, and our ears hear their words, instructing us in the right way, and exhorting us to walk therein, and that we turn not to the right hand or to the left. Give us grace, we beseech thee, to profit by their ministry; may thy word spoken in our ear sink deep in our heart, and bring forth in us the fruit of good living.

And, O gracious God, wilt thou send down upon the ministers of thy gospel, and upon the congregations committed to their charge, the healthful spirit of thy grace. Pour upon them the continual dew of thy blessing. Give grace, O heavenly Father, to all bishops and other ministers, that they may, both by their life and doctrine, set forth thy true and lively word, and rightly and duly administer the ordinances of thy gospel. And especially, O Lord, and most earnestly do we ask thy blessing upon him who is appointed to be our spiritual ruler and guide; who labors among us in word and doctrine, and breaks to us the bread of life. Thou hast commanded us to remember those who have the rule over us, and have spoken unto us thy word; for they watch for our souls, as they who must give account to thee of their fidelity. Him who rules over us, and watches for our souls, would we, O blessed Lord, remember in these our prayers; beseeching thee to rule his heart, to strengthen his hands and bless his labors. His best gifts and acquirements are our gain: should he lose his labors, we must lose our souls. Do thou, the God of all mercy and grace, who hast given this treasure in earthen vessels, and who alone canst make the frailty of man sufficient for such a ministry, endue him, our beloved pastor, with every gift and grace necessary to the full and faithful performance of all the duties of his office. Awaken in his mind a holy zeal for thy glory, and for the salvation of men. Help him to devote himself, and all his powers and faculties, to thee, in the work of his ministry. Enlighten his mind with the truths of thy word, and with the doctrines of eternal life. May thy Holy Spirit be his teacher, and bring to his remembrance whatever is profitable for doctrine, for reproof, for correction and for instruction in righteousness. Wilt thou, O gracious God, be ever with him in performing the duties of his ministry. Support him under all the discouragements which may intercept his way. Give him patience and strength in all the painful labors of his office, and wisdom rightly to divide the word of truth, and to give to all their portion of meat in due season. Remove from him the fear of man; and give him utterance that he may open his mouth boldly to make known the mystery of the gospel, and shun not to declare all the counsel of God. Grant him the comfort of seeing thy work prosper in his hand; may many souls, by his labors and thy blessing converted to thee, be his crown of rejoicing.

And wilt thou, O Lord, watch over him for good. May his life be precious in thy sight. Preserve, we beseech thee, his health and strength. Shield him from sorrows and perils and calamitous events, and grant him such temporal comforts as may be convenient and useful, and encourage him in his labor of love. Bless him in his house, [in his family,] and in his connections. May he long continue to labor successfully in building up the Redeemer's kingdom and turning many to righteousness; and at last, having fought a good fight, and finished his course with joy, may he receive the crown of righteousness laid up for him in thy heavenly kingdom.

And give us grace, O Lord, we beseech thee, rightly and truly to profit by his ministry, and to do all that is in our power to hold up his hand, and aid him in the arduous duties of his pastoral care, that he may do them with joy and not with grief. May his patient labor, for our benefit, fill our hearts with grateful affection, and with that love which is not in word and tongue only, but in deed and in truth.

Hear us, O Lord, we beseech thee, for the sake of thy Son, our Savior, Jesus Christ, in whose name and words we further pray:—

Our Father who art, &c. *Amen.*

The following prayers are more general, and may be used in Families, or by companies of Christians in meetings for Prayer, and on other occasions.

Righteous, adorable and everliving God, in whom we live and move and have our being; whose goodness is, like thy power, unbounded, behold in mercy the souls who are here before thee. We approach thee, O God, as fallen, sinful creatures, unworthy to lift our eyes to a righteous God in prayer. Trusting not in our own righteousness, but in thy manifold and great mercies, and the infinite merits of a Savior's blood, we beseech thee to cleanse us from sin, and behold us in love. Help us, with humble reverence, religious awe, and praying hearts, in his prevailing name, to come before thee. Grant us, O Lord, such a right view of thy justice and thy mercy, that we may fear without despair, and hope without presumption.

Let thy Holy Spirit be with us to help our infirmities, to enliven our devotion, to reclaim our wandering thoughts, and raise our affections from the world to thee. Assist us mercifully, O Lord, in our supplications and prayers; raise our hopes and dispose our ways towards the attainment of everlasting salvation. May we love the things which thou commandest, and desire those which thou dost promise; that so, among the manifold changes of this world, our hearts may surely there be fixed, where true joys are to be found. Give us grace to cast away the works of darkness and put upon us the armor of light. In all time of our tribulation, in all time of our prosperity, in the hour of death, and in the day of judgment, support us with thy grace, preserve us from pride, uphold us with thy spirit, and save our souls, in Jesus Christ.

We beseech thee, O God, to hear our prayers, and accept of our intercessions for all who desire, and all who need them. Extend the light of thy gospel through the darkness of this sinful world, and grant that the knowledge of Christ, and the doctrines of life eternal, may spread more and more, till all the ends of the earth shall see the salvation that is in Jesus Christ.

We beseech thee, O God, to inspire continually the universal church with the spirit of truth, unity and concord; and grant that all they who do confess thy name may agree in the truth of thy holy word, and live in harmony and godly love; may they hold the true faith in unity of spirit, in the bond of peace, and in righteousness of life. And we beseech thee so to dispose the hearts of all Christian rulers, that they may truly and impartially administer justice, to the suppression of wickedness and vice, and to the maintenance of true religion and virtue. May peace and harmony, and the blessings of true liberty, equal laws, and pure and undefiled religion, be extended to all the nations of the earth.

Bless, O Lord, we beseech thee, the people of this our country with prosperity and peace. Inspire them with thankfulness to thee, for thy manifold and great mercies, and cause them to show their sense of thy goodness by living according to thy righteous laws. May thy heavenly wisdom, and thy holy, protecting providence, guide and govern those who are in authority over us. May it please thee to bless and prosper all their ministrations, to the advancement of thy glory, the good of thy church, and to the honor, safety, and welfare of thy people: and grant that peace and happiness, truth and justice, religion and piety may be established among us for all generations.

Extend, O Lord, thy heavenly benediction to the spiritual rulers set in thy church. Give grace, we humbly beseech thee, to all the ministers of thy gospel of every grade, and in all their various fields of labor; and grant that they may, both by their life and doctrine, set forth thy true and lively word; rightly and truly administer all the ordinances of our Savior, Christ; and be instruments, through thy grace, of turning the hearts of the disobedient to the wisdom of the just, and of declaring to all who have ears to hear, the whole counsel of God.

May it please thee, O Lord, to give to all thy people increase of grace, to hear meekly thy word, and to receive it with pure affection, and to bring forth the fruits of the spirit. May it please thee to bring into the way of truth all such as have erred and are deceived; to strengthen such as do stand; to comfort and help the weak-hearted; to raise up those who fall, and to subdue our spiritual enemies. And we most humbly beseech thee of thy goodness, O Lord, to comfort and succor all those who, in this transitory life, are in trouble, sorrow, need, sickness, or in any other adversity; giving them patience and resignation under their sufferings, and wisdom and grace to make a right improvement from their afflictions.

May thy gracious ears, O Lord, be open to all who seek thy face in prayer. We pray thee to enlighten and comfort those who are too fearful of thy terror, and distrustful of thy mercy. The bruised reed thou wilt not break; a broken and contrite heart thou wilt not despise. May all who mourn in Zion find thee a God of refuge; may they dwell in peace, feeling thy pardon, supported by thy Spirit, absolved by thy sentence, and saved by thy mercy. O may we not, for any troubles of life, or for any allurements of the world, cast away our confidence in thee, or place it in any other. We offer these our supplications and prayers in the name of Jesus Christ; and conclude them with the words which he has taught us:

Our Father who art, &c. *Amen.*

ALMIGHTY and everliving God, unto whom all hearts are open, all desires known, and from whom no secrets are hid, behold in mercy thy dependent creatures, who desire, with all humility and adoration, to approach thy gracious throne. We beseech thee to hear our prayers, and pardon our sins. Create and make in us new and contrite hearts, and give us such sincere repentance, that we may obtain of thee, the God of all mercy, perfect remission and forgiveness.

We adore thee, O God, for thine infinite perfections; we bless thee for thy great and manifold mercies. With hearts united, we would render unto thee humble and hearty thanks, for all thy goodness and loving kindness to us and to all mankind. We thank thee for our life, and for all the blessings which add to our comfort: that our lives, so unprofitable to thee, are still continued; that we have been preserved, through various perils, and conducted, by unnumbered mercies, safely to the present time. We thank thee for this present opportunity and privilege of assembling in thy name and presence; and for the comforting doctrines of life and peace contained in thy holy word. We praise thee, O God, that thou hast laid help on one who is mighty; that thou hast so loved the world; hast had such compassion upon the fallen race of men, as to give thine only Son to be our Savior; that through the merits of his sacrifice thou canst be just, and yet be the justifier of those who believe in Jesus Christ; and that we are called to a knowledge of thy grace and faith in thee. Make us sensible of thy goodness in giving us such gracious means and frequent opportunities of religious improvement. Blessed be thy name for thy forbearing mercy; for thy patient goodness to creatures so undeserving: for the invitations of thy word, and for thy promises of salvation and eternal life in Jesus Christ. We beseech thee to impress thy saving truth upon our minds; grant us that lively, holy faith which renews the heart; and whilst we live, may we live to thee. Do thou, the Lord of all power and might, the author and giver of all good things, graft in our hearts the love of thy name; increase in us pure and undefiled religion; nourish us with the lively truth of thy holy word, filling our soul with goodness; and of thy great mercy dispose our hearts, and direct our ways, towards the attainment of everlasting salvation.

Give us grace, O Lord, to love thy statutes, and to walk faithfully in the way of thy commandments. Incline our heart unto thy testimonies. Turn away our eyes from all sinful vanities, and quicken us in the way that we should go. Assist us in all we do with thy heavenly grace, and dispose our ways towards the attainment of everlasting salvation, that among all the perils of this changing world, our hearts may be steadfastly fixed upon the unchanging glories of the world to come. May we follow the steps of our blessed Savior who once came into this world to visit us in great humility; like him be unwearied in well doing; that when he shall come again, in his glorious majesty, to judge the quick and the dead, we may be found acceptable in thy sight, and receive the blessing which he shall pronounce to those who love and fear thee.

And accept, O Lord, of our intercessions for all our fellow-men. Extend, we beseech thee, the knowledge of Jesus Christ, and the saving truths of thy blessed word, through all the nations of the earth. May thy gospel be spread till it is preached to every creature, and in an honest and good heart by all received. O may thy kingdom come and its power increase, till thy will is done on earth as it is in heaven. Awaken in the impenitent a just sense of thy power and of thy mercy. Let the wicked forsake his way, and the unrighteous man his thoughts; may they return unto the Lord, who will have mercy upon them, and to God, who will abundantly pardon. May we and all men seek thee while thou mayst be found, and call upon thee while thou art near, and partake in the benefits of thy everlasting covenant, even the sure mercies of David.

Give us hearts, O Lord, to feel, and to pray for all the sons and daughters of sorrow. May they remember the exhortation. not to despise the chastening of the Lord, nor faint when rebuked of him; and, knowing that whom the Lord loveth he chasteneth, may they trust in thy mercy and be resigned to thy will. Behold, O Lord, in mercy them who are visited with sickness. May they bow with submission under thy rod, knowing who hath appointed it, and be enabled, through thy grace, to see wisdom and goodness in all thy dealings May they know, in a holy, lively faith, that to live is Christ, to die is gain.

We commend ourselves, O heavenly Father, to thy holy, protecting providence. Wilt thou watch over us for good, and direct and bless us in all we do.

O thou blessed Savior of a sinful world, who for us men and for our redemption came down from heaven; lived for our example; was delivered for our offences, and raised for our justification, help us to walk in thy steps, and to serve thee as our Lord and Master, doing the things which thou commandest.

O thou Holy Spirit of the Father, and Spirit of the Son, Sanctifier of the faithful, visit us, we pray thee, with thy love and favor. Open our understanding, that we may know and receive the truth as it is in Jesus Christ. Dwell in our hearts, and sanctify our desires and all our affections.

O blessed Lord God and Savior, who hast given us grace at this time to make our common supplications unto thee, and dost promise, that when two or three are gathered together in thy name, thou wilt grant their requests; fulfil now, O Lord, we humbly beseech thee, the desires and petitions of thy servants, as may be most expedient for them, granting us in this world knowledge of thy truth, and in the world to come life everlasting, through Jesus Christ, our blessed Lord and Redeemer. *Amen.*

O ETERNAL God, whose wise and unfailing providence orders all things in heaven and on earth, who hast compassion upon the sons of men, and hast graciously promised to hear the prayers of those who ask in the name of Jesus Christ, we desire, with reverence and adoration, to present before thee our humble supplications. Let thy merciful ears be open to our petitions, and that we obtain our requests, help us, we beseech thee, to ask for such things, and with such hearts, as shall please thee. We are unworthy, through our manifold sins, to offer unto thee any sacrifice. We have daily offended against thee, who art holy, just and good. We have sinned and done wickedly in departing from thy precepts and thy judgments. We have erred and strayed from thy righteous ways, and have followed too much the evil devices and desires of our own hearts. We have left undone what our duty required, and have done those things which thy law forbids. Do thou, O heavenly Father, who hast promised forgiveness to those who confess and forsake their sins, have mercy upon us; pardon our offences, and deliver us from the condemnation and the power of sin. Sanctify our hearts, and, by thy Holy Spirit, work in us to will and to do what is pleasing in thy sight.

We bless thy holy name, that to the Lord our God belong mercies and forgiveness; that through the merits of a righteous Savior thou art ever ready to receive a returning, penitent sinner. We praise thee for thy adorable attributes of power and wisdom, benevolence and mercy. We thank thee for unnumbered favors vouchsafed to us and to all mankind; for the gospel preached to sinful creatures, and for the day and means of grace and salvation. (We thank thee that our lives are still preserved; and that we are permitted, once more, to lay aside our worldly cares; to meet here in thy presence; [to read thy word;] to talk of thy mercies, and to address thee in prayer and praise. Grant, O Lord, that we may pass this time of our being together as becometh weak and dependent creatures, in the presence of a righteous, holy, and heart-searching God.) Sanctify all our affections; give us right views of thy character, of the Savior's merits, and of our duty. Preserve us from all self-righteousness, vanity and pride. May it be our chief desire to honor thee, and to save ourselves and others. Grant that all things may be done decently and in good order, to thy glory and to our edification. May our mouth be exercised in wisdom, and our talking be of thy judgments. In every duty of prayer or praise; of reading thy word or speaking of thy mercies, let thy Holy Spirit be with us, to strengthen our faith, to restrain our wandering thoughts, to enliven our devotion, and to fix our attention and our desires on spiritual things, and to unite our hearts in Christian love. Our hearts are in thy hand; our wants and our infirmities are all before thee. Thou knowest our desires and our necessities before we ask, and our ignorance in asking. O gracious God, wilt thou do for us and work in us whatever thou seest fitting for our present need, and our eternal good. Increase in us faith and hope and charity, and may we never forget that the greatest of these is charity. O shed abroad thy love in our hearts; may that spirit be in us which was in our Savior Christ; that meekness and humility, that forgiving temper and spirit of love. May our benevolent affections be raised in thankfulness to thee, and fall, as the dew of heaven, upon our fellow-men.

Assist, O Lord, and hear our supplications for all mankind. Bless thy church universal, wherever dispersed, throughout the world. May mercy and peace be upon the whole Israel of God. Prosper thy word, wherever it is spoken, and send it where it is not heard. Cause thy face to shine upon thy chosen people, and grant that thy way may be known through all the earth, and thy saving health among all nations. May the borders of Zion be enlarged, till the kingdoms of the earth become the kingdoms of the Lord and of his Christ, and all shall know thee from the least to the greatest. Bless all who name the name of Christ, with every gift and every grace. Revive thy work in the midst of the years. Pour out of thy Spirit, O blessed Lord, amongst us. Awaken the zeal of thy people: bless the labors of thy ministering servants. May all our churches arise and shine, and be the salt of the earth; and may the light of gospel truth dispel the darkness of sin and unbelief. Increase and bless the means which are used to extend the knowledge of Christ and the doctrines of life. Wilt thou, O Lord, add to thy church daily and in great numbers such as should be saved. May they who are now living in sin be renewed in heart, awakened to righteousness, and saved in Christ forever. Awaken in our minds a deep concern for the perishing souls of our fellow-men. O blessed Lord, who died for their sins, save them from perdition.

We beseech thee, O Lord, mercifully to hear these our supplications and prayers. Pardon our cold affections and wandering thoughts, and fulfil our desires and petitions in such manner as may be most expedient for us; granting us, in this world, knowledge of thy truth, and in the world to come life everlasting. These, our petitions, we present in the name of our Lord Jesus Christ.

And unto thee, who art able to keep us from falling, and to present us faultless before the throne of thy glory, be ascribed all majesty, dominion and power, both now and ever. *Amen.*

Adorable and everliving God, the Father of all mercies, the Giver of all good, we, thine unworthy creatures, who are still, by thy patient goodness, preserved, and permitted once more to meet before thee, desire, with heart and voice united, to lift our souls to thee in adoration and praise. Thou art the Lord, by whom we escape death, and enjoy the things which pertain to life and godliness. We bless thee as the Author of our being, and the Giver of life, and of all that makes life desirable. Thou hast holden us up ever since we were born, and may our praise be always of thee. Impress upon our hearts a lively and lasting sense of what thou hast done for us, and work in us that which is pleasing in thy sight.

We acknowledge, O God, our sinfulness, and beseech thee to give us that true repentance which is not to be repented of, and that faith towards the Lord Jesus Christ which renews the heart, worketh by love and overcometh the world. Through the merits of his blood, may our sins be forgiven; and through thy sanctifying grace, may we be created again unto good works. O may thy Spirit help our infirmities and make intercession for us. Let the words of our mouth and the meditation of our heart be acceptable in thy sight. May our prayers be set forth before thee as incense, and the lifting up of our hands as the evening sacrifice.

Great, O Lord, are thy mercies vouchsafed to us, while our hearts are worldly, forgetful of thy goodness, and neglectful of thy great salvation. Shut not thy merciful ears to our prayers; but spare us, O Lord God, most mighty; thou holy, just and merciful Savior, permit us not, for the vanities of life, to err from thee, nor, for any things of time and sense, to lose our souls.

Teach us, O thou God of mercy, to realize how short and uncertain is the life of man. The Son of man cometh as a thief in the night, and thou only knowest how soon we shall be called to another world, and our souls be fixed in their eternal state. And yet we live in this world as though we were never to leave it; forgetful of our latter end, and unprepared for judgment. How wasteful are we of our precious time! how careless of our souls!

how thoughtless of eternity! Justly mightest thou call us away in the midst of our sins. O quicken us that we may live. Awaken us to righteousness, that we sin not. Remember not, Lord, our sins against thee, but thy love to us in Jesus Christ; not weighing our merits, but pardoning our offences.

And wilt thou, O merciful God, awaken in our minds a deep concern for the salvation, not of ourselves only, but of others. Hear our prayer, we humbly beseech thee, for those who do not pray for themselves. Arrest, by thy grace, those who are going along the broad way to ruin; turning a deaf ear to the calls of mercy and of a bleeding Savior, and unmindful of the judgment which awaits them. O may thy quickening Spirit convince them of sin, of righteousness and of judgment, and turn their hearts to the wisdom of the just.

Extend thy mercy to all for whom we ought to pray. Bless our churches and our country. Behold, O Lord, in mercy, this little flock of thy worshipping people here before thee. Bless the church of God which Christ has purchased with his blood, and especially that branch of it with which we are particularly connected. Keep us, O Lord, by thy perpetual mercy. Unite our hearts in Christian love. Enrich our minds with true wisdom and heavenly grace. May we be steadfast and immovable; always abounding in the work of the Lord, through Jesus Christ, to whom, with the Father and Holy Spirit, be endless praise. *Amen.*

For the Closing of a Religious Meeting.

Almighty and everlasting God, unto whom all hearts are open, all desires known, and from whom no secrets are hid, cleanse the thoughts of our hearts by the inspiration of thy Holy Spirit, that we may address thee with reverence and godly fear, and with hearts duly thankful for thy unnumbered mercies. We thank thee for thy goodness in preserving our unprofitable lives from day to day, and from week to week; that seasons of spiritual refreshment often return, and that time and opportunity are given us to know thy word and to do thy will. We bless thee, O God, especially for thy favors vouchsafed us during the past day and this present evening. To the praise of thy patient goodness we thankfully acknowledge it, that we have had this pleasing opportunity of meeting together; that we have been permitted with social affections to unite our hearts and voices in prayer and praise to thee, the Lord God of our salvation; that we may talk of thy loving kindness early in the morning, and of thy faithfulness in the night season. O may we be duly thankful for this, and for all thy mercies: may we realize the blessedness of gospel truth; of seeing the things which we see, and of hearing the things which we hear. May the counsels of thy word sink deep in our hearts, and bring forth the fruits of pure and undefiled religion. Like thy servants of old who feared the Lord, may we speak often one to another on the subject of our salvation in Jesus Christ; and may a book of remembrance be written, a remembrance, not of our sins and unworthiness, but of thy mercy, and of the love of Christ, which passeth man's understanding. May a sense of thy goodness increase our love of thy law, and make us more faithful in serving thee.

Let thy fatherly hand, we beseech thee, ever be extended to preserve us from sin and danger, and to guide our steps in the way of righteousness and peace. Though, through the frailty of our nature, and amidst the busy cares of life, we are prone to be forgetful of thee, our God and Savior, O be not thou unmindful of us: may thy kind and watchful providence ever be over us: may thy Holy Spirit be ever with us, and so lead us in the knowledge and obedience of thy word, that in the end we may obtain everlasting life.

Shed abroad thy love in our hearts. May we all be united in the bands of a holy affection, and strive together for the faith of the gospel, in unity of spirit, in the bond of peace, and in righteousness of life. Dispose our minds to every good word and work, that we may abound in mercy and good fruits. Make us thankful in prosperity; patient in tribulation; resigned in adversity. and faithful in every duty.

Wilt thou, O gracious God, revive thy work among this people. May the knowledge of Christ, and an awakened concern for the salvation of their souls, be more widely extended. O may multitudes be inquiring what they shall do to be saved; how they shall flee from the wrath to come, and save themselves from this untoward generation. With sincere penitence and lively faith, may they come into thy church as doves to their windows.

Inspire, O Lord, the ministers of thy gospel with holy zeal; and of thy great mercy so direct and govern them in their labor of love, that the comfortable gospel of Jesus Christ may be truly preached, truly received, and truly followed. Have mercy upon those who are still in the ways of sin, impiety and unbelief: take from them all ignorance, hardness of heart and contempt of thy word; and fetch them home, blessed Lord, to thy flock, that they may be saved among the remnant of the true Israelites, and be made one fold under one Shepherd.

Bless the people of our country with union, prosperity and peace; shield them by thy holy protecting providence. Surely trusting in thy defence, may we not fear the power of any adversary.

Make us, we beseech thee, a happy people, having the Lord for our God, and thy word for our guide. Do thou, O God, mercifully incline thine ear unto us who have now made our prayers and supplications unto thee, and grant that what we have asked according to thy will may effectually be obtained. Have compassion, we beseech thee, upon us and our infirmities; pardon us wherein we ask amiss; and those good things which for our unworthiness we dare not, and for our blindness we cannot ask, vouchsafe to give us for the worthiness of thy Son, our Savior, Jesus Christ.

O Lord, bless us and keep us, be gracious unto us, and give us peace, both now and evermore. *Amen.*

The Lord's Prayer, Paraphrased.

MOST merciful and gracious God, we, thy sinful, dependent creatures, in the name and words of our Savior, Christ, look unto thee in prayer, as

Our Father, who art in heaven, exalted above all worlds, and invisible to mortal eyes; who humblest thyself to behold the things that are in the earth: who so lovedst the world as to give thine only Son, that through faith in him we may be heirs of eternal life. We adore thee for that unspeakable manner of love, which, through him, thou hast bestowed upon us, that we should be called the sons of God; and, because sons, heirs of God and joint heirs with Christ; and, by the spirit of adoption, are permitted to cry, Abba, to thee, as unto a reconciled Father. In his name, and through his merits, we rejoice to say,

Hallowed be thy name. May we truly sanctify and reverence the Lord God in our hearts and our lives; and may all the earth keep silence before thee. To thee may every knee bow, and every tongue swear by thy name, as that of the only true and living God. May the nations of the earth, with angels and archangels, and all the company of heaven, laud and magnify thy glorious name. May a thankful sense of thy boundless goodness continually swell our notes of praise. As thou, who hast called us to a knowledge of thy grace, art holy; so may we be holy in all manner of conversation; as it is written, Be ye holy, for I am holy. May thy name be hallowed for thy glorious attributes; for thy righteous providence, and for the redemption of mankind in Jesus Christ. Ever adored be thy name, that thou canst be just, and yet justify those who have sinned against thee; and that our hopes are raised from sorrow, sin and death, to life immortal.

Thy kingdom come. May the truth of thy blessed gospel be established in every heart, and the King whom thou hast set on thy holy hill of Zion, be by all acknowledged, as both Lord and Christ. May there be added daily to thy church such as should be saved. Grant that the ministers of thy gospel, and thy word spoken by their mouth, may be instrumental, through the mighty power of the Holy Ghost, in the conversion of souls, till the King of saints shall have the utmost parts of the earth for his possession. O hasten on those glorious days of the Redeemer's kingdom, when the mountain of the Lord's house shall be established in the top of the mountains, and be exalted above the hills, and all nations shall flow unto it: when wars and strifes shall cease, and the earth shall be full of the knowledge of the Lord, as the waters cover the sea.

Thy will be done on earth, as it is in heaven. We pray, that through the power of thy grace, all who name the name of Christ may depart from iniquity, and hold the true faith in unity of spirit, in the bond of peace, and in righteousness of life. Be gracious unto thy church, and grant that every member of it may truly and godly serve thee. May all divisions and discord cease. As the blessed angels in heaven, and the spirits of just men made perfect, unite in love and praise; so may thy people here on earth be joined together in one heart and one mind, striving together for the faith of the gospel, and endeavoring to be perfect, as our Father in heaven is perfect. Help us to follow the example of Christ's humility, patience and love, till we come, in the unity of the faith, and of the knowledge of the Son of God, unto the perfect man; unto the measure of the stature of the fulness of Christ.

Give us this day our daily bread. Do thou, O Lord, who knowest our wants and our dependence, give to us and to our brethren what is needful and convenient, and give us grace with thankful hearts to receive and rightly to use it. Make us contented with what thy goodness shall bestow; and may we desire, above all earthly things, that our souls may be fed with the bread of life—with the heavenly manna of thy word and doctrine.

Forgive us our trespasses. We have erred and strayed from thy righteous ways, and have followed the evil devices of our own hearts. Do thou, the God of mercy, forgive our sins; sanctify our hearts, and renew a right spirit within us. We beseech thee, O Lord, to blot out our transgressions.

As we forgive those who trespass against us. If there be any who injure us, or wish us evil, give us grace, O Lord, truly to forgive them; and, as far as in us lies, to overcome evil with good. May the spirit of meekness which was in our blessed Savior be in us; may we forgive, as we hope to be forgiven, knowing that vengeance is thine and that thou wilt judge the world in righteousness.

Lead us not into temptation. Such is the frailty

of our nature, that without thee we cannot but fall. Keep us, we beseech thee, both outwardly in our bodies and inwardly in our souls; defend us from adversity and preserve us from all temptation to sin. Give us wisdom and grace to avoid that which will entice us to transgress thy holy laws. In times of peril suffer us not to fall into sin.

But deliver us from evil. When, for the trial of our steadfastness, or for other purposes of thy providence, we are exposed to temptation, mercifully look upon our infirmities, and in all such dangers stretch forth thy hand to help and defend us. Grant that we may never be tempted above what we are made able to withstand; but that, through thy grace, a way may be opened to escape the snare.

For these great blessings we look unto thee, our heavenly Father, through the merits and mediation of thy blessed Son.

For thine is the kingdom of the whole world, both of nature and grace, *and the power* to support us in trial, and to save with an everlasting salvation. *And* to thee only, as thy just due, be ascribed all *the glory forever and ever. Amen.*

A Hymn to the God of Christians.

1. *Holy* Father, great Creator,
   Source of mercy, love, and peace,
Deign to bless thy sinful creature,
   Through the Savior's righteousness;
      Heavenly Father,
   Through the Savior, hear and bless.

2. *Holy* Jesus, Lord of Glory,
   Whom angelic hosts proclaim,
Be with us, who, here before thee,
   Meet and worship in thy name.
      Dear Redeemer,
   In our hearts thy peace proclaim.

A Hymn to the God of Christians.

3. *Holy* Spirit, Sanctifier,
Come with unction from above,
Touch our hearts with sacred fire;
Fill them with the Savior's love;
Source of comfort,
Cheer us with the Savior's love.

4. God the Lord, through every nation,
Let thy wondrous mercies shine;
In the song of thy salvation,
Every tongue with rapture join.
Great Jehovah,
Form our hearts, and make them thine.

PART THIRD.

PRAYERS WHICH MAY BE USED IN MISSIONARY MEETINGS, AND ON OTHER OCCASIONS.

A Prayer for the Church.

Adorable and everliving God, who hast built thy church upon the foundation of apostles and prophets, Jesus Christ himself being the chief corner-stone, and hast promised to be with its ministers to the end of the world, we beseech thee to behold it with thy favor and blessing, and keep it with thy perpetual mercy. Grant, we beseech thee, that, by the operation of thy Holy Spirit, all Christians, in their vocation and ministry, may truly and godly serve thee. May they be so joined together in unity of spirit and in the bond of peace, that they may be a holy temple, acceptable unto thee. With one heart may they desire the prosperity of the Redeemer's kingdom, and with one mouth profess the faith once delivered to the saints. Defend them from heresy and schism. Bring into the way of truth all who have erred and are deceived. Strengthen such as do stand; comfort and help the weak-hearted; raise up those who fall; preserve us in the hour of temptation, and deliver us from evil.

Enlarge, we beseech thee, the borders of Zion, and add to thy church daily, and in vast numbers, such as should be saved. O may thy kingdom come with power, till all shall know thee, from the least to the greatest, and thy will be done on earth as it is in heaven.

And grant, O Lord, that the course of this world may be so peaceably ordered by thy governance, that thy people, being hurt by no persecutions, may serve thee without fear, in holiness and righteousness, all their days; through Jesus Christ, our Lord and Savior. *Amen.*

A Prayer for the Clergy.

Almighty and everliving God, who, of thy infinite love to mankind, hast given thy Son Jesus Christ to be our Redeemer, and the Author of everlasting life; who, after he had died for our sins, and risen for our justification, sent forth his apostles and prophets and other ministers to preach his gospel and make disciples of all nations; for these, so great benefits of thy eternal goodness, and that thou art still sending laborers into thy vineyard, and calling men to the knowledge of thy salvation in Jesus Christ, we render thee most hearty thanks; we bless and praise thy holy name. We bless thee, O God, that thou didst so love the world, as to send into it thy blessed Son to be our Savior; and that thou hast commanded the good tidings of his gospel to be proclaimed to all the nations of the earth. Give us grace to manifest our thankfulness for this thy great goodness, by endeavoring, as thou shalt give us grace and means, to spread the knowledge of Christ, and to extend the ministrations of his religion to all who need them.

Teach us, O Lord, to pray, and graciously hear our humble prayers for those who are ordained to preach the gospel of Christ, and to minister in holy things. Wilt thou, O God, who alone canst, make them sufficient for these things; rule their hearts, strengthen their hands and bless their labors. Endue them with wisdom from above; inspire them with a holy, heavenly zeal, and grant that thy word, spoken by their mouth, may have such free course and be so blest, that it may never be spoken in vain. Send down upon our bishops and other clergy, and upon the congregations committed to their charge, the healthful spirit of thy grace; and, that they may truly please thee, pour upon them the continual dew of thy blessing. Let all thy ministers be clothed with righteousness, and be wholesome examples and patterns to the flock of Christ. Grant that they may, both by their life and doctrine, set forth thy true and lively word; that they may rightly and duly administer the sacraments and other ordinances of Jesus Christ, and be faithful to declare all the counsel of God. Make them, O Lord, we beseech thee, instruments of thy grace, in awakening sinners to righteousness; in turning the hearts of the disobedient to the wisdom of the just, and extending the borders of the Redeemer's kingdom.

And wilt thou, O merciful God, behold with compassion the perishing souls of thy sinful creatures. Raise up, we beseech thee, and send into thy harvest, able ministers of thy word; pastors and teachers after thine own heart, who shall labor faithfully and successfully in word and doctrine; whose meat and drink it shall be to know and do thy will.

And may it please thee, O thou Lord of the harvest, to convince the people among whom thy ministers labor, of sin, of righteousness and of judgment. Open their minds that they may understand the things of thy law: give them grace to hear meekly thy word, to receive, in an honest and good heart, the doctrines of eternal life, and bring forth the fruits of the spirit. May the light of thy truth and the power of thy grace be extended to the remotest regions of the earth, and all who do confess thy name live according to the precepts of thy holy word. Hear us, O Lord, we beseech thee, and grant our requests, for the sake of thy Son, our Savior, Jesus Christ. *Amen.*

A Prayer suitable for Associations, and other Meetings of the Clergy.

Most gracious Lord God, the Author of all blessedness and Giver of all good, who, by thy Son, Jesus Christ, hast appointed divers orders of ministers in thy church, and promised to be with them to the end of the world, look down, we beseech thee, with thy favor and blessings, upon us, thy unworthy servants, who are called to be thy mouth to the people, and to minister before thee in sacred things. Without thee nothing is strong, nothing holy, nothing good. Without the aid of thy Holy Spirit, and the wisdom which is from above, no man is sufficient for such a work. Increase and multiply upon us thy mercy, and be thou our ruler and guide. Awaken in our minds a just estimate and lively sense of the nature and duties and importance of the office and ministry to which we are called; to be messengers, watchmen and stewards of the Lord Jesus Christ; to teach and feed and provide for his family; to seek for his sheep who are dispersed abroad, that they may be saved in him forever. Though unworthy to loose the latchet of his shoes, we are called to labor in his name, and to pray men, in Christ's stead, to be reconciled to God. Preserve us, O Lord, from being deceived in regard to our call to this ministry, and from all unfaithfulness in the discharge of it. O thou God of mercy, may thy presence and thy grace be ever with us. Open our minds that we may understand the Scriptures and the true doctrines of eternal life. Awaken in our hearts a holy zeal for the honor of thy name, for the prosperity of thy church, and for the salvation of ourselves and others. May it be our meat and drink, and the supreme desire of our hearts, to walk in the steps of our Savior, Christ, and to do his work. Remove from us the fear of man and all undue regard to worldly things; may we truly and faithfully declare to all who have ears to hear the whole counsel of God, and so plant and water that thou mayst give increase, and our labor be not in vain.

In all trials and difficulties do thou, O blessed Lord, be our guide and support. Though bonds or afflictions abide us, may none of them move us from our steadfastness: may it be our chief desire to finish our course with joy, and the ministry which we have received, and to testify the gospel of the grace of God. To thee, our God and Savior, would we devote ourselves, our soul and body and spirit, with all our faculties. Fill our memory with the words of thy law and the truth of thy gospel. Help us to minister the doctrine and sacraments and discipline of Christ, according as thou hast commanded, and to banish and drive away from thy church all erroneous and strange doctrines which are contrary to thy word. Help us to be earnest and faithful in prayers for ourselves and for others; and to be diligent in reading and studying the Scriptures, and in the use of all other means which, through thy blessing, will help us in the performance of all the duties which appertain to our office and ministry.

And help us, O Lord, we beseech thee, so to

fashion our lives and to walk before the people, that we may be wholesome examples to the flock of Christ. Help us to follow after charity, which is the bond of perfectness, and to maintain and set forward as much as lieth in us, quietness, peace and love among all Christian people, and especially among them who are or shall be committed to our charge.

Be gracious, O Lord, to thy church. May the borders of Zion be enlarged, till the kingdoms of the earth shall become the kingdom of the Lord, and all the ends of the world shall rejoice in thy salvation. And wilt thou, O gracious Lord, behold, with thy favor and blessing, the churches and congregations with which we are severally and more particularly connected. We beseech thee to pour out thy spirit and revive thy work amongst them. Bless to their edification the ministry of thy word. By thy mighty power may sinners be converted, and the careless awakened to righteousness. Strengthen those who stand; comfort and bless the weak-hearted; raise up those who fall, and add to thy church such as should be saved.

Direct us, O Lord, in all that we do and ought to do, with thy most gracious favor, and further us with thy continual help, that in all our works, begun, continued and ended in thee, we may be instrumental in building up the Redeemer's kingdom, to the glory of thy great name, and the salvation of ourselves and others.

These things, and whatever else thou seest to be necessary and convenient to us, and to the flocks committed to our care, and to thy whole church, we humbly ask, through the merits and mediation of Jesus Christ, in whose name and words we further pray:—

Our Father who art in heaven, &c.

The two following forms of Prayer, to be used, the one at the opening, the other at the closing of a meeting, are chiefly from some forms compiled for the use of THE PROTESTANT EPISCOPAL CLERICAL ASSOCIATION OF THE CITY OF NEW YORK.

Prayers to be used at the Opening of a Meeting.

ALMIGHTY God, unto whom all hearts are open, and from whom all holy desires and all good counsels do proceed, cleanse the thoughts of our hearts, by the inspiration of thy Holy Spirit, that in all the exercises for which we are now gathered together in thy name, the words of our mouth and the meditations of our hearts may be acceptable in thy sight, through Jesus Christ, our strength and our Redeemer. *Amen.*

WE presume not to come to thy throne of grace, O merciful Lord, trusting in our own righteousness, but in thy manifold and great mercies. We are not worthy so much as to lift up our eyes unto heaven. We acknowledge the manifold sins which we have committed by thought, word and deed, against thy divine majesty. We beseech thee, O God, to behold us in mercy, not weighing our merits, but pardoning our offences. In the name of our Lord and Savior, Jesus Christ, and through his merits, we would come before thy gracious throne, beseeching thee, for his sake, to hear our supplications and prayers.

O Lord, show thy mercy upon us;
Ans. *And grant us thy salvation.*

O God, make clean our hearts within us;
Ans. *And take not thy Holy Spirit from us.*

O Lord, unto us, who are but dust, and unworthy sinners, is this grace given, that we should preach the unsearchable riches of Christ: that we are separated unto the gospel of thy Son; made overseers of the flock which he hath purchased with his own blood. Thou hast committed unto us the word of reconciliation, that we should show unto men the way of eternal life. Having received this ministry, as we have obtained mercy of thee, O Lord, we faint not, but earnestly desire, by manifestation of the truth, to commend ourselves to every man's conscience, in the fear of God. We feel, O heavenly Father, that we are not sufficient for these things: that our wisdom is but foolishness; our strength but weakness; our love. too cold; our faith too feeble, and our zeal too languid. Without thee we can do nothing good. Unspeakably precious are the souls committed to our trust; and if we are not faithful to warn them of their wicked way, their blood wilt thou require at the watchmen's hands. To whom can we look for succor but unto thee, O merciful Lord, whose grace is sufficient for us, and whose strength is made perfect in the weakness of thy ministers. Without thee, O blessed Jesus, who hast promised to be with them to the end of the world, we can do nothing; but in thy strength we can do all things which appertain to our office and ministry. Pour upon us the abundance of thy grace, that we may be strong in thee, O Lord, and in the power of thy might be able ministers of the New Testament. Increase our faith and trust in thee, and put upon us the whole armor of God, that we may withstand all the fiery darts of the wicked. These mercies we humbly beg, for the sake of Jesus Christ, our blessed Lord and Savior. *Amen.*

ALMIGHTY God, in thy great goodness to thy sinful creatures, be pleased to endue our souls with the spirit of love. May we love thee with all our heart and soul and mind, and follow after charity which is the bond of perfectness. Let the love of Christ so constrain us, that we may live not to ourselves, but unto Him, who died for our sins, and rose again for our justification; and grant us such fervent affection for the souls of men, and desire for their salvation, that we may be ready to impart, not the gospel only, but our lives also to those among whom we labor. May the weapons of our warfare be not carnal, but mighty, through God, to the casting down every thing that exalteth itself against thee, and bringing every thought into captivity to the obedience of Christ. Let not our speech and our preaching be with enticing words of man's wisdom, but in demonstration of the Spirit and of power. Open thou our understanding, that we may know the way of salvation as revealed in the gospel, and be wise to win souls to Christ. Teach us to declare, in his spirit, the whole counsel of God, keeping back nothing that is profitable; that sinners may be humbled, the Savior exalted, and God glorified in all things. These things we also ask in the name of our Lord and Savior, Jesus Christ. *Amen.*

O MERCIFUL God, unto whom we must all render an account of our stewardships, deliver us, we beseech thee, from the fear of man. May we count it a small thing to be judged of man's judgment, knowing that he who judgeth us is the Lord. May all our glorying be in the cross of Christ. May we never be ashamed to confess him before men; but have great boldness in the faith, and speak boldly, as we ought to speak, to make known the mystery of the gospel, that Christ may be magnified in us, whether by life, or by death. May it be our chief desire to make known among men Jesus Christ and him crucified, willing for his sake to be accounted fools, and to suffer reproaches and persecutions and distress. May we never think of ourselves more highly than we ought to think, nor be unduly influenced by the love of praise or filthy lucre; but be humble and meek, gladly becoming the servants of all, that men may be saved in Jesus Christ, through whom alone we offer these our humble prayers. *Amen.*

O Lord, we are encompassed with infirmities; whatever hindrances and difficulties beset us, enable us, in humble, steadfast faith, to look still to thee for guidance and strength. In patience may we possess our souls. Inspire us with such zeal as becometh those who bear the message of salvation to perishing sinners. May we have our people in our hearts, and long after them all, in the bowels of Jesus Christ; not ceasing to pray for them; warning every man, and teaching every man in all wisdom, that we may present every man perfect in Christ Jesus. Though the fruit of our labor do not soon appear, give us faith and patience to wait in hope, and with a holy confidence to trust in thee: relying upon thy promises, may we be steadfast, unmovable, always abounding in the work of the Lord, forasmuch as we know that our labor is not in vain in the Lord. May we never be forgetful of our dependence upon thee, but always remember that neither is he that planteth nor he that watereth any thing, but God that giveth the increase. Give, we earnestly beseech thee, O give thy blessing to our labors; let not thy word return unto thee void, but prosper it in the thing whereto thou sendest it. Be with us in season and out of season. Bear witness, by thy Spirit, to thy word, making it a savor of life to the hearers, awakening the careless, establishing the wavering, recovering those who err from the truth; comforting those who mourn, and building up thy people in their most holy faith. Grant these blessings, O gracious God, through Jesus Christ, our Lord and Savior. *Amen.*

WE humbly beseech thee, O heavenly Father, in behalf of the flocks which thou hast appointed us to feed, that thou wouldst grant them, according to the riches of thy glory, to be strengthened with might in the inner man, that Christ may dwell in their hearts by faith; that, being rooted and grounded in love, they may be able to comprehend, with all saints, what is the breadth and length, and depth and height, and know the love of Christ, which passeth knowledge, that they may be filled with all the fulness of God. From all ignorance, hardness of heart, and neglect of thy holy word, good Lord, deliver them. Give them grace to receive with meekness the ingrafted word, which is able to save their souls; and to be doers of the word, and not hearers only. Have mercy, O gracious Lord, upon the impenitent: alarm the careless, and awaken them to righteousness. Open the eyes of the blind; guide the inquiring; pity those who are deceived; be gracious to all who mourn for their sins, and defend thy people in every danger, and from every sin.

We beseech thee, O merciful God, to hear our prayers. Vouchsafe thy blessing upon our present meeting. May our coming together be for the better. We beseech thee, according to thy gracious promise, to be with us, who have met in thy name, and, we humbly trust, according to thy will. May this social interview tend to the good of thy church, and to the spiritual refreshment of our own souls. Preserve us from all error, levity, pride, and prejudice. May we love as brethren; be humble, affectionate and kind; and in all we think and speak and do, have a solemn sense of thy presence, and a single eye to thy glory. All these our humble petitions we offer and present unto thee, O heavenly Father, in the name and through the mediation of Jesus Christ, to whom, with thee, and the Holy Ghost, be all glory and praise, now and for evermore. *Amen.*

Our Father who art, &c.

Prayers to be used at the Conclusion of a Meeting.

Almighty God, the Father of all mercies, we, thine unworthy servants, do give thee most humble and hearty thanks for all thy goodness and loving kindness to us and to all men. Praised be thy glorious name for thine inestimable love in the redemption of the world by our Lord Jesus Christ. Wonderful are the mercies through him vouchsafed to thy sinful creatures; unspeakably precious the blessings which thou hast given us through his death and resurrection. We bless thee, O God, especially for this opportunity of talking of thy loving kindness, and for the delightful fellowship and communion which, by thy goodness, we have now been permitted to enjoy. Grant, O Lord, that great and permanent good, to ourselves and to others, may ensue from this meeting. Whatever lessons we have learned,—whatever impressions we have received, may they be sanctified and abiding. May brotherly love continue. May our love to Christ, and for his church, be increased: may we be more devoted to his service, and more heartily determined, in the sufficiency of his grace, to make full proof of our ministry. Enable us to endure hardness, as good soldiers of Jesus Christ; to be instant, in season and out of season: may we follow after righteousness, faith, meekness and love, and the gospel, which we preach, come to the hearers, not in word only, but also in power, to the purifying of the heart by faith.

But before thee, O God, who searchest the heart, and triest the reins of men, and while we rejoice in believing that thou hast been in the midst of us, we bow with self-abasement, and a sense of unworthiness, and ask thy forgiveness of the sins which we may have committed in thy presence. We feel that our holiest things have need of pardon. Have mercy upon us, O Lord, have mercy upon us and pardon our offences, for his sake who died for our sins and rose again for our justification, Jesus Christ our Lord. *Amen.*

O God, who hast commanded us to make intercession for all men, have mercy, we beseech thee, upon the whole church of Christ on earth. Let thy continued pity cleanse and defend it; and especially that portion of it with which we are particularly associated. Preserve it from all perils and adversities, and cause it to shine in the light of thy blessing, as a city set on a hill. Defend it from all heresy and schism. Take away every root of bitterness, that all its ministers and people may be kindly affectioned one to another; in honor preferring one another; not slothful in business; fervent in spirit, serving the Lord. On all our congregations and their pastors pour out a spirit of active and self-denying zeal; that they may labor in unity of spirit and in the bond of peace, to promote the spread of the gospel throughout our land, and to the uttermost parts of the earth. And to all the means of grace, and all the efforts of benevolence, in the churches in which we minister, vouchsafe thy favor, to guide, to govern and to prosper them, that thy glory may be advanced, and the kingdom of Christ enlarged. We humbly pray for thy blessing upon the bishops of our church, and especially upon him who has the spiritual superintendence of the churches under our care. Endow them richly with all the wisdom, love, tenderness, firmness and zeal necessary to the faithful discharge of the duties of their office. Deeply imbue their hearts with the spirit of Christ. May all their influence be holy. May they lay hands suddenly on no man; and may all those whom they do ordain to the sacred ministry, be such as will do the work of evangelists. May they labor in hope, and so fight the good fight of faith, and finish their course, that finally they may receive a crown of righteousness, which fadeth not away, through Jesus Christ, their Lord and Master.

Ans. *O Lord, we beseech thee to hear us.*

To all who are or shall be ordained to the various orders of the ministry in thy church, give thy grace and heavenly benediction. May they take heed to themselves and to their doctrine, and be examples to the flock, in word, in conversation, in charity, in spirit, in faith and purity, giving no offence in any thing, that the ministry be not blamed. May they avoid questions which do but gender strife, and be gentle unto all men, apt to teach and patient; in meekness instructing them who oppose themselves. In doctrine may they show uncorruptness, gravity, sincerity: not being ashamed of the testimony of the Lord, but ready to be partakers of the afflictions of the gospel, according to the power of God. May they show themselves workmen who need not be ashamed, rightly dividing the word of truth. Increase, O Lord, we humbly beseech thee, the number of pious, faithful ministers: thou gracious Lord of the harvest, send into it laborers qualified and disposed truly to do thy work. If thou give the word, great will be the company of the preachers. Do thou, in thy merciful goodness, give shepherds to all destitute flocks, and build up the waste places of Zion. We pray thee to give thy blessing to those institutions, in which candidates for the ministry are educated for the work whereunto thou shalt be pleased to call them. Enlighten the understanding, sanctify the hearts, and prosper the efforts of those who conduct them; and so enrich the youth connected with them, that they may become apt and meet to exercise the ministry, to the glory of God, and to the edifying of his church.

Ans. *O Lord, we beseech thee to hear us.*

We pray, O gracious Lord, that all Christians may have more and more of the mind of Christ, and be diligent in all good works. May all their endeavors to do thy will be sanctified by thy Spirit, guided by thy wisdom, and prospered by thy blessing. May an ardent desire for the coming of thy kingdom unite the hearts, increase the prayers, and multiply the exertions of all who name themselves of Christ. May they pray earnestly and strive diligently, that the gospel may be preached to every creature. May we deeply lament the weakness of our faith, and the coldness of our love and our zeal for thee and for thy church. O Lord, we beseech thee, pour out upon all Christian people the spirit of missions;—the earnest desire, by all proper means, to spread to all the nations of the earth the knowledge of Christ, and the doctrines of eternal life. May the treasury of the Lord be filled with the means of supporting those who do the work of evangelists. May thy blessing be with those servants of Christ who have gone forth to preach the gospel to the destitute, whether in heathen or in Christian lands, and let the power of thy grace be manifested in their success. Have mercy upon all idolaters and unbelievers. For the children of Israel, unto whom pertained the adoption and the covenants, and of whom, as concerning the flesh, Christ came, we offer our earnest intercession. Our hearts' desire and prayer to thee for Israel is, that they may be saved. From the rising of the sun unto the going down of the same, let thy name be great among the Gentiles, and in every place may incense be offered unto thy name and a pure offering. O take the heathen for thine inheritance, and the utmost parts of the earth for thy possession.

Ans. *O Lord, we beseech thee to hear us.*

Finally, O Lord, we beseech thee to have mercy on us, unworthy sinners. Whatever we need in time, and for eternity, vouchsafe to grant; and when we have served thee in our generation, may we sleep in Jesus, and meet at thy right hand, having our garments washed and made white in the blood of the Lamb. And unto the Father, the Son and the Holy Ghost, three persons and one God, be all honor and glory, world without end. *Amen.*

The grace of our Lord Jesus Christ, and the love of God, and the fellowship of the Holy Ghost, be with us all evermore. *Amen.*

A Prayer for the Success of Missionary Labors.

O Lord God, our heavenly Father, who, in thy mercy, hast so loved the world as to give thine only Son to be our Savior, and hast commanded that the good tidings of pardon and peace and life, through faith in him, should be proclaimed to all mankind, give us hearts, we beseech thee, to be duly thankful for this thy unspeakable goodness, and hear our supplications and prayers. May a thankful sense of thy mercy to our fallen, sinful race, awaken in our hearts a deep concern for the salvation of those for whom the Savior died. Give thy blessing, we beseech thee, to the means and efforts used for the propagation of the gospel, and for extending the light of thy word through the darkness of this sinful world.

Accept, O Lord, of our supplications for those nations and people of the earth who are sitting in the shadow of death, having no hope, and without God in the world; and for all who are in error or ignorance or unbelief. May the Sun of righteousness rise upon them, with healing in his wings. Take from them all blindness and hardness of heart, and give them repentance unto life. Bless thy word wherever it is spoken, and send it to all places where it is not heard. Look with favor upon the ministers of thy gospel: give them wisdom and faith and zeal, and so bless thy word spoken by their mouth, that the renovating doctrines of eternal life may be truly taught, truly received and truly followed, and the earth be filled with the knowledge of the Lord. Give thy blessing, we beseech thee, to Bible and Missionary societies, and to all who assist and labor and contribute for the spread of the gospel, and for the promotion of truth and godliness. Remember them, O Lord, for good, and prosper and reward their labor of love.

Grant, O God, we beseech thee, that thy ministering servants, who have left their homes, their friends, and their country, to publish thy truth in foreign climes, may be under thy special care and keeping. Preserve them, O thou Father of mercies, from perils by land and perils by water; from sickness, from enemies, and from every evil to which they may be exposed. Give them such wisdom and such success that they may be instruments of turning many to righteousness, and hereafter shine as the brightness of the firmament, and as the stars, forever and ever. Guide and bless them, we beseech thee, in every effort to extend the knowledge of Jesus Christ.

And be merciful, O Lord, we beseech thee, to the perishing souls among whom they labor. Do thou, who desirest not the death of a sinner, but rather that he should be converted and live to thee, have mercy upon all who are living in sin, and give them repentance towards thee, the true God, and faith towards the Lord Jesus Christ, that they may be saved among the true Israelites, and become one fold under one Shepherd.

And grant, O blessed Lord, that the stewards of thy mysteries who labor among us in word and doctrine, may be endued with wisdom from on high; and that we may so profit by their ministry, that in the last day, when our Savior Christ shall come in glorious majesty to judge the world, we may rise to life immortal, through him who liveth and reigneth with thee and the Holy Ghost, ever one God, world without end. *Amen.*

A Prayer for Missionary Societies, and suitable to be used in their Meetings.

O blessed Lord God, who art exalted above the heavens, and yet, through thine infinite mercy, hast so loved the world, as to give thine only Son to be our Savior, and the author of everlasting life; who, after he had made perfect our redemption by his death and resurrection, sent abroad into the world apostles and prophets and other ministers, to preach the gospel to every creature, and to make disciples of all nations; for these, so great benefits of thy eternal goodness, and that thou art still calling thy ministering servants to the same labor of love, and dost inspire in the hearts of many people a pious desire to strengthen their hand, and to promote the spread of thy gospel, and the salvation of mankind, we render thee most hearty thanks; we bless and praise thy holy name.

Accept, O Lord, we beseech thee, our prayers and supplications for the ministers of thy gospel; give them such wisdom and faith and zeal, and so bless thy word spoken by their mouth, that thy work may prosper in their hands, and that humble, believing souls may in vast numbers fly to thy church as doves to their windows. Behold in mercy all those throughout the world who are in the darkness of error or of unbelief. Take from them, we beseech thee, all ignorance, hardness of heart, and opposition to thy holy word; and so fetch them home, blessed Lord, to thy flock, that they may be saved among the remnant of the true Israelites, and become one fold under one Shepherd, Jesus Christ.

Give thy blessing, O Lord, we beseech thee, to all Missionary associations, and to all those who contribute to support the preaching of the gospel, and labor to extend the borders of the Redeemer's kingdom. Wilt thou rule their hearts, enlarge their means, bless them in their pious labors, and remember them for good.

We beseech thee, O God, to look down with thy favor and blessing upon us, who, through thy merciful goodness, are here assembled. Help us to know thy truth, to do thy will, and to live to thy glory. Direct us in our humble efforts to extend the knowledge of thy truth, and the ministrations of thy gospel to those who need them. [Accept, O Lord, our alms and oblations.] Grant that what is cast into thy treasury may be so disposed of and applied, as to aid in extending the knowledge of thy salvation, and increasing the practice of pure and undefiled religion. May all we do be by us designed, and by thee directed, to the setting forth of thy praise, and to the salvation of ourselves and others. Assist us mercifully, O Lord, with thy heavenly grace, and dispose all our ways towards the attainment of everlasting salvation; and in all the changes and perils of this mortal life, may we ever be defended by thy most gracious and ready help, through Jesus Christ our Lord. And may the grace of our Lord Jesus Christ be with us evermore. *Amen.*

Another for a Missionary Society.

ALMIGHTY and everliving God, unto whom all hearts are open, all desires known, and from whom no secrets are hid, cleanse the thoughts of our hearts by the inspiration of thy Holy Spirit, that we may perfectly love thee, and on this occasion, with thankful hearts and holy affections, come before thee with prayer and praise. We bless thy holy name that thou hast given thine only Son

Jesus Christ to be the Savior of the world, and that thou hast commanded the good tidings of pardon and life, through him, to be proclaimed and taught to all mankind. Praised be thy name that thou hast vouchsafed to call us to the knowledge of thy grace and faith in thee. We bless thee, O God, that we live in a land where the gospel is preached and thy word is known. Make us, we beseech thee, duly thankful for these and for all thy mercies; and give us grace to show forth thy praise, by a holy zeal for enlarging the borders of the Redeemer's kingdom, and imparting the light of thy holy word to those who are in spiritual darkness, and in the ignorance of unbelief. Be gracious unto thy church; grant that every member of it may serve thee faithfully. May it be so guided by thy good Spirit, that all who profess and call themselves Christians may be led into the way of truth, and hold the faith, once delivered to the saints, in unity of spirit, in the bond of peace, and in righteousness of life. Send down, we beseech thee, upon our bishops and other clergy, and upon the congregations committed to their charge, the healthful spirit of thy grace; and that they may truly please thee, pour upon them the continual dew of thy blessing. Bless thy word wherever it is spoken, and send it to those places where it is not heard. Inspire with heavenly wisdom and holy zeal all the ministers of thy gospel, and those especially who, as missionaries and evangelists, labor to extend the borders of the Redeemer's kingdom.

And we implore thy blessing upon those who associate and who contribute of their substance to support and to extend the preaching of thy word and the ministrations of the Savior's gospel; and especially upon thy people who are now, by thy gracious permission, here assembled. Accept, O Lord, our alms and oblations; and grant that what has been and shall be cast into thy treasury, or given for missionary purposes, and other pious use, may be so disposed of and applied, as to be the means of extending the knowledge of thy saving truth, and of turning the hearts of the disobedient to the wisdom of the just. And vouchsafe, O Lord, so to rule the hearts and bless the labors of all thy people, that the comfortable gospel of Christ may be truly preached, truly received and truly followed, till all the ends of the earth shall rejoice in thy salvation.

Awaken within us a prudent, godly zeal, in promoting our own and others' salvation. Give thy blessing to all Bible and Missionary societies. May we never be weary in well doing, but ever rejoice to be instrumental in extending to others those religious privileges which through thy blessing we enjoy. Direct us, O Lord, in all our doings, with thy most gracious favor, and further us with thy continual help, that in all our works and all our efforts, we may seek thy glory and do thy will; and finally obtain everlasting life, through Jesus Christ, our Lord and Savior. *Amen.*

Another Prayer suitable for Clerical or Missionary Associations.

O HOLY, just and merciful God, unto whom all hearts are open, all desires known, and from whom no secrets are hid, mercifully incline thine ears to the prayers and supplications which we desire humbly to ask in the name of Jesus Christ. Behold us in mercy; forgive our sins; sanctify our hearts, and renew a right spirit within us. Impress upon us a just and deep sense of thy goodness to us and to all men. Make us duly thankful for the inestimable gift of a divine Savior, and for the knowledge of thy grace and faith in him. Make us thankful that our lot has fallen in a Christian land; that the Holy Scriptures, containing a revelation of thy will, are in our hands; that the gospel of salvation is preached in our ears; that means, and ordinances, and opportunities are given to teach the doctrines of life, and build us up in thy holy faith and fear. Make us thankful, O Lord, for these great blessings, and give us grace to make a right use of them. May we love the things which thou commandest, and desire those which thou dost promise; and among the manifold changes of this world, may our hearts be surely fixed where true joys are to be found.

May the light of thy gospel shine throughout the world, and they who have received it live as becomes it. Revive, O Lord, thy work amongst us, and extend the light of thy truth to all who are still living in sin and in the darkness of unbelief. Inspire with holy zeal the ministers of the gospel; give them such knowledge and utterance, and so bless thy word spoken by their mouth, that the saving doctrines of the cross may be truly preached, truly received, and truly followed, and the earth be filled with the knowledge of the Lord.

Awaken in the hearts of thy people an earnest desire to hold up the hands of thy ministers, and help them in fulfilling their Master's command, to preach the gospel to every creature. Give thy blessing, we beseech thee, to all those who associate for this purpose, and by their substance, their counsel, and their prayers, endeavor to aid in this pious work. May they never be weary in well doing. Pour upon them the abundance of thy blessings: may they never want the consolations of the faith and hope which in love they would extend to others.

Be merciful, O Lord, to all mankind. May sinners be awakened to righteousness, and turn to thee with penitence and prayer. May they who are seeking thy love, find thee in a time accepted. Wilt thou, O Lord, reveal thyself to them, as thou dost not to the world. Direct their hearts into the love of God, and into the patient waiting for Christ. Comfort and encourage them by thy gracious promises of pardon and acceptance. Those who come to thee in faith thou wilt not reject. O give unto them who ask; let them who seek, find; open the door of thy blessed kingdom to those who knock, that they may find pardon and peace and rest for their souls.

Keep, we beseech thee, O Lord, thy church with thy perpetual mercy. Grant that the course of this world may be so peaceably ordered by thy governance, that thy people may joyfully serve thee in all godly quietness. Being hurt by no persecutions and discouraged by no trials, may we evermore give thanks unto thee in thy holy church. And because the frailty of man without thee cannot but fall, keep us ever, by thy help, from all things hurtful, and lead us to all things profitable to our salvation.

Do thou, O merciful God, who hast permitted us at this time to unite in supplications unto thee, and dost promise that when two or three are gathered together in thy name, thou wilt grant their requests; graciously hear and fulfil these our desires and petitions, which we ask and present in the name and through the mediation of Jesus Christ, our blessed Lord and Savior. *Amen.*

A Prayer that may be used in Meetings on Charitable Occasions, after a Sermon and Contribution.

ADORABLE and everliving God, who, by thy righteous providence, orderest all things in heaven and on earth, and whose mercies are, like thy years, unnumbered, we desire humbly to adore thee for thy infinite perfections; we bless thy holy name for thy manifold favors daily bestowed upon us and upon all mankind, both spiritual and temporal; and chiefly we adore thee for thy mercy in Jesus Christ. Praised be thy name, that thou hast been pleased to call us to the knowledge of thy grace and faith in thee; that we live in a land where the gospel is preached; and that we are permitted still to hear it. We bless thee especially for this opportunity of uniting in prayer and praise before thee, and of hearing the counsels of thy word. May thy truth be grafted inwardly in our hearts, and bring forth in us the fruit of good living.

Thou hast taught us that all our doings without charity are nothing worth; send thy Holy Spirit, and pour into our hearts that most excellent gift of Christian love, which is the bond of peace and of all virtues, and without which whosoever liveth is counted as dead before thee. Accept, O Lord, the alms and oblations and the prayers which we have offered before thee, not weighing our merits, but pardoning our offences. Inspire us with that love which is the fulfilling of the whole law. May we, through thy grace, be ready to every good work, and never be weary in well doing.

Behold, we beseech thee, with thy compassionate mercy, all the sons and daughters of sorrow. Provide for the fatherless children and widows, and all who are poor and needy; and dispose us to be bountiful according to our means, and to pity those who need the comforts which, through thy goodness, we enjoy. And when we shall have served thee in our generation, may we be found acceptable in thy sight, and receive that blessing which thy well beloved Son shall pronounce to all who love and serve thee, saying, Come, ye blessed of my Father, receive the kingdom prepared for you from the beginning of the world. Grant this, we beseech thee, O merciful God, through Jesus Christ, our Mediator and Redeemer. *Amen.*

Another, more general.

O Lord, our heavenly Father, whose blessed Son, Jesus Christ, in tender love to mankind, did take our nature upon him, and did spend his life in works of mercy, and went about doing good; grant that the spirit may be in us which was in him, the like benevolence and tender love for mankind. Make us pitiful, inclined to mercy and good works. According to our means and opportunities, make us ready to give and glad to distribute, desiring through thy mercy and our Savior's merits to lay up treasures in heaven, where moth and rust cannot corrupt them. May we love our neighbors as we love ourselves, and do to all men as we would have them do to us. May we be ready and disposed to extend to the destitute and needy such charitable aid as, in a like situation, we should reasonably desire to receive. May we be merciful as we hope to obtain mercy, and freely give, from the consideration that we freely receive.

Behold us, O Lord, with thy favor and blessing on this present occasion, and prosper the work which our hands now find to do. Favorably, with mercy, hear our prayer, and graciously accept what we contribute to honor thy name, and to benefit our fellow-men. May all our offerings be made with pure hearts and charitable affections; may they be blest to the promotion of the objects for which they are given, and be accepted of thee, O thou God of all mercy and grace, as a sacrifice with which thou art well pleased.

We are sensible, O God, and may we never forget, that our best deeds are without merit before thee; we would not put our trust in any thing that we do. We are unworthy, through our manifold sins, to offer unto thee any sacrifice; yet we beseech thee to accept this our bounden duty and service, not weighing our merits, but pardoning our offences, and receiving our humble offerings, through the merits and mediation of thy Son, our Savior, Jesus Christ. *Amen.*

Another Prayer for the Meeting of a Charitable Society.

O Lord and merciful God, who hast taught us in thy holy word that the end of the commandment is charity, and hast promised that the merciful shall obtain mercy; we beseech thee favorably to behold and bless thy servants, the members of the society here present, who have associated for the benevolent purpose of benefiting their fellow-creatures. [*The particular object of the society may here be expressed.*] We beseech thee, O Lord, to strengthen, direct and prosper them in this, their pious work and labor of love. Enlarge still more their hearts and their means for doing good. Direct them in all they do with thy most gracious favor; prosper them with thy continual help, and pour upon them the abundance of thy grace, that their benevolent labors may be extensively useful, to the glory and praise of thy great name, and to the relief and comfort of those who need. Wilt thou, O blessed Lord, remunerate their kindness and remember them for good. Bless them in their houses and their stores. The Lord deliver them in the time of trouble: the Lord preserve and keep them, that they may be blest upon the earth, and be prepared to dwell with thee in life everlasting, through Jesus Christ, our Lord. *Amen.*

For Improvement in Sickness.*

O God and merciful Father, who despisest not the sighing of a contrite heart, nor the desires of those who are afflicted or distressed, mercifully assist us in the prayers which we would now make before thee. Thou knowest, Lord, our necessities before we ask, and the imperfection of our sincerest prayers. We beseech thee to cleanse our hearts from the defilement of sin, and to sanctify our thoughts by the inspiration of thy Holy Spirit. With pity behold our infirmities and sorrows, and assist us in the supplications and prayers which we desire, with all due reverence and humility, to offer before thee. Turn from us the evils that we have justly deserved; and help us, in all dangers and afflictions, to put our whole trust and confidence in thy mercy, and patiently submit to thy holy will. Remember not, Lord, our offences, but thy mercy to us in Jesus Christ. Grant us that peace which

---

* In the English "Clergyman's Companion," is a great variety of prayers for the sick, collected from many eminent divines of the English church; which, with extracts on other subjects, were republished in New York in 1806, by the Rev. J. H. Hobart, D. D.; and in 1828, being then bishop of that diocese, he published another edition, with alterations and additions. As those excellent compilations are probably in the hands of most of our clergy, I have inserted in this work fewer prayers for the use of the sick.

the world cannot give, and that comfort of hope which we are not worthy to ask, but in his most holy name.

Trusting not in ourselves, but in his merits, and in thy gracious promise to hear our prayers for the sick and afflicted, we humbly beseech thee to look down, with favor and compassion, upon [this family visited with affliction. With pity behold their fears and their sorrows, and support and comfort and bless them, according as they have need. Prepare them, we beseech thee, for every event of thy providence. And wilt thou, O merciful God, visit with the consolations of thy comfort and peace] this thy servant, visited with sickness. [*Here the particular case may be named.*] Look upon *him* with the eyes of thy mercy. If it be consistent with thy goodness, preserve *him*, we beseech thee, from bodily pains and distress, and from all needless doubts and fears and faithless apprehensions. May *his* reason be clear, *his* mind composed, and *his* thoughts occupied with spiritual things; and whatever trials and sufferings it may seem good to thee to inflict, grant *him*, we beseech thee, patience to bear the rod, and grace to know who hath appointed it. According to *his* day, so may *his* strength be. May *his* soul, being awakened to righteousness and renewed by grace, rely upon thy mercy, confident that thou art wise and good in all thy dealings, and that thou lovest those whom thy hand correcteth. Give *him* a deep sense of thy power and authority over all the works of thy hand. Knowing that the Lord is just, may every murmuring thought be suppressed, and patience have its perfect work in a cheerful resignation to thy unerring will. May *he* wait thy pleasure with humble submission, knowing that thou art patient with a returning sinner, and that all things work for good to those who love and fear thee.

And grant, O Lord, that *he* may be more desirous that this affliction should be sanctified, than that it should be removed. Give *him* grace to profit by this visitation, as an occasion of spiritual improvement. May it awaken in *his* mind a more lively sense of the shortness and uncertainty of this present life, and of the vast importance of being prepared for a future state. Grant *him* that repentance which is not to be repented of, and that faith in the Lord Jesus Christ which reneweth the heart, worketh by love, and overcometh the world. May *he* look unto Jesus as the author and finisher of *his* faith, and the end of the law for righteousness to those who believe. O visit *him* with thy salvation; support *him* by thy grace; do for *him*, and work in *him*, whatever is necessary for *his* present comfort and eternal good; and grant *him* such a lively hope of thy mercy in Jesus Christ, that *he* may say with thy apostle, For me to live is Christ, and to die is gain.

But thou knowest, Lord, the weakness of our nature, and how little it is that we can bear. That *his* patience fail not, and for the glory of thy great name, wilt thou return in mercy and say to this affliction, It is enough. All medicines act by thy decree; all means prevail if thou shalt bless them. Bless, we beseech thee, the means and remedies used and applied for restoring our *brother* to health and ease. Give wisdom to those who minister, and strength to *him* who receives them. But let no confidence in natural means or human skill diminish *his* hope and trust in thee. If it be thy good pleasure that *his* health may be restored, may *his* love to thee increase, and a thankful sense of thy goodness induce *him* to devote the residue of *his* life to the God who giveth it. May the remainder of *his* days be spent in thy service and to thy glory. And whatever may be thy wise purpose respecting *his* term of days here on the earth, give *him* grace, we beseech thee, so to take thy visitation, that, after this painful life is ended, *he* may dwell with thee in life everlasting. Dispose *his* heart to return *his* spirit willingly to thee who gavest it, as into the hands of a faithful Creator; and with great humility and a deep sense of thy goodness, to look and hope for thy salvation in Jesus Christ.

And grant, O Lord, that each and all of us, in our best estate of health, may seriously consider, and continually remember, how frail and sinful and mortal we are. May we not boast ourselves of to-morrow, nor forget our dependence upon thee. May we not abuse thy patience and long-suffering by sinful vanities, nor incumber our minds with needless cares, deceitful pleasures, or unprofitable pursuits of this present world. Grant us grace to pass the time of our sojourning here in thy faith and fear; and to live so righteously, soberly and godly in this present world, as becometh those who must shortly die; as becometh those who are redeemed from death by the precious blood of Jesus Christ; as becometh those who must soon appear before thy judgment seat. Hear us, O merciful God, we humbly beseech thee, for thy mercy's sake in Jesus Christ. *Amen.*

For a Person in a Decline, or dangerously sick.

O MOST merciful and gracious God, who art the hope of all the ends of the earth, and our only refuge in distress, with great reverence and humility, and a deep sense of our unworthiness, we would bow ourselves in the dust before thee. To thee belong mercies and forgiveness, though we have sinned and done wickedly. Remember not, Lord, our offences, but thy mercy to mankind in Jesus Christ. For his sake we beseech thee to blot out our offences, and forgive our multiplied transgressions.

Most just art thou, O Lord, in all thy dealings with the sons of men. Affliction cometh not of the dust; thy righteous providence governeth all things here below. Sickness and pains and sorrows are the dispensations of thy hand, and are less than our sins deserve. In the midst of life we are in death; to whom can we fly for help and salvation but unto thee who for our sins art justly displeased!

Trusting in thy compassionate mercy, we beseech thee, O God, to accept our prayers and intercessions for this thy servant. Do thou, to whom belong the issues of life and death, and in whom alone dwelleth all the fulness of mercy and grace, strengthen, support and comfort *him* according to the necessity of *his* case. Give *him* unfeigned repentance for all the errors of *his* life past, and a steadfast faith in thy Son Jesus Christ. Endue *his* soul with patience and resignation to thy holy will. Enable *him* to see love in thy rod and justice in thy dealings, and to bow in submission before thee. May *he* neither despise thy chastening nor faint under thy rebukes, but make improvement from this visitation, as an opportunity for *his* soul's benefit. May *his* heart be raised in hope and love to thee. Reveal to *his* soul the comforts of thy mercy in Jesus Christ, and of thy reconciled countenance. Forsake *him* not in this momentous trial of *his* faith and patience, but visit *him* with thy salvation. Preserve *him*, if such be thy good pleasure, from bodily pains, and discouragement of mind. Whatever of good is fitting for us to ask and for *him* to receive, we beseech thee in thy mercy to bestow. Prolong *his* days here on the earth, for the comfort of *his* friends, and that *he* may do good in *his* generation. Bless the food and the remedies administered to the increase of *his* bodily strength, and, if it be thy good pleasure, to *his* restoration to perfect health. Do thou, who heardst the prayers of Hezekiah on the bed of sickness, lengthen *his* years on earth, and help *him* to devote them to thee in a holy and obedient walking before thee.

But if thou hast in thy wisdom otherwise appointed, and whether sooner or later it shall be thy pleasure to remove *him* from this life, fit and prepare *him*, we humbly beseech thee, for immortal blessedness. Reform whatever is amiss in the temper and disposition of *his* mind. Give *him* unfeigned repentance for all the sins of *his* past life; mercifully forgive whatever offences *he* may have committed against thee. Grant *him* a sound and steadfast and victorious faith in our Savior Christ. Raise *his* affections from the things of this world to the joys of immortality. Make *his* repentance perfect, *his* faith lively and strong, *his* hope steadfast, *his* reason clear, *his* patience unshaken, *his* submission humble, and *his* resignation complete. And when the lamp of life shall expire, when the time shall come, whether soon, or at some distant period, that *his* soul shall be freed from its mortal prison, may it find a safe and easy passage to the world above; and, being washed and sanctified in the blood of Christ, be numbered among the spirits of just men made perfect.

And now, what, Lord, is our hope? truly our hope is in thee. Whom else have we in heaven, and what is there on earth that we can reasonably desire in comparison of thee, our God and Savior? Make us ever mindful of the time when we shall lie down to sleep in the dust. May we so apply our hearts unto true wisdom, that we may die the death of the righteous, and our last end be like his. Thou knowest, Lord, the secrets of our hearts; shut not thy merciful ears to our prayers, but spare us, good Lord, spare the people whom thou hast redeemed with thy precious blood. O holy, just and merciful God, thou righteous Savior of a sinful world, deliver us not into the bitter pains of eternal death. Preserve us through life from the peril of temptation, and suffer us not, at our last hour, for any fear of death, to fall from thee. Raise us, we beseech thee, from the death of sin to a life of righteousness, that when we depart this life we may rest in Jesus Christ; and at the general resurrection, in the last day, be found acceptable in thy sight, and receive, through the merits of the Savior's blood, the rewards and felicity prepared for the righteous in heaven. With those who have departed this life in thy faith and fear, may we have our perfect consummation and bliss, in thy eternal kingdom of life and glory, through the merits of our Lord and Savior, Jesus Christ. *Amen.*

A Prayer for a Sick Person, when there appeareth but little or no hope of recovery.

O FATHER of mercies and God of all comfort, with whom belong the issues of life and death, and who art our only hope in time of danger or distress, with deep reverence and humility we would look unto thee for succor in behalf of this thy servant here lying under thy hand in great weakness of body. Behold *him*, O Lord, in mercy, and support *him* with thy heavenly grace; though the outward man decay and nature fail, strengthen *him*, we beseech thee, with thy Holy Spirit. Remember not, Lord, *his* offences past; grant *him*, O merciful God, through the merits of a righteous Savior, repentance unfeigned and sincere for all *his* sins, and that righteousness which is by faith in Jesus Christ.

Shouldst thou be extreme to mark iniquities, O Lord, who could stand! but there is forgiveness with thee, that thou mayst be feared. Let thine ears be attentive to our humble supplications; may thy forgiveness be extended to this our *brother*, who, in this hour of bodily weakness, and in this momentous trial of *his* faith and hope, would look unto thee who alone canst save. With confidence in thy mercy, and trusting in thy gracious promises, we would commend *him* into thy hands, as into the hands of a faithful Creator, and a merciful Savior; praying that thou wilt work in *him* and do for *him* what shall be best for *his* present comfort, and for *his* eternal good. Preserve *him*, O God, if it be consistent with thy wisdom, from bodily pains, and bless whatever shall be ministered for *his* comfort and ease. May *he* have strength and patience to bear whatever thy just hand shall inflict, and grace to make all the improvement from this sickness which thy wisdom intendeth.

There is nothing, O Lord, impossible with thee. Shouldst thou speak the word, *he* would be restored to health; and we beseech thee, O God, if it be consistent with thy unerring wisdom, that thou wilt raise *him* up and grant *him* a longer continuance on the earth. O spare *him* a little, before *he* go hence and be no more seen! If thy wisdom has otherwise appointed, O be thou merciful to *his* soul, and fit and prepare *him* for a happier state. Sanctify *his* heart, and renew a right spirit within *him*. Preserve *him* from the temptations of the enemy, and from all desponding fears. May *he* know and feel that thou art a God, mighty to save; and plead with thee, in a lively faith, the merits of an infinite Savior. And when thou shalt call *him* hence, may *he* depart in peace, and *his* soul be received into those heavenly mansions which the Savior has prepared for those who love him.

And teach those of us, O God, who survive amidst the daily scenes of mortality which surround us, to realize how short and uncertain is human life, that whatever our hands find to do, we may do it with all diligence and care, before that night cometh in which no man can work. Teach us to watch and to pray, and to remember that the Son of man cometh at an hour which we know not. Thou, Lord, only knowest how soon we shall be as water spilt on the ground. May we ever be mindful of the one thing needful, and finish our work before our course is done. Hear us, O Lord, we beseech thee, for thy mercy's sake in Jesus Christ. *Amen.*

A Prayer for a Sick Person, when there is reason to hope that he is convalescent.

MERCIFUL and gracious God, the Giver and the Preserver of our lives, we desire to approach thee, in humble confidence that thou wilt hear the prayer of faith, and impart thy grace to those who need. We know, and we thankfully acknowledge, that all things, in heaven and on earth, are at thy just and wise disposal, and that not a sparrow falleth except the Lord permit. We beseech thee, O God, to pardon our sins, and to accept the supplications and prayers which, with all due reverence and submission, we desire now to present before thee. May we come before thee with penitence and faith; with a thankful sense of thy unnumbered mercies, and with a holy confidence in thy word and promises, revealed in Jesus Christ. Permit us, O Lord, [again] to plead with thee in behalf of this our sick *brother*, who [still] would look unto thee for succor. Most cordially do we unite with *him* in humble, grateful and devout acknowledgments of thy great and manifold goodness vouchsafed to *him* at all times, and especially during *his* present sickness. We bless thee, O Lord, that thou hast not forsaken *him* in this trial of *his* faith and patience; but hast visited *him* with many comforts, [and enabled *him* to bear this visitation with resignation to thy holy will; that thou hast, as we humbly hope and trust, brought *him* nearer to thyself, and revealed to *his* soul the comforts of thy love in Jesus Christ.] We thank thee that *he* is surrounded with kind friends, and with many temporal comforts. [We bless thee, O thou God of all mercy, that, as we have reason to hope, thou hast sent *him* relief, and that *his* sickness has abated.] Thou art able to give *him* full strength, and to raise *him* up to perfect health. We beseech thee, O Lord, if it be consistent with thy wisdom, that thou wilt extend to *him* this great blessing; that thou wilt give medicine to heal *his* sickness, and prosper the means and remedies ministered and applied, to *his* entire relief. *He* is weak, but thou art almighty: *he* is brought low, but speak the word only, and *he* shall be made whole. Restore *him*, we beseech thee, to health of body, vigor of mind, and cheerfulness of spirit, that *he* may go to thy house, and offer thee, with great gladness, the sacrifice of praise and thanksgiving, the fruit of *his* lips, and the oblation of *his* heart: may he pay *his* vows in the presence of all thy people, and spend the remainder of *his* days in a holy and obedient walking in the way of thy commandments.

And wilt thou, O God, refresh *his* mind with spiritual comforts. Dispose *him*, in all things, to submit to thy righteous will. May *he* not be impatient under thy hand, but, through thy grace, behave suitably in every trial, and perform every duty which thou requirest. Sanctify this visitation, to the purifying of *his* heart from all sinful affections, and building *him* up in thy holy faith, till *he* arrives at the perfect stature of the fullness of Christ. Grant *him* a lively hope in thy heavenly promises, which shall be a helmet of salvation upon *his* head. O may *his* whole heart and soul be more and more conformed to the Savior's image. May the uncertainty of life and the frailty of this mortal nature, raise the more earnestly *his* hopes and desires to the immortal glories of the Redeemer's kingdom, and the endless joys of the world to come.

And we beseech thee, O Lord, to behold, with thy favor and blessing, all the sick and afflicted, bestowing upon them temporal comforts and spiritual consolations. Awakened by the visitations of thy mighty hand to a deep sense of the one thing needful, may their thoughts and their hopes be raised to thee. Give them repentance towards God, and faith towards the Lord Jesus Christ, that their sins may be done away by thy mercy, and their pardon sealed in heaven before they depart to the eternal world. May they whom thy rod correcteth neither despise thy chastenings, nor faint under thy rebukes, but make improvement from their sorrows to the benefit of their souls.

And we bless thy holy name for all thy servants departed this life in thy faith and fear, beseeching thee to give us grace so to follow their good examples, that with them we may be partakers of thy heavenly kingdom. Hear us, O Lord, we beseech thee, for Christ's sake, and hear the prayer which he has taught us:

Our Father who art, &c. *Amen.*

A Prayer for one who, from the nature of his sickness or other cause, is not able to unite understandingly in it.

O God and merciful Father, who despisest not the sighing of a contrite heart, nor the humble desires of those who look to thee for aid, mercifully behold our sorrows and hear our prayers. In the midst of life we are exposed to sickness, pains and death. To whom can we fly for refuge in distress but unto thee, O God, who, for our sins, art justly displeased, and art of purer eyes than to behold evil. Holy and just art thou in all thy ways, and righteous and merciful in thy dealings with the children of men. Humbly we implore thy forgiveness of our manifold transgressions. With pity behold the sorrows of our hearts and the infirmity of our nature, and turn from us those evils which we justly have deserved.

May we be duly thankful, that amidst the manifold sorrows of this mortal state, thou art a God of refuge, hearing prayer and pitying the distressed. In the confidence of this faith, we beseech thee, O Lord, to accept our supplications and prayers for those who are unable to pray for themselves; who by reason of mental disorder, or bodily weakness or distress, are not able to call on thee for what they need. Though we are unworthy, by reason of our sins, to pray on our own behalf, and to offer unto thee any sacrifice, yet we beseech thee, O God, to permit us to intercede particularly for this thy *servant*, beseeching thee to compassionate his infirmity. Whatever good is fitting for us to ask, and for *him* to receive, we beseech thee, in thy merciful goodness, to bestow. Write not *his* sins against *him*, O thou Preserver of men, but remember thy love in Jesus Christ. Thou knowest, Lord, *his* case, and *his* thoughts, and what *he* needs; we beseech thee to strengthen and relieve *him*, according to his necessities. So far as *he* is now capable of knowing thy will and *his* duty, may *he* be resigned and submissive; trusting in the merits of a righteous Savior. Enlighten *his* mind with thy heavenly grace. Hear the prayers of *his* friends. The less able *he* is to pray for *himself*, the more earnest should be our supplications on *his* behalf. Preserve *him*, we beseech thee, from bodily pains. Bless to *his* use and benefit the food and medicine which may be administered. Restore *him*, if it be consistent with thy unerring wisdom, to health of body and to soundness and vigor of mind, that *his* soul may bless thy holy name. Sanctify *his* sufferings to the benefit of *his* soul, and to the promotion of *his* salvation in Jesus Christ.

Blessed be thy holy name, that in the midst of judgment thou rememberest mercy; that thou lovest those whom thy rod correcteth; that thou givest ease to torturing pains, mingling many comforts with life's bitterest portion. Shall we receive good at thy hand, and shall we not receive evil? Help us, in all the sufferings and other trials of life, to say with our blessed Savior, Not as we will, but as thou wilt.

All flesh is as grass, and passeth away as the flower of the field. Make us deeply sensible of the shortness and uncertainty of human life, and let thy Spirit guide and support us through this vale of misery in holiness and righteousness, that when we have served thee in our generation, we may depart this life in peace; having the testimony of a good conscience; in the communion of thy holy church; in the confidence of a true faith; in the comfort of a sure religious hope; in favor with thee our God, and in perfect charity with all the world.

Assist us mercifully, O Lord, and hear us in these

our supplications, and dispose our ways towards the attainment of everlasting salvation. Among all the changes and sorrows of this mortal life, may we ever be defended by thy most gracious and ready help.

These things, and whatever else thou seest necessary for us, for our sick *friend*, [for this family,] and for the whole family of mankind, we humbly ask, in the name, and through the merits of our Lord and Savior, Jesus Christ. *Amen.*

A Prayer for a Sick Child.

ALMIGHTY God and most merciful Father, the Giver and the Preserver of our lives; to thee belong the issues of life and death; to thee alone can frail and sinful mortals fly for refuge in distress. Thou hast taught us by thy Son, Jesus Christ, that if we ask in true faith we shall receive; that if we seek, we shall find; that if we knock, the gates of thy mercy shall be opened unto us. With humble reverence we bow before thee, beseeching thee graciously to look upon our afflictions; with pity to behold the sorrows of our hearts; mercifully to forgive our sins, and favorably to hear our prayers. Graciously hear us, we humbly beseech thee: O blessed Lord, graciously hear our prayers, and grant the petitions which, in the name of Jesus Christ, we humbly present before thee. Look with thy compassionate favor upon this child visited with sickness. Visit *him*, O Lord, with thy salvation. *His* life is in thy hand; may it be precious in thy sight. Thou hast but to speak the word, and this child shall be well from the same hour. Deliver *him*, O Lord, we beseech thee, in thy good appointed time, from bodily pain and sickness, and save *his* soul for thy mercy's sake. Behold with pity the fears and sorrows of those who acknowledge their dependence, and rejoice that they are dependent upon a righteous, merciful and prayer-hearing God, whose tender mercies are over all thy works; who dost not willingly afflict or grieve the children of men; who intendest good in thy severest chastisements, and lovest the soul whom thy hand correcteth. If it be thy good pleasure that this child may live, and *his* days be prolonged on the earth, relieve *him*, we beseech thee, from bodily distress: bless the means which are used for restoring *him* to health. All medicines act by thy decree, and none can fail if thou shalt bless them. Grant that this child may live to thee. Guide and preserve *him* through all the dangers of life, both of soul and body. Make *him* a comfort to his friends, a blessing to the earth, and an instrument of thy glory, by serving thee faithfully, and doing good in *his* generation.

But if in thy wisdom thou hast otherwise appointed, and it be thy purpose to remove *him* from this world of pain and sins and sorrows, receive *him*, O God, we humbly beseech thee, into those heavenly habitations of life and glory, where the souls of those who rest in Jesus Christ enjoy perpetual felicity. May *his* soul be washed and sanctified in the Savior's blood. Give now unto us who ask; let us who seek, find; open to us who knock, that this child may enjoy thy heavenly benediction, and rest in the arms of that blessed Savior who has said, "Of such is the kingdom of God."

And wilt thou behold with compassion the distressing anxiety of the afflicted *parents*. Relieve them from their fears and apprehensions. Restore, we beseech thee, *their* beloved child to *their* arms in health; and may *he* long live to *their* comfort and to thy glory, a member of Christ, a child of God, and an inheritor of the kingdom of heaven. Or give *them* grace to submit with patience to thy superior wisdom, sensible that the Lord gave what he taketh away. Prepare *them* for every event of thy providence. In all *their* sorrows help *them* to say with thy servant of old, "It is the Lord, let him do what seemeth to him good." Give *them*, O Lord, in the abundant fruition of thy grace, a better portion than *sons* or *daughters*—an unfading inheritance among thy saints in light, where the righteous shall be forever happy. Hear us, O Lord, we beseech thee, for the worthiness of thy Son, our Savior, Jesus Christ. *Amen.*

A Prayer that may be used with a Family and their Friends on a Funeral Occasion.

O ETERNAL and everliving God, whose wise and just providence governeth all things in heaven and on earth; who hatest nothing that thou hast made, and hast compassion upon the children of men; we lift our eyes to thee as the Father of mercies, and our only help in time of sorrow and distress. With great reverence and humility, and with a deep sense of our unworthiness, we desire on this occasion to bow before thee in penitence and prayer.

Most just art thou, O Lord, in all thy dealings with mankind: affliction cometh not of the dust: the sorrows which visit the hearts of men receive commission all from thee. Sickness and pains and death are the dispensations of thy righteous hand, and they are less than our sins deserve. Thou art faithful and true in all thy ways: equity and judgment are the habitation of thy seat. We acknowledge the justice of that sentence which thou hast pronounced upon our fallen race, "Dust thou art, and unto dust shalt thou return." It is of thy mercy, and because thy compassion faileth not, that we are not consumed: that we yet remain living monuments of thy forbearing mercy, and are permitted to address thee in supplication and prayer. Graciously, O Lord, look upon us, in this season of affliction; mercifully forgive our sins; with pity behold the sorrow of our hearts; favorably hear our prayers, which, on this mournful occasion, we desire to offer before thy gracious throne.

Awakened by this painful visitation of thy providence, which hath called us [again] to the house of mourning, we adore thy justice; we would bow with submission and reverential awe. Extend, O Lord, thy compassionate mercy to each and all of us, who are here present. Forgive us our sins, and renew a right spirit within us. Spare us, O Lord, spare the people whom thou hast redeemed. Teach us so to number our days upon the earth, and so to apply our hearts unto true wisdom, that amidst all the changes and sorrows of this world, our hearts may surely there be fixed, where true joys are to be found.

Grant, O heavenly Father, that the occasion, on which we are now assembled, may cause us to reflect upon our mortality, and truly to repent of our sins. May our mourning be after a godly sort; may we consider that death is the lot of all men, and must soon be ours; and, through thy grace, may we so lay it to heart, that we may never be afraid, nor unprepared to die. While we sympathize in the sorrows of our mourning friends, and weep with those whom thou hast called to weep, may our thoughts be raised to a better hope in a better world. Amidst these painful proofs that the wages of sin is death, may we rejoice in the consolation, that the gift of God is eternal life through Jesus Christ; that this corruptible shall put on incorruption, and that, through the mighty power of

Him who is the resurrection and the life, the faithful shall rise to life immortal.

We bless thee, O God, that thou didst so love the world as to give thine only-begotten Son, that all who believe in him should not perish, but have everlasting life: that he took not the nature of angels, but the seed of Abraham; and lived and died and rose from the dead, that we may live through him. We praise thee that life and immortality are brought to light, and that our hopes are raised from this our fallen state of sorrow and death, to glorious mansions of rest and peace. Raise, we beseech thee, our affections and our desires from the world to thee, and our hearts from the death of sin to a life of righteousness. Dispose our thoughts and direct our ways towards the attainment of everlasting salvation, that, amidst all the cares and sorrows of this mortal state, we may ever be defended by thy most gracious and ready help. Sanctify to our religious improvement this mournful dispensation of thy just providence, that when we are called to leave this world, we may die the death of the righteous, and our last end be like his.

In thy word hast thou taught us, O heavenly Father, that thou dost not willingly afflict or grieve the children of men; look with pity, we beseech thee, upon the sorrows of thy *servants*, who on this occasion are called to mourn. [We commend to thy compassionate goodness the sorrows of the *parents* for *their* child deceased.] In thy wisdom hast thou seen fit to visit *them* with sorrow, and to bring this great distress upon *them*. Remember *them*, O Lord, in mercy, and sanctify thy fatherly correction to *them*. Endue *their* soul with patience under *their* affliction, and with resignation to thy blessed will. Comfort *them* with a sense of thy goodness, and give peace to *their* troubled mind.

Grant, O Lord, that *they* [the *brothers* and *sisters*

of the deceased] may be blest with the comforting support of thy grace. While following the remains of so dear a connection from the house of mourning to the house of death, may thy Spirit and the comfort of thy peace be with *them.* May *they* not mourn without hope: viewing the grave as the place where the Lord Jesus lay, may *their* desires be raised to the high and holy place where he in glory forever reigns.

[Extend, we beseech thee, thy compassionate goodness to the surviving companion of the deceased. In this distressing sorrow may thy heavenly grace be with *him*, and so sanctify, O righteous God, this severe affliction, that what seems so great a loss may conduce to *his* eternal gain. With pious submission to thy unerring wisdom, may *he* resign this dear friend to thy superior claim; may *he* know and feel that the Lord gave what he taketh away; that thou art just and good in all thy ways, and that thy mercy endureth for ever.]

And for all whom this event of thy providence has called to mourn, whether present or absent, be pleased, O God, to hear our supplications. Prepare them to make, and assist them in making all suitable improvement from this affliction. Give them grace to bear this bereavement with such humility and resignation as becometh the gospel of Jesus Christ. May they neither despise thy chastening, nor faint under thy rebukes; but say, with thy servant of old, "It is the Lord, let him dowhat seemeth to him good." May their hopes and desires be so raised to thee and to heavenly things, that, when they depart this life, they may rest in God, through Jesus Christ.

Assist us, O Lord, in what remains of the mournful duties to which we are now called. May the comforts of thy truth, and power of thy grace, be with thy people, while, with decent solemnity, they commit these earthly remains to the ground; looking, with the eye of faith, to the resurrection of the dead, and the life of the world to come.

And grant, O merciful God, that the mournful solemnities of this day may awaken us to righteousness. Let us not be forgetful that our days are swiftly passing away, and that every hour shortens our scanty span. Give us grace to live as those who are born to die, and whose spirits must soon depart to the eternal world. Grant that the shortness of life may continually remind us of its importance, and the uncertainty of its continuance make us ever ready and prepared for its end.

And we bless thy holy name for all thy servants who have departed this life in thy faith and fear, beseeching thee to give us grace so to follow their good examples, that with them we may be partakers of thy heavenly kingdom. Hear us, O Lord, we beseech thee, for the sake of thy Son, our Savior, Jesus Christ.

And may the grace of our Lord Jesus Christ be with us all, now and evermore. *Amen.*

A Prayer that may be used at a Funeral, when there is not to be a Service at the Grave.

O God and merciful Father, who despisest not the sighing of a contrite heart, nor the humble desires of those who are visited with sorrow, graciously assist our prayers which we make before thee in our present afflictions. In mercy behold our sorrows and hear our supplications. In the midst of life we are in death: to whom can we flee for succor but to thee, O God, who for our sins art justly displeased! To whom can sinners fly for refuge but to thee, to whom belong mercies and forgiveness: to thee, who art always more ready to hear than we to pray, and art wont to give more than we desire or deserve. Favorably and in mercy hear our supplications; with pity behold the infirmity of our nature and the sorrow of our hearts, and pardon our manifold offences.

Man that is born of a woman hath but a short time to live, and is full of misery: he cometh up and is cut down like a flower; he fleeth, as it were a shadow, and never continueth in one stay. Our days at the longest are short, and at the strongest are frail; and when we feel the most secure, we know not what a day or an hour may bring forth. We consume away in thy displeasure, and are afraid at thy wrathful indignation. When thou art angry, all our days are gone; we bring our years to an end as it were a tale that is told. Yet, O Lord most holy, O God most mighty, O merciful Savior, deliver us not into the bitter pains of eternal death. Thou knowest, Lord, the secrets of our hearts: shut not thy merciful ears to our prayers, but spare us, Lord most holy: thou worthy Judge eternal, suffer us not, at our last hour, to fall from thee. Support us, O Lord, through life by thy free Spirit, and direct our ways towards the attainment of everlasting salvation, that, among all the changes and trials of this mortal state, we may ever be defended by thy most gracious and ready help, and finally be received into thy heavenly mansions of glory and peace, through Jesus Christ our Lord.

It hath pleased thee, O righteous God, to take out of this world the soul of *our deceased friend;* help us, we beseech thee, with due submission to thy unerring providence, decently to commit *his* body to the ground, earth to earth, ashes to ashes, dust to dust: and help us to look forward in faith and hope to the general resurrection in the last day, and the life of the world to come, through our Lord Jesus Christ, at whose second coming in glorious majesty to judge the world, the earth and the sea shall give up their dead, and the corruptible bodies of those who sleep in him shall be changed and made like unto his own glorious body, according to the mighty working, whereby he is able to subdue all things unto himself. Thou hast taught us, by a voice from heaven, that blessed are the dead who die in the Lord. Grant us grace so to live, that when it shall please thee to call us hence, we may die the death of the righteous, and our last end be like his. Thou has taught us, O heavenly Father, in thy holy word, that thou dost not willingly afflict or grieve the children of men; look with pity, we beseech thee, upon the sorrows of thy *servants*, who, by this event of thy providence, are called to mourn. In thy wisdom thou hast seen fit to visit *them* with sorrow, [to take from *them*, &c. *Here the particular case of the mourners may be mentioned.*] Remember *them*, O Lord, in mercy. Sanctify thy fatherly correction to *them*. Endue *their* souls with patience under *their* affliction, and with resignation to thy blessed will. Comfort *them* with a sense of thy goodness; lift up thy countenance upon *them* and give *them* peace, through Jesus Christ our Lord.

Raise us, O merciful God, from the death of sin to a life of righteousness, that when we shall depart this life, we may rest in him who is the resurrection and the life; and in the last and great day of the Lord, may we be found acceptable in thy sight, and receive that blessing which he shall then pronounce to all who love and fear thee; saying, Come, ye blessed children of my Father, receive the kingdom prepared for you from the beginning of the world. Hear us, O Lord, we beseech thee, for the sake of the same, thy Son, our Savior; and hear the prayer which he hath taught us to use:

Our Father, who art in heaven, hallowed be thy

name. Thy kingdom come; thy will be done on earth, as it is in heaven. Give us this day our daily bread. And forgive us our trespasses, as we forgive those who trespass against us. And lead us not into temptation; but deliver us from evil. For thine is the kingdom, and the power, and the glory, forever and ever. *Amen.*

May the grace of our Lord Jesus Christ, and the love of God, and the fellowship of the Holy Ghost, be with us all evermore. *Amen.*

A Prayer for a Family in Affliction.

O MOST mighty God and merciful Father, who hast compassion upon all men, and hatest nothing that thou hast made; who despisest not the humble desires of those who fly to thee for succor, behold our afflictions, and mercifully hear our prayers. Encompassed as we are by sorrows, pains and death, to whom can we look for succor but unto thee, O God, whom we are daily offending by our manifold sins, and who art of purer eyes than to behold evil. Create and make in us new and contrite hearts, that we may truly repent of our sins, and obtain of thee, the God of all mercy, perfect remission and forgiveness.

Righteous art thou, O God, and just in all thy dealings; equity and judgment are the habitation of thy seat; goodness and mercy are in all thy dealings with the children of men. We acknowledge, O Lord, that our sufferings are less than our sins deserve; that it is of thy mercy, and because thy compassion faileth not, that we are not consumed. But thou knowest, O Lord, the weakness of our nature, and how little it is that we can bear. That our strength fail not, and for thy mercy's sake, behold us with compassion, and turn from us those evils which we too justly have deserved.

We are unworthy, through our manifold sins, to offer unto thee any sacrifice; yet, we beseech thee to hear these our supplications and prayers, not weighing our merits, but pardoning our offences. May we be thankful that there is a merciful God, to whom the afflicted and the weak may look for comfort and support. Confiding in thy mercy and thy gracious promises, we implore, O heavenly Father, thy compassionate favor upon *this family*, who desire, in humble supplication, to look to thee for aid. To thee, O Lord, it seemeth fitting to visit *them* with *sorrow and distress*. [*The particular affliction may here be mentioned.*] Thou knowest, O Lord, *their fears*, *their* sorrows, and what *they* need. Wilt thou relieve, comfort and support *them*, according to the necessities of *their* case. Forsake *them* not, we humbly beseech thee; forsake not the *souls* whom thy hand correcteth. Thou art able to turn mourning into gladness, and to give songs of joy for the heaviness of sorrow. O remember *them* in mercy; relieve *them* from distress, and sanctify *their fears* and *their* sorrows to the benefit of *their* souls. Prepare *them*, O Lord, for every event of thy providence: turn from *them* the evils of life, and sustain *them* under those trials of *their* faith and patience, to which it may seem to thee good to call *them*. In all the changes and disappointments of life, help *them*, with becoming resignation, and a deep sense of thy righteous dealings, to submit to thy will, and to say in *their* hearts, Thy will be done. Help *them*, O Lord, to see love in thy dealings, and to know that temporal afflictions, through thy blessing, tend to spiritual good. Help *them* to say with thy servant Job, Shall we receive good at the hand of God, and shall we not receive evil? O may this evil, this weight of sorrow, which rests so hard upon *them*, through thy blessing, be turned to good; and may *they* know and feel from happy experience, that all things work together for good, to those who love and fear thee.

Do thou, O God, who art the fountain of all wisdom, mercy and grace, who knowest our necessities before we ask, and our ignorance in asking, have compassion upon our infirmities; pardon us wherein we ask amiss; grant the petitions which we have now offered; and all those good things which, through blindness or neglect, we do not ask for, vouchsafe to give us, for the worthiness of thy Son, our Savior, Jesus Christ. *Amen.*

A Prayer for a Prisoner, or Prisoners, under Sentence of Death.

O Father of mercies, and God of all comfort, the only hope of all the ends of the earth, we, thy sinful, unworthy creatures, desire, with great and reverential awe, to bow before thee, and to look unto thee for succor, in behalf of *this* thy *servant*, under sentence of condemnation. According to human appearance, *his* days on earth are numbered, and the time of *his* departure is at hand. Remember not, Lord, *his* offences, but thy mercy to mankind in Jesus Christ. In the midst of life we are in death; to whom can sinful, dying mortals look for aid, but unto thee, O God, who, for our sins, art justly displeased. Yet, O Lord God, most holy, thou worthy Judge eternal, deliver *him* not into the bitter pains of eternal death. O holy and merciful Savior, accept *his* tears and supplications. Grant *him* sincere and true repentance for all the sins and transgressions of *his* life past, that *he* may obtain of thee, the God of all mercy, perfect remission and forgiveness, and *his* pardon be sealed in heaven, before *he* go hence, and be no more seen. Do thou, who of thine infinite goodness didst accept the penitential prayer of a sinner on the cross, extend thy mercy to *this* thy *servant;* accept *him*, O thou Savior of men, for thy mercy's sake, and wash away *his* guilt by thy most precious blood. Support *him*, O Lord, in this momentous trial, by the comforts of thy Holy Spirit. May *he* look, with a true faith and sure confidence, to Him who, while we were yet sinners, died for us. Grant *him* such a view of thy mercy in Jesus Christ, that *he* may not fear the approach of death; but, looking beyond the grave, to the high and holy place where the Savior reigns, may *he* rejoice in the hope of eternal life. May *he* depart this life in a religious and holy hope, in favor with thee our God, and in perfect charity with all mankind.

Thou knowest, Lord, the secrets of *his* heart: shut not thy merciful ears to our prayers on *his* behalf. Spare *him*, O Lord God most holy, and help *him* in *his* last hour to trust in thee. To thee, O heavenly Father, with whom do live the spirits of those who depart this life in thy faith and fear, we humbly commend the soul of *this* our *brother*, as into the hands of a faithful Creator and merciful Savior, praying that it may be washed in the blood of that Lamb of God which taketh away the sins of the world.

And grant, O Lord, that the ministrations of justice may awaken men to righteousness, and be instrumental, through thy blessing, in turning the hearts of the disobedient to the wisdom of the just. May all remember that their precious hours are swiftly wasting; and that every passing moment shortens our scanty span. Help us, O Lord, to be prepared to die the death of the righteous, and that our last end may be like his.

These our supplications, O heavenly Father, we humbly offer in the name and through the merits of Jesus Christ, who taught us, when we pray, to say, Our Father, who art, &c. *Amen.*

A Prayer for Courts of Justice.

ADORABLE and everlasting God, the high and mighty Ruler of the universe, who dost from thy throne behold all the dwellers upon the earth, and who canst order the wills and control the affections of sinful men, with reverence and humility we would present ourselves before thee, sensible that thou art in heaven, and we upon the earth. Righteousness and judgment are the habitation of thy throne. To thee all hearts are open, and all desires known. Thou knowest, O God, our need before we ask; our hearts are in thy hands, and our sins are not hid from thee. Wilt thou pardon our sins, sanctify our hearts, and hear our prayers. Behold, we beseech thee, with thy favor and blessing, the people and government of these United States; and of this state, especially, in which we live. Bless all those who are in authority; endue them with wisdom, and so guide their counsels, and strengthen their hands, that the hearts of the disobedient may be turned to the wisdom of the just; that peace and happiness, truth and justice, holiness and piety, may be established in our land; and that thy people, secured by the protection of equal laws and the administration of impartial justice, may serve thee in quietness and godliness of living.

More particularly do we offer our prayers to thee, the only wise God, in behalf of this court, by the permission of thy good providence here assembled, for the administration of justice to thy people.

Grant to the judges and other officers thy heavenly benediction. Give them the spirit of wisdom and understanding; of counsel and of right knowledge; and so enlighten their minds with the just principles of law and of equity, that they may truly and impartially administer justice, restrain wickedness, suppress vice, promote righteousness and maintain peace. May the sword which they are appointed to bear be such a terror to evil works, that it may not be borne in vain. From the equity of their judgments may men learn righteousness; honoring them as the ministers of God for good, and submitting to every ordinance of man, for the Lord's sake.

And grant, O Lord, that they who shall come before this court to obtain justice and maintain their rights, according to the wise and equitable laws of our country, may be in their hearts disposed to do justly, to love mercy, and to render that measure to others which they seek for themselves. Preserve us from all envy, hatred and malice, and from all uncharitableness. May we do to others as we would have them do to us, and endeavor to owe no man any thing, but to love one another; and may we ever remain a happy and united people, having justice for our guide, and the Lord for our God.

And, O thou righteous Judge of all the earth, may the solemnities of an earthly tribunal awaken in our minds a lively apprehension, and impress upon our hearts a constant remembrance of that day of the Lord, when we must all appear before the bar of thy judgment seat, and receive the doom which is to fix our eternal state. May we consider well and wisely, and in a time accepted, what testimony our passing hours may give, at that time, when all hearts shall be laid open, and no secrets can be hid. Give us grace to cast away the works of darkness and to walk in the light of truth and according to thy righteous laws, that we may receive the approbation of our final Judge, and inherit the kingdom prepared for the righteous from the beginning of the world.

Extend, O Lord, we beseech thee, the blessings of civil freedom and the administration of impartial justice to all the people of the earth. Give peace and harmony to contending nations, and so rule their hearts and enlighten their minds, that they may live in unity and godly love. Give thy blessing to the preaching of the gospel, till the Redeemer's kingdom shall be spread to the utmost bounds of the habitable globe, and all the ends of the world shall see the salvation of our God.

These things, O heavenly Father, and whatever of good thou seest fitting for us, for this court of justice, for our state and country, and for all mankind, we humbly ask in the name, and through the merits of our Lord and Savior, Jesus Christ.

And may the Lord bless and keep us, and give us peace, now and evermore. *Amen.*

A Prayer for a Legislative Assembly.

O God, the King immortal, invisible, who art exalted above all thrones and dominions, King of kings and Lord of lords; whose wise and just providence ordereth all things in heaven and on earth; with all due reverence and adoration, we look unto thee, as the author of our being, and the giver of all good. Without thee, nothing is stable, nothing holy, nothing secure: except the Lord keep the city, the watchman waketh in vain. Without thy blessing, it is but labor lost that we rise early, and are careful and troubled about many things. We look unto thee, as the only hope of all the ends of the earth.

We adore thee as the God in whom our fathers trusted and were delivered. We have heard with our ears what thou didst in their days, and in times of old. They got not this land in possession by their own sword, neither did their own arm save them; but thy hand and thy arm achieved for them the victory. We desire, O God, to put our trust in thee; and humbly beseech thee to behold us with thy favor and blessing, to pardon our sins, sanctify our hearts and hear our prayers. We beseech thee, O God, to bestow thy blessing upon our country, and upon all the people of these United States. May thy paternal and holy protecting providence be over them for good: may they ever be thy people, and the Lord be their God: preserve and keep them by thy perpetual mercy. Behold, we beseech thee, with thy favor and blessing, the president of the United States, the governor and *council* of this state in which we live, and all others who are lawfully set in authority over us; and so replenish them with thy heavenly wisdom, that they may always incline to thy will, and walk in thy ways; grant that they may rule with uprightness, execute justice and maintain truth. And may all the people respect and obey the civil magistrates, as ministers of God, appointed for the public good. Preserve them, we beseech thee, from selfishness and party spirit; may they be influenced by benevolence and the love of their country; and, according to the wisdom given them, promote its prosperity and peace.

And we humbly beseech thee, O gracious God, more especially, to behold with thy favor and blessing *the General Court and Legislature of this state*, now assembled before thee. Give them wisdom to know and to ordain whatever shall be best for the general good of all thy people. Be pleased, O God, we beseech thee, to direct and prosper all their deliberations and measures to the advancement of thy glory, the promotion of pure and undefiled religion, and to the safety, honor and welfare of thy people. Grant that all things may be so ordered and settled, by their endeavors, upon the best and surest foundations, that peace and happiness, truth and justice, religion and piety may be established among us for all generations; and that the people of this our country, being enlightened by the knowledge of thy word, and secure, through the protection of wise and equal laws, and the administration of impartial justice, may serve thee without fear, in holiness and righteousness, all the days of their life.

And grant, O Lord, that the whole course of this life may be so peaceably ordered by thy governance, that thy people may joyfully serve thee in all godly quietness; that they may walk in the ways of truth and peace, and at last be numbered with thy saints in glory everlasting, through Jesus Christ our Lord. And to thee, the only wise God, our Savior, be glory and majesty, dominion and power, both now and ever. *Amen.*

A Prayer suitable to be used in a Town or Freemen's Meeting.

ADORABLE and everliving God, the Creator and Preserver of all mankind, who dost, from thy throne, behold all the dwellers upon the earth, and hast the hearts and the wants of all thy creatures before thee, we implore thy favor and blessing upon thy people here assembled. We adore thee for thy infinite perfections; we praise thy holy name for all thy dispensations of goodness and mercy to us and to all mankind. Our fathers put their trust in thee and were not forsaken. May the remembrance of mercies, which have ever been of old, inspire our hearts with gratitude and praise to thee, who hast graciously blest the people of this our country with prosperity and increase, and given us a great name among the nations of the earth. May a sense of thy goodness ever engage us in thy faith and fear. May we so love that which thou commandest, and desire the things which thou dost promise, that among all the manifold changes and temptations of this mortal life, our hearts may surely there be fixed, where true joys are to be found. Without thee, nothing is strong, nothing holy; increase and multiply upon us thy mercy, and be our ruler and guide. Vouchsafe to direct, sanctify and govern, both our hearts and bodies in the ways of thy laws, and in the works of thy commandments. Pour down the abundance of thy blessings upon this our favored country. Give wisdom and strength and union to our rulers and magistrates. Bless the people and the government of the United States; and of this state, particularly, in which we live. May our legislature and courts of justice, and all who are appointed to give laws and execute them, be endued with wisdom, and equity, and with the love of their country. Assist them in all the various administrations of justice and right which appertain to the offices respectively committed to their trust. We beseech thee to bless all who are in authority over us, and so rule their hearts and strengthen their hands, that truth and happiness and peace may be established in all our borders; that righteousness and prosperity may increase, and that all thy people may serve thee in virtue and godliness of living. Make us duly thankful for the inestimable blessing of civil liberty, good government and equitable laws; and for the security of our religious rights and privileges. May we so use as never to abuse, nor forget from whom we receive them. We pray that thy watchful eye and holy protecting providence may be over us for good; guide us continually by thy unerring counsel: prosper us in all our lawful pursuits; and preserve us from desolating judgments and all calamitous events.

More particularly do we look unto thee, the only wise God, for thy favor and blessing upon the people of this town, and the important occasion on which we are here assembled. May we justly view and duly appreciate the blessing of our enfranchisement: the high privilege of choosing those who shall be our rulers, and of making appointments to offices of trust. May thy blessing, O Lord, be with us; the blessing of wisdom, harmony and love. Preserve us from the evils of party feeling, selfishness and contention. May it be the sincere desire of each and every one to promote the public welfare. In this important exercise of the rights of freemen, may they be directed to the choice of such persons as are best qualified for the offices to which they shall be elected. And give grace, we beseech thee, and wisdom to all those who are or shall be thus called to serve their town or state or country; may they willingly and faithfully perform the important duties of their office, sincerely endeavoring to promote equity, union and peace.

And may we all be disposed to harmony and love, and to give that measure to others which we expect from them. May the people of this town be continually united, as a happy society, with interests and feelings in common. May they who are strong support the weak, and every member of the community, according to his means and station, bear his just part of the public burthens, and contribute his due proportion to the general good. And grant, O Lord, that our land may still enjoy, and better appreciate the light of thy truth and the blessings of thy bountiful hand. Remove from us all spiritual ignorance, and preserve us from an evil heart of unbelief, in departing from thee, the living God. May we ever remain a happy, united people, having truth for our guide, and the Lord for our God. Hear us, O Lord, and bless us for the worthiness of thy Son, our Savior, Jesus Christ. And may his grace, and thy love, and the communion of the Holy Spirit, be with us all, evermore. *Amen.*

A Prayer suitable for a Temperance Meeting.

O MERCIFUL God, who art the Giver of all good, and orderest all things in heaven and on earth; who hast compassion upon mankind, and hast graciously promised to hear the prayer of those who ask in the name of Jesus Christ, mercifully forgive our sins, and accept our humble supplications. Shouldst thou be extreme to mark iniquities, no man living could be justified. For the glory of thy name, turn from us all those evils which we too justly have deserved. Increase and multiply upon us thy mercy. Let thy ears be open to our petitions; prepare our hearts to come worthily before thee, not in our own name, nor trusting in our own righteousness, but in the name of Jesus Christ, and trusting in thy mercy through his merits. Help us, O Lord, we beseech thee, to fulfil the duties of our respective stations in life, and to go forward in our Christian course. Open our eyes, that we may see the excellency of thy law; give us understanding that we may know thy testimonies, and write the truths of thy gospel on our hearts. Direct and bless us in all our endeavors to know and to do thy will. Thou knowest, O God, that we are set in the midst of manifold and great dangers, and that our nature is weak; grant to us such strength and protection as may support us in all perils, and carry us safely through all temptation. Keep us both outwardly in our bodies, and inwardly in our souls, that we may be defended from all adversities which may happen to the body, and from all evil thoughts which may assault or hurt the soul. Purify our hearts from all inordinate and sinful affections. Give us grace to be temperate in all things; in our meats and drinks, and in all that we do: may we use the world as not abusing it. Grant that the good things which thou givest may by us and by all people be thankfully received, and used with sobriety and moderation; that we may give good examples to others; that the flesh may be subject to thy Holy Spirit, and that, denying ungodliness and worldly lusts, we may live soberly, righteously and godly in this present world. Whether we eat or drink, or whatever we do, may we do all to thy glory in Jesus Christ.

Give thy blessing, O Lord, we beseech thee, to those who associate, and to all who labor to suppress intemperance, ungodliness and vice. Give success to their benevolent efforts, and so rule their hearts and strengthen their hands, that they may be instrumental in promoting sobriety and good morals. Cause them to be unwearied in well doing, and reward their labor of love. Grant that our coming together at this time may tend to the good of ourselves and others. Give to us and to all men grace, that we may not abuse ourselves nor injure others by an improper use of the things of time and sense; deliver us from all inordinate and sinful affections, and help us to pass the time of our sojourning here in thy fear, and to live as they should live who expect shortly to give an account to thee, who wilt judge all men according to their works. Preserve us from idleness in what concerns the welfare of our bodies and of our souls; may we not be slothful in business, but fervent in spirit, serving the Lord. Help each and all of us to do our duty in the state of life to which it shall please thee to call us. Direct us in all our doings with thy most gracious favor; prosper us with thy continual help, that in all our works, begun, continued and ended in thee, we may glorify thy holy name; and finally, by thy mercy, obtain everlasting life, through our Lord and Savior, Jesus Christ. *Amen.*

The grace of our Lord Jesus Christ, the love of God, and the fellowship of the Holy Ghost, be with us all, evermore. *Amen.*

A Form of Service that may be used at the laying of the Corner Stone of a Church.

The several Parts of the following Service, as they are numbered, may be divided among the Clergy who are present, as shall be judged expedient.

1. *Sentences of Scripture.*

Except the Lord build the house, their labor is but lost that build it; except the Lord keep the city, the watchmen waketh but in vain.

The same stone which the builders refused, is become the head-stone in the corner. This is the Lord's doing, and it is marvellous in our eyes.

O give thanks unto the Lord; for he is gracious, and his mercy endureth forever.

2. *Introductory Address.*

Friends and brethren: Devout men of old, under the law and under the gospel, have erected houses for the public worship of Almighty God, and have separated them from common use, for the more decent celebration of the christian ordinances, and to fill men's minds with greater reverence for God. We cannot doubt but such pious works are approved of God. King David was commended for his desire to perform such a work; that it was in his heart to build God a house. The building of churches tends very much to the promotion of his holy worship, and the practice of good morals and true religion. We humbly trust that He will favorably accept of this our present purpose of laying, with suitable solemnities, the foundation of a house, to be erected to the honor of His great name, and dedicated to His holy worship. Let us then unite in asking His blessing upon this our undertaking.

3. *Then may be offered the following Prayers, or other Collects, at discretion, from the Book of Common Prayer.*

Our Father, who art in heaven, hallowed be thy name. Thy kingdom come; thy will be done on earth as it is in heaven. Give us this day our daily bread. And forgive us our trespasses, as we forgive those who trespass against us. And lead us not into temptation; but deliver us from evil. For thine is the kingdom, and the power and the glory, forever and ever. *Amen.*

Direct us, O Lord, in what we do, with thy most gracious favor, and further us with thy continual help; and grant that in this and all our works, we may glorify thy holy name, through Jesus Christ, our Lord. *Amen.*

O blessed Lord, who art the giver of all good, visit, we pray thee, this people with thy love and favor; enlighten their minds with the truths of the everlasting gospel; graft in their hearts the love of thy name; increase in them true religion; nourish them with all goodness; and of thy great mercy, keep them steadfast in thy faith and fear, through Jesus Christ, our Lord and Savior. *Amen.*

Grant, O Lord, we beseech thee, that the course of this world may be so peaceably ordered by thy governance, that thy church may joyfully serve thee in all godly quietness, through the same, our Lord and Savior, Jesus Christ. *Amen.*

4. *Then may be read responsively the* 84*th and* 132*d Psalms.*
5. *The following Lesson from Ezra iii.* 8, 9, 10, 11, *may here be read.*

Now in the second year of their coming unto the house of God at Jerusalem, in the second month, began Zerubbabel, the son of Shealtiel, and Jeshua, the son of Jozadak, and the remnant of their brethren, the priests and the Levites, and all they that were come out of the captivity unto Jerusalem; and appointed the Levites, from twenty years old and upward, to set forward the work of the house of the Lord. Then stood Jeshua with his sons and his brethren, Kadmiel and his sons, the sons of Judah, together, to set forward the workmen in the house of God: the sons of Henadad, with their sons and their brethren the Levites. And when the builders laid the foundation of the temple of the Lord, they set the priests, in their apparel, with trumpets, and the Levites, the sons of Asaph, with cymbals, to praise the Lord, after the ordinance of David, king of Israel. And they sung together, by course, in praising and giving thanks unto the Lord, because he is good, for his mercy endureth forever towards Israel. And all the people shouted with a great shout, when they praised the Lord, because the foundation of the house of the Lord was laid.

6. *Then may be sung the* 25*th Hymn,* 1, 2, 6, 7, 8.
7. *The Inscription on the Stone, or Deposites under it, may here be read.*

8. *The person who officiates, having found that the Stone is rightly laid, may strike it three times with a hammer, saying as follows:*

In the name of the Father, and of the Son, and of the Holy Ghost, I lay this corner-stone as the foundation of an edifice to be erected for a house of prayer, and to be dedicated to the worship of Almighty God, according to the canons and liturgy and usages of the Protestant Episcopal Church in the United States. *Amen.*

Other foundation can no man lay, than that on which standeth the house of God, which is the church of the living God, the pillar and ground of the truth; even the foundation of apostles and prophets, Jesus Christ himself being the chief corner-stone.

Let us pray. O eternal God, mighty in power and of majesty incomprehensible, whom the heaven of heavens cannot contain, much less the walls of temples made with hands, and who yet didst command thy servants of old to build houses to the honor of thy great name, and for the purpose of setting forth thy praise; look down, we beseech thee, with thy favor and blessing upon us, thy unworthy servants, who are here assembled in thy name and presence, to lay the foundation of a house, with thy permission, to be erected to thy name, and sacred to thy worship. Accept, O Lord, we beseech thee, the pious intention of this thy people, and give thy blessing to the work which they have taken in hand. Preserve them, O thou God of mercy, from all untoward accidents and calamitous events. Sanctify their hearts and enlarge their means. May they rejoice to honor the Lord with their substance; may their barns be filled with plenty, and their stores with increase. Unite them in harmony, peace and love. Enable them, with joy and gladness, to bring this work to a happy issue, that this edifice may be completed and adorned in a manner and style decent, and suitable to the honor of thy name, and convenient for the various parts of thy holy worship. Wilt thou, O Lord, watch over them for good, and direct and bless them in all the work. May this consecrated spot which they have chosen, whereon to build their altar and erect a house to thee, the living God, be to them a happy Bethel, where they and their descendants, for many generations, may worship thee, their God and Savior, in spirit and in truth. To this house, when erected, as to thy courts, may their hearts incline: may they be sensible that the Lord is in this place; and may it be to them as the house of God and the gate of heaven. May their thoughts and desires be raised to thy spiritual house not made with hands, of which Jesus Christ is the chief corner-stone; to him coming, as unto a living stone, chosen of God and precious, may all who in this place shall call upon thy name, as lively stones, be built up a spiritual house, a holy priesthood, offering sacrifices acceptable to God by Jesus Christ. Grant, O God, that all those who, through thy merciful goodness, shall be permitted and inclined hereafter to serve thee in this place, may be so joined together in unity of spirit and in the bond of peace, that they may be a holy temple acceptable unto thee. And to all thy people, O God, give thy heavenly grace, and especially to us who are here present, that with one heart we may desire and labor to promote the prosperity of thy holy apostolic church, and with one mouth may profess that true faith which was once, by the inspiration of thy Holy Spirit, delivered to the saints. And keep, O Lord, we beseech thee, thy whole household, the church, in continual godliness; that, through thy protection, it may be free from all adversities, and devoutly given to serve thee in good works, through Jesus Christ, our Lord, to whom, with thee and the Holy Ghost, be all honor and glory, world without end. *Amen.*

9. *Here may be the Address, if any is to be delivered.*
10. *Then may be sung a portion from the Psalms or Hymns.*
11. *Conclude with the Benediction.*

May the blessing of God Almighty, the Father, the Son, and the Holy Ghost, be amongst you and remain with you always. *Amen.*

PART FOURTH.

OFFICES AND PRAYERS, THAT MAY BE USED IN CHURCHES, OR IN PUBLIC WORSHIP.

A Form of Prayer allowed to be used on days appointed by the Civil Authority as Public Fasts.

The Service is to be as usual, excepting the alterations hereby permitted.

The Venite Exultemus may be omitted.

Proper Psalms. Morning—25*th and* 51*st; Evening*—86*th*, 130*th and* 143*d. The Officiating Minister, at his discretion, instead of the above may select other Psalms, which, in his judgment, are more appropriate to the particular occasion.*

Lessons. Morning—First, Isaiah, 58*th chapter; Second, Matthew,* 6*th chapter; Evening—First, Ezekiel,* 18*th chapter; Second, James,* 4*th chapter.*

The Litany is not to be omitted.

Immediately before the General Thanksgiving, in both the Morning and the Evening Service, a part or all of the following Prayers may be used.

Almighty and everlasting God, who hatest nothing that thou hast made, and dost forgive the sins of those who are penitent, create and make in us new and contrite hearts, that we, worthily lamenting our sins, and acknowledging our wretchedness, may obtain of thee, the God of all mercy, perfect remission and forgiveness, through Jesus Christ our Lord. *Amen.*

O Lord God and merciful Father, who hast compassion upon mankind, and wouldst not the death of a sinner, but rather that he should turn from his wickedness and live; look down, we beseech thee, in mercy upon us, thy unworthy creatures, who humbly confess before thee our trespasses and sins. Do thou, to whom alone it appertaineth to forgive sins, spare the people, whom, in thy mercy, thou hast redeemed with the Savior's blood. Enter not into judgment with thy servants, O Lord, nor visit us according to our iniquities. Help us truly to acknowledge our vileness, and give us that repentance which is not to be repented of. Turn us, O Lord our God, to thee; and we shall be turned. Be merciful, O be merciful, to those who humbly desire, with weeping, fasting and prayer, to turn to thee. Thou art a God full of compassion and long-suffering, and of great pity, sparing those who deserve punishment, and in thy righteous wrath remembering mercy. Hear us, O Lord, we beseech thee, and after the multitude of thy mercies blot out our offences, and cleanse us from the defilement of sin; sanctify our hearts, and save our souls, we beseech thee, through the merits and mediation of thy only Son, our Savior, Jesus Christ. *Amen.*

Almighty and everlasting God, whose wise and righteous providence governeth all things in heaven and on earth, look down, we humbly beseech thee, in mercy upon our country, and upon all the people of these United States. Restrain thine indignation against our multiplied sins, and turn thine anger from us. Remember not, Lord, our offences, but thy love to us in Jesus Christ: O call to mind thy mercies, which have ever been of old. From the judgments of thy hand may the people learn righteousness, and may thy patient goodness and long-suffering lead us to repentance. May peace, through thy merciful goodness, ever reign in our borders, and our land continue to bring forth its increase. We beseech thee, O God, to bless the governor and other rulers of this state, and all those who are set in authority over us; and so rule their hearts and strengthen their hands, that vice may be suppressed and godliness abound. In all dangers and difficulties, may we ever look unto thee as our only helper and sure defence. We pray that thy watchful care, and holy, protecting providence, may be over us for good. Guide us continually with thy unerring counsel; direct and prosper us in all we do, and preserve us from desolating judgments and calamitous events. Grant, O God, to us and to all thy people, that we may so love the things which thou commandest, and desire those which thou dost promise, that, among the sundry and manifold changes of the world, our hearts may surely there be fixed where true joys are to be found. These and all other necessaries for us, and for our rulers, and for all estates of thy people in this our favored country, we humbly beg in the name, and through the mediation, of Jesus Christ, our most blessed Lord and Savior. *Amen.*

THE COMMUNION SERVICE.

The Collects. O blessed Lord, who didst direct that thy disciples should fast when the bridegroom should be taken from them, and who for our sakes and for our example didst thyself fast upon the earth, give us grace, we beseech thee, to use such abstinence and self-denial, that our flesh may be subdued to the spirit, and that we may ever obey thy godly motions in righteousness and true holiness, to thy honor and glory, who livest and reignest with the Father and the Holy Ghost, one God, world without end. *Amen.*

O holy, eternal and gracious God, whose ways

are all righteous, and whose mercies cannot be numbered, we, thy sinful people, this day assembled, in thy name and presence, to bow before thee with fasting, humiliation and prayer, do humbly confess our manifold sins, and acknowledge that it is of thy mercies that we are not consumed. Great and manifold have been, and still are, thy blessings bestowed upon us, and upon our country, whilst, by our sins and wickedness, we have provoked thy just wrath and indignation against us. O be thou merciful to us, thy unworthy creatures; enter not into judgment with those who, in thy sight, must be condemned. Make us deeply sensible of our evil hearts and sinful ways. Work in us a hearty contrition; give us that godly sorrow for sin which worketh true repentance. O take not thy Holy Spirit from us; work in us, we beseech thee, to will and to do what is pleasing in thy sight. Turn us from the error of our ways; renew us in the spirit of our minds, and create us again unto good works, that we may walk before thee in faith and righteousness, and finally be inheritors of thine everlasting kingdom. And grant, O Lord, that our land may still enjoy the light of thy truth, and the blessings of thy bountiful hand. Remove from us all spiritual ignorance, and preserve us from an evil heart of unbelief, that we may never depart from thee, the only living God. Be thou with us, as thou wast with our fathers; and bless us, our God, even as thou blessedst them, to thy honor and glory, and to our comfort and salvation in Jesus Christ. *Amen.*

The Epistle. Ephesians iv. 17. This I say, therefore, and testify in the Lord, that ye henceforth walk not as other Gentiles walk, in the vanity of their mind; having the understanding darkened; being alienated from the life of God, through the ignorance that is in them, because of the blindness of their heart; who, being past feeling, have given themselves over unto lasciviousness, to work all uncleanness with greediness. But ye have not so learned Christ; if so be that ye have heard him, and have been taught by him, as the truth is in Jesus; that ye put off, concerning the former conversation, the old man, which is corrupt, according to the deceitful lusts; and be renewed in the spirit of your mind; and that ye put on the new man, which after God is created in righteousness and true holiness. Wherefore putting away lying, speak every man truth with his neighbor; for we are members one of another. Be ye angry and sin not; let not the sun go down upon your wrath; neither give place to the devil. Let him that stole steal no more; but rather let him labor, working with his hands the thing which is good, that he may have to give to him who needeth. Let no corrupt communication proceed out of your mouth, but that which is good to the use of edifying, that it may minister grace unto the hearers. And grieve not the Holy Spirit of God, whereby ye are sealed unto the day of redemption. Let all bitterness, and wrath, and anger, and clamor, and evil-speaking be put away from you, with all malice; and be ye kind one to another, tender-hearted, forgiving one another, even as God, for Christ's sake, hath forgiven you.

The Gospel. St. Luke xiii. 1. There were present at that season some who told him of the Galileans, whose blood Pilate had mingled with their sacrifices. And Jesus, answering, said unto them, Suppose ye that these Galileans were sinners above all the Galileans because they suffered such things? I tell you nay; but, except ye repent, ye shall all likewise perish. Or those eighteen on whom the tower in Siloam fell and slew them, think ye that they were sinners above all men who dwelt in Jerusalem? I tell you nay; but, except ye repent, ye shall all likewise perish. He spake also this parable: A certain man had a fig-tree planted in his vineyard; and he came and sought fruit thereon, and found none. Then said he unto the dresser of his vineyard, Behold, these three years I come seeking fruit on this fig-tree, and find none: cut it down; why cumbereth it the ground? And he, answering, said unto him, Lord, let it alone this year also, till I shall dig about it and dung it: and if it bear fruit, well; and if not, then after that thou shalt cut it down.

Churches who desire, in their public worship, to pray particularly for the Governor and Legislature of their State, may, in the Prayer for the President of the United States, and all in civil authority, after the words the President of the United States, *add,* the Governor of this State.

When Congress and the Legislature of the State are in session at the same time, after the words in the Prayer for Congress, in Congress assembled, *may be added,* and for the Legislature of this State (or General Court of this Commonwealth) in their present session.

When the Legislature of the State is in session, and the Congress not so, the prayer for Congress may be used; but instead of the words, as for the people of these United States in general, so especially for their Senate and Representatives in Congress assembled, *may be substituted,* as for the people of this State (or Commonwealth) in general, so especially for our Legislature (or General Court) in their present session.

A Prayer to be used in Seasons of much Sickness, or Epidemic Diseases.

O God and merciful Father, who despisest not the sighing of a contrite heart, nor the humble supplications of those who fly to thee for succor and seek thy face in prayer, look down, we beseech thee, with pity upon us thy dependent, unworthy creatures. We acknowledge, O God, that we have sinned and done wickedly in departing from thy precepts and thy judgments, provoking thy just wrath and indignation against us. We would humbly bewail our ingratitude and forgetfulness of thy goodness; that our affections towards thee are so cold, while thy mercies to us are so abundant. Help us, O heavenly Father, earnestly to repent; and work in us a godly sorrow for all our misdeeds. It is of thy mercy that we are not consumed; in the midst of life we are in death; to whom can we fly for aid but to thee, the God of mercy, and the Father of our Savior Christ. Look with compassion upon us, and upon our country: while thy judgments are abroad in the earth, may the people of this land learn righteousness, and so turn to thee with penitence and prayer, that thou wilt turn from us all those evils which our sins have deserved. Preserve us, O thou God of mercy, from the pestilence which walketh in darkness, and from the desolating scourge now visiting the earth [our country] and approaching our borders. Remember not, Lord, our offences; spare in mercy those whom in love thou hast redeemed. From all pestilential diseases, and the sickness which destroys at noon-day, good Lord, deliver us and the inhabitants of this our country.

And we beseech thee, O God, in the plenitude of thy mercy, to behold with pity all the countries and parts of the earth which are visited with distressing sickness and prevailing mortal diseases. O stay the hand of the destroying angel, and say to the affliction, It is enough. And grant that the visitations of thy righteous providence may cause us, and all the inhabitants of the earth, to remember that the Lord ruleth, and that sickness, and pains, and death, are the dispensations of thy righteous hand, and less than our sins deserve. Awakened by thy warning voice, may we turn to thee, the Lord God of our salvation, and put our trust in thee alone. And grant that thy forbearing mercy, so long extended to this our favored country, may fill our hearts with gratitude and love. Assist us mercifully with thy heavenly grace, and dispose all our ways towards the attainment of everlasting salvation; and among all the changes, and perils, and other trials of this mortal life, direct and support us by thy most gracious and ready help, through Jesus Christ, our blessed Lord and Savior. *Amen.*

A Thanksgiving for Deliverance from great Sickness and Mortality.

Almighty and immortal God, who art the giver of all good, and whose mercy is over all thy works, we adore thee for thy great goodness, and for all the wonders which thou dost for the children of men. To thee belong mercy and forgiveness, though we have sinned against thee. Thou art patient and long-suffering, and in the midst of judgment rememberest mercy, turning from us many evils which we most justly have deserved. We render thee, O God, our humble thanks and praise, that thou deliverest thy people from the pestilence that walketh in darkness, and from the sickness which destroyeth at noon-day. We give thanks to thee, the God of all mercy, for having preserved us, thy unworthy creatures, through the late distressing sickness and mortality, with which, for our sins, thou hast visited our land. The sorrows of death encompassed us: we called upon thee in the time of trouble; we besought thee to save our soul, and found thee gracious and merciful. Thou hast delivered our soul from death, our eyes from tears, and our feet from falling. Though many have fallen beside us, and are now resting in their graves, our lives are yet prolonged, and we are permitted to praise thee for thy goodness. Give us grace to be duly thankful for this thy great mercy, and grant that the lives which thou preservest may be devoted to thee. Help us to walk before thee in the land of the living; to take the cup of salvation; to offer thee the sacrifice of thankful hearts and holy lives. We would pay our vows unto thee, in the sight of all thy people, acknowledging it to be of thy mercy that we are not consumed, and beseeching thee to give us grace to show our thankfulness by obedience to thy laws, and by lives devoted to thee, through Jesus Christ, our Lord, to whom, with thee and the Holy Ghost, be all glory and praise, world without end. *Amen.*

The following Office for the Burial of the Dead is allowed to be used when the Corpse is carried into the Church.

The Minister shall begin the service by reading the following sentences of Scripture.

I AM the resurrection and the life, saith the Lord; he that believeth in me, though he were dead, yet shall he live; and whosoever liveth and believeth in me shall never die. *St. John* xi. 25, 26.

I know that my Redeemer liveth, and that he shall stand at the latter day upon the earth; and though after my skin worms destroy this body, yet in my flesh shall I see God; whom I shall see for myself, and mine eyes shall behold, and not another. *Job* xix. 25, 26, 27.

We brought nothing into this world, and it is certain we can carry nothing out. 1 *Tim.* vi. 7.

The Lord gave, and the Lord hath taken away; blessed be the name of the Lord. *Job* i. 21.

The Minister may then say, Let us pray, *and proceed with the General Confession.*

Almighty and most merciful Father, we have erred, and strayed from thy ways like lost sheep. We have followed too much the devices and desires of our own hearts. We have offended against thy holy laws. We have left undone those things which we ought to have done, and we have done those things which we ought not to have done; and there is no health in us. But thou, O Lord, have mercy upon us miserable offenders. Spare thou those, O God, who confess their faults. Restore thou those who are penitent; according to thy promises declared unto mankind, in Christ Jesus, our Lord. And grant, O most merciful Father, for his sake, that we may hereafter live a godly, righteous, and sober life, to the glory of thy holy name. *Amen.*

Our Father who art in heaven, hallowed be thy name. Thy kingdom come; thy will be done on earth as it is in heaven. Give us this day our daily bread. And forgive us our trespasses, as we forgive those who trespass against us. And lead us not into temptation; but deliver us from evil. For thine is the kingdom, and the power, and the glory, for ever and ever. *Amen.*

Then likewise may be added:

Minister. O Lord, open thou our lips.

Answer. And our mouth shall show forth thy praise.

Then shall be said the following selection from the 39*th and the* 90*th Psalms.*

Lord, let me know my end, and the number of

my days, that I may be certified how long I have to live.

Behold, thou hast made my days as it were a span long, and mine age is even as nothing in respect of thee; and verily, every man living is altogether vanity.

For man walketh in a vain shadow, and disquieteth himself in vain: he heapeth up riches, and cannot tell who shall gather them.

And now, Lord, what is my hope? Truly my hope is in thee.

Deliver me from all mine offences, and make me not a rebuke unto the foolish.

When thou with rebukes dost chasten man for sin, thou makest his beauty to consume away, like as it were a moth fretting a garment: every man, therefore, is but vanity.

Hear my prayer, O Lord, and with thine ears consider my calling: hold not thy peace at my tears.

For I am a stranger with thee, and a sojourner, as all my fathers were.

O save me a little, that I may recover my strength, before I go hence, and be no more seen.

Lord, thou hast been our refuge, from one generation to another.

Before the mountains were brought forth, or ever the earth and the world were made, thou art God from everlasting, and world without end.

Thou turnest man to destruction; again thou sayest, Come again, ye children of men.

For a thousand years in thy sight are but as yesterday; seeing that is past as a watch in the night.

As soon as thou scatterest them, they are even as a sleep, and fade away suddenly like the grass.

In the morning it is green and groweth up; but

in the evening it is cut down, dried up and withered.

For we consume away in thy displeasure, and are afaid at thy wrathful indignation.

Thou hast set our misdeeds before thee, and our secret sins in the light of thy countenance.

For when thou art angry, all our days are gone; we bring our years to an end, like a tale that is told.

The days of our age are threescore years and ten; and though men be so strong that they come to fourscore years, yet is their strength then but labor and sorrow; so soon passeth it away, and we are gone.

So teach us to number our days, that we may apply our hearts unto wisdom.

Glory be to the Father, and to the Son, and to the Holy Ghost.

As it was in the beginning, is now, and ever shall be, world without end. *Amen.*

Then shall be read the following Lesson.

1 *Corinthians* xv. 20. Now is Christ risen from the dead, and become the first-fruits of them that slept. For since by man came death, by man came also the resurrection of the dead. For as in Adam all die, even so in Christ shall all be made alive. But every man in his own order; Christ the first-fruits; afterwards, they that are Christ's at his coming. Then cometh the end, when he shall have delivered up the kingdom to God, even the Father; when he shall have put down all rule, and all authority and power. For he must reign till he hath put all enemies under his feet. The last enemy that shall be destroyed is death; for he hath put all things under his feet. But when he saith, all things are put under him, it is manifest that he is excepted which did

put all things under him. And when all things shall be subdued unto him, then shall the Son also himself be subject unto him that put all things under him, that God may be all in all. Else what shall they do who are baptized for the dead, if the dead rise not at all? Why are they then baptized for the dead? And why stand we in jeopardy every hour? I protest by your rejoicing, which I have in Christ Jesus our Lord, I die daily. If after the manner of men I have fought with beasts at Ephesus, what advantageth it me if the dead rise not? Let us eat and drink, for to-morrow we die. Be not deceived; evil communications corrupt good manners. Awake to righteousness and sin not; for some have not the knowledge of God. I speak this to your shame. But some man will say, How are the dead raised up? and with what body do they come? Thou fool, that which thou sowest is not quickened except it die; and that which thou sowest, thou sowest not that body which shall be, but bare grain; it may chance of wheat, or of some other grain. But God giveth it a body as it hath pleased him; and to every seed its own body. All flesh is not the same flesh; but there is one kind of flesh of men, another flesh of beasts, another of fishes, and another of birds. There are also celestial bodies, and bodies terrestrial; but the glory of the celestial is one, and the glory of the terrestrial is another. There is one glory of the sun, and another glory of the moon, and another glory of the stars; for one star differeth from another star in glory. So also is the resurrection of the dead. It is sown in corruption, it is raised in incorruption; it is sown in dishonor, it is raised in glory; it is sown in weakness, it is raised in power; it is sown a natural body, it is raised a spiritual body. There is a natural body, and there is a spiritual body. And so it is written, The first man, Adam, was made a living soul; the last Adam was made a quickening spirit. Howbeit, that was not first which is spiritual, but that which is natural; and afterwards that which is spiritual. The first man is of the earth, earthy; the second man is the Lord from heaven. As is the earthy, such are they also that are earthy; and as is the heavenly, such are they also that are heavenly. And as we have borne the image of the earthy, we shall also bear the image of the heavenly. Now this I say, brethren, that flesh and blood cannot inherit the kingdom of God; neither doth corruption inherit incorruption. Behold, I show you a mystery: we shall not all sleep; but we shall all be changed, in a moment, in the twinkling of an eye, at the last trump: for the trumpet shall sound, and the dead shall be raised incorruptible, and we shall be changed. For this corruptible must put on incorruption, and this mortal must put on immortality. So when this corruptible shall have put on incorruption, and this mortal shall have put on immortality, then shall be brought to pass the saying that is written, Death is swallowed up in victory. O death, where is thy sting! O grave, where is thy victory! The sting of death is sin, and the strength of sin is the law: but thanks be to God, who giveth us the victory, through our Lord Jesus Christ. Therefore, my beloved brethren, be ye steadfast, unmovable, always abounding in the work of the Lord; forasmuch as ye know that your labor is not in vain in the Lord.

The Minister may add any of the following Prayers, saying,

Let us pray. O God and merciful Father, who despisest not the sighing of a contrite heart, nor the desire of those who are visited with sorrow, mercifully hear the prayers which we offer before thee in all our troubles and adversities Look, we humbly beseech thee, upon our infirmities; and, for the glory of thy name, turn from us all those evils which we most justly have deserved; and grant that in all the troubles and afflictions which thou, in thy unerring wisdom, seest it fitting to lay upon us, we may put our whole trust and confidence in thy mercy, and continually serve thee in holiness and pureness of living, to thy honor and glory, through our only mediator and advocate, Jesus Christ, our Lord. *Amen.*

Almighty God, who, through thine only begotten Son, Jesus Christ, hast overcome death, and opened unto us the gate of everlasting life, quicken us, we beseech thee, by thy Holy Spirit, and raise our thoughts and desires to thee; that, among all the sorrows, and the manifold changes of this world, our hearts and hopes may surely there be fixed where true joys are to be found. Strengthen our faith by the knowledge of Christ, and the power of his resurrection; dispose our ways towards the attainment of everlasting salvation, that in all the trials of this mortal life thy grace may be our help and comfort, through Jesus Christ, our Savior. *Amen.*

O merciful God and heavenly Father, who hast taught us in thy holy word that thou dost not willingly afflict or grieve the children of men, look with pity, we beseech thee, upon the sorrows of thy *servants*, who, on this occasion, are called to mourn for the death of a *near relative* and dear friend. It has seemed good to thy unerring wisdom to visit *them* with sorrow, and to bring this *great* distress upon *them*. Remember *them*, O Lord, in mercy; sanctify this affliction to *their* spiritual benefit. Endue *their* soul with patience under *their* suffering, and with resignation to thy holy will. Comfort *them* with a sense of thy goodness; lift upon *them* the light of thy reconciled countenance, and give *them* peace, through Jesus Christ our Lord. *Amen.*

Almighty and everliving God, the giver and the preserver of our lives; the aid of all who need; the helper of all who fly to thee for succor; the life of those who believe, and the resurrection of the dead, with reverence and adoration we desire to approach thy throne. Assist us, we beseech thee, in our supplications and prayers. Mercifully look upon our infirmities, and comfort and support us in all the various changes and sorrows of this mortal, sinful state. We know, and acknowledge, that all things in heaven and on earth are at thy wise and just disposal, and that not a sparrow falls except the Lord permit. Sickness, and pains, and death, are the dispensations of thy righteous hand, and are less than our sins deserve. Grant us grace, in every affliction, to confide in thy merciful goodness. Make us duly thankful that, in the gospel of Jesus Christ, life and immortality are brought to light; and that thou hast prepared, for those who love thee, such good things as pass man's understanding. Raise our affections and our desires from the world to thee, and our souls from the death of sin to a life of righteousness.

Sanctify, O Lord, we beseech thee, this instance of mortality to all of us who, through thy forbearing mercy, still survive. May it awaken in our minds serious thoughts upon our latter end, and quicken our diligence in preparing for the same important change. May we find, from blessed experience, that it is better to go to the house of mourning than to the house of feasting; and when it shall please thee to call us hence, may we die the death of the righteous, and our last end be like his.

Accept, O Lord, of our humble intercessions for

our mourning *friends* who *are* following the lifeless remains of *their* dear *relative* [*or, as the case may be,*] to the grave. Hear us, O Lord, for *them*, though unworthy to ask for ourselves; and so regard *their* sorrows, that *they* may find, in the bosom of *their* God, that comfort and peace which the world cannot give. Support *them* in *their* afflictions, and direct *their* hearts and *their* hopes to that Savior of *their* souls who has said, Blessed are they who mourn, for they shall be comforted. May *their* mourning be after a godly sort; may *they* know from blessed experience that the Lord loveth those whom he chasteneth, and be enabled to say, Thy will be done. Help *them* to see justice in thy dealings, wisdom in thy providence, and love in thy correction; and to be sensible that it is good for *them* that *they* have been afflicted. Endue *them* with patience under this distressing bereavement, and with pious resignation to thy blessed will; and help *them* to make such improvement from *their* sorrows, that what seemeth to *them* so great a loss, may, through thy blessing, tend to *their* eternal gain. While following the remains of *their friend* to the house appointed for all flesh, may the consolations of thy peace be with *them;* and, viewing the grave as the place where the Lord Jesus lay, may *their* hopes be raised to the high and holy place where he forever reigneth. These things, and whatever else thou seest fitting for us, for our mourning *friends*, and for all mankind, we humbly ask in the name and through the merits of him who is the resurrection and the life, our Lord and Savior, Jesus Christ. *Amen.*

The following may be used when the last of the above is omitted; especially at the Funeral of a Child.

O Father of mercies and God of all comfort, who

art our only hope in time of need, we look unto thee in the name of Jesus Christ, confident that thou wilt hear the prayer of faith, and impart thy grace to those who need. We beseech thee to behold us in mercy; to forgive our sins, and to hear our prayers. Righteous art thou, O God, in all thy ways, and merciful and good in thy dealings with the children of men. Our sufferings are less than our sins deserve: it is of thy mercy, and because thy compassion faileth not, that we are not consumed. But thou knowest, Lord, our weakness, and how little it is that we can endure; that our faith fail not, and for the glory of thy name, turn from us, we beseech thee, the evils of life, or give us grace to bear them with due submission to thy holy will. Behold, and bless us on this occasion, when called to weep with those whom thy righteous providence has called to weep. Let thy Holy Spirit be with us, to sanctify our hearts, and inspire us with a just sense of thy character, and of our duty. Cause us to know our end, and the number of our days, how few they are, that we may duly reflect how short a time we have to live. Thou hast made our days but few, and our age is as nothing, compared with thee. In middle age, and in youth, and in childhood, is man cut down like a flower. May the shortness of the time allotted us make us more diligent in performing what our hands find to do; remembering that no work can be done in the grave whither we go. While we sympathize in the sorrows of our mourning friends, raise, we beseech thee, our thoughts and our hopes to those heavenly things which thou hast promised to the faithful in a better world; and while we see and feel that the wages of sin is death, may we rejoice and be thankful that the gift of God is eternal life, through Jesus Christ; who, by rising from the dead, hath become the first-fruits of those who sleep, that in him this mortal shall put on immortality; that he will change these our perishing bodies, and make them like unto his own glorious body, and death shall be swallowed up in victory. Make us duly thankful that there is a place of refuge, a God hearing prayer, to whom the afflicted may fly for comfort and peace. In the confidence of this belief, and trusting in thy mercy, through the merits of our Savior, we commend to thy compassionate goodness the afflicted *family* from whom thou hast taken a beloved *child*. Behold *them*, O Lord, in mercy, and sanctify *their* sorrows. Make *them* sensible that thou art just and good, and give *them* grace to be resigned to thy holy will. May *they* say in *their* heart, It is the Lord; let him do what seemeth to him good. May *they*, on this distressing occasion, be still and know that thou art God, and that thou makest all things work together for good to those who love thee. May *they* think, with thankfulness, on the many blessings which *they* still possess; and chiefly may *they* rejoice, with consolation, in the day and means of grace. Help *them*, we beseech thee, O God, and help us all to make suitable improvement from this mournful event; to see the vanity of earthly hopes, and the uncertainty of terrestrial things. What, Lord, is our hope? Truly our hope is in thee. And having this hope, may we purify ourselves, even as thou art pure. May we live to thy glory in this world, and finally, by thy mercy, obtain everlasting life, through Jesus Christ our Lord, to whom, with thee and the Holy Ghost, be all honor and glory, world without end. *Amen.*

Instead of the above Prayers, which follow the Lesson, or any of them, may be selected such Collects from the Prayer Book as shall be thought more suitable.

The Sermon or Exhortation, if there be one at the time, may here follow.

The Service may be concluded with the following Prayer and Blessing:

O God, whose days are without end, and whose mercies cannot be numbered, make us, we beseech thee, deeply sensible of the shortness and uncertainty of human life, and let thy Holy Spirit lead us through this vale of misery in holiness and righteousness all the days of our lives; that when we shall have served thee in our generation, we may be gathered unto our fathers, having the testimony of a good conscience; in the communion of thy holy church; in the confidence of a certain faith; in the comfort of a reasonable, religious, and steadfast hope; in favor with thee our God, and in perfect charity with all the world. All which we ask through Jesus Christ our Lord. *Amen.*

The blessing of God Almighty, the Father, the Son, and the Holy Ghost, be amongst you, and remain with you always. *Amen.*

When it is not convenient to carry the corpse into a church, the above Service may be used in a private dwelling-house, or other building.

Public Thanksgiving.

In addition to the Form of Prayer and Thanksgiving to Almighty God for the Fruits of the Earth, &c. *the following Prayer may be used, at the discretion of the minister.*

Adorable and everliving God, who art the Author and Giver of all good things; who visitest the earth and blessest it, making it very plenteous; who sendest rain into the valleys, makest the grass to grow upon the mountains, and crownest the year with thy goodness, thou art the God of all the earth; all creatures wait upon thee that thou mayst give them their meat in due season. We would praise thee, O Lord, for thy unbounded goodness, and declare the wonders which thou dost for the children of men. Our fathers hoped in thee; they trusted in thee, and thou didst deliver them. We thank thee, O God, for the good land which thou gavest to them and to us, their children, and for blessings unnumbered, both temporal and spiritual, which, through thy patient goodness, we still enjoy. Thou, O God, hast proved us; thou didst remember us in our low estate, and redeemedst us from our enemies. Thou givest peace in our borders, and blessest our labors with increase. We yield thee thanksgiving and praise for thy great and manifold blessings vouchsafed to the government and people of these United States; that we have the enjoyment of civil and religious liberty, and are protected by the administration of just and equal laws. Grant that a sense of thy goodness to us and to our country may engage our hearts and lives in thy service. Give wisdom, and strength, and union to our public councils. Bless the governor and other rulers of this state, and all who are in authority over us. Bless our churches, and all our religious institutions. May the gospel spread, and godliness more and more prevail; and may all who profess the faith of Christ walk worthy of their vocation. We pray that the blessings of that liberty wherewith Christ has made us free, may be extended and preserved among all people. Enlarge the borders of the Redeemer's kingdom, till all the ends of the earth shall rejoice in his salvation. Increase and multiply upon us thy mercy, that, thou being our Ruler and Guide, we may so pass through things temporal, that finally we lose not the things eternal. These things, and whatever else thou seest to be good for us and our country, and for all the people and nations of the earth, we ask, through the merits and mediation of Jesus Christ, our blessed Lord and Savior. *Amen.*

Another, which may be used after the Sermon.

ADORABLE and everliving God, who art the Giver of all good, grant, we beseech thee, that the words which we have now heard, and the occasion on which we are permitted at this time to meet together, may, through thy grace, awaken in our minds a thankful sense of thy great goodness. Accept our repeated thanks for the goodly heritage which thy bounty has bestowed upon us; for the civil and religious privileges which we enjoy, and for all the benefits still continued to this our favored country. We thankfully acknowledge that it is of thy goodness that these United States have been preserved through many perils, and advanced in prosperity to an honorable name among the nations of the earth. We praise thee for the many blessings vouchsafed to us, and to the people of this state in which we live, during the year which is now drawing towards an end. May a deep and permanent sense of thy goodness engage our hearts and lives in thy fear and service. Help us to enjoy the bounty which thy hand bestows, with temperance, and sobriety, and with thankfulness to thee. Bless, O Lord, our churches, and all our religious institutions, and enlarge the borders of the Redeemer's kingdom till all the ends of the earth shall see and rejoice in thy salvation. We present these our thankful offerings in the name, and through the merits, of our Lord and Savior, Jesus Christ; to whom, with thee and the Divine Spirit, be rendered unceasing praise. *Amen.*

A Prayer that may be used on the Fourth Day of July.

O HOLY, righteous, and immortal God, King of kings and Lord of lords, who dost, from thy heavenly throne, behold and govern all the people and kingdoms of this lower world, thou art a strong tower and defence to those who fear and trust in thee; thou art the Giver of all good, and the only hope of all the ends of the earth. With humble adoration we would lift our heart and voice to thee, in praise and prayer. We adore thee as the God in whom our fathers trusted; as the God whose holy, protecting arm has preserved the people of these United States through many and great perils; has distinguished them by unnumbered blessings, and given them a great name among the nations of the earth. We praise thee for the dispensations of thy bountiful hand, and for all thy goodness vouchsafed to us thy favored people. Through thy blessing, and because thy compassions fail not, we are brought again to behold this anniversary of our national Independence. May its return call to our remembrance thy mercies, which have ever been of old; and may we be sensible that not for our own righteousness, or the uprightness of our own heart, hast thou brought us in to possess this good land; nor has the might of our own arm given us victory in battle. Not unto us, O Lord, not unto us, but unto thy name be the praise, for thy mercy, and for thy truth's sake. Grant unto us, we beseech thee, such sense of thy blessings to us, and to the people of our country, that our hearts may be unfeignedly thankful, and our lives be devoted to thee. And we pray, O God, that we and our country may still be under thy holy care and protection. Be thou our shield and our buckler, that we, surely trusting in thy defence, may not fear the power of any adversaries. We beseech thee to continue thy merciful goodness to us and to our country. Give wisdom, and strength, and union to the government and people of these United States, and this state especially in which we live. Bless all who are set in authority over us, and so enlighten their minds, direct their counsels, and strengthen their hands, that righteousness and peace may dwell in our land. May they who are appointed to give laws, and to execute them, be endued with wisdom and equity, and a just regard to the public good, that, through their impartial ministrations, peace and happiness, truth and justice, religion and piety may increase, and the safety and welfare of thy people be promoted. Grant, O Lord, that a deep sense of thy providential care may preserve us from pride and self-dependence. While we are thankful for the great blessings of civil liberty and political independence, may we be preserved from a trust in ourselves, and from all vain confidence of boasting. May we never forget who it is that makes us to differ from others, nor use our liberty for a cloak of maliciousness; but follow after charity, and the things which make for peace. Much reason have we to fear that the sins which prevail in our country, and our ungrateful returns for thy unnumbered mercies, should provoke thy indignation, and call thy judgments upon us. We beseech thee mercifully to look upon our infirmities, and turn from us the evils which we justly have deserved. Preserve us, O Lord, from desolating judgments; from selfishness, discord, and contention. O grant, we beseech thee, that we may be united and happy; ever rejoicing in thy holy protection. And wilt thou, O Lord, be merciful to those who need the blessings which we enjoy. May light and liberty, and pure and undefiled religion, be more and more extended, till all the nations of the earth shall rejoice in thee their God. And may all who shall assemble on occasion of this anniversary, be duly sensible from whom our blessings flow. Help us to enjoy the bounty which thy hand bestows, with temperance and sobriety, and in thy faith and fear. May this day be so celebrated as not to increase the sins of the nation; but rather, through thy blessing, be so observed as to diffuse the comforts of rational freedom, social affections, and pious gratitude throughout the community. Extend thy blessing to our churches; to our religious institutions, and to all our efforts to spread the knowledge of Christ, and the comforts of his gospel. May thy kingdom come, and thy will be done on earth, as it is in heaven. May the days come quickly, when the mountain of the Lord's house shall be established in the top of the mountains, and be exalted above the hills, and all nations flow unto it; when the Redeemer's kingdom shall overspread the earth, and all the ends of the world shall see and rejoice in the salvation of our God. We ask these things in the name and through the merits of our Lord and Savior, Jesus Christ. *Amen.*

A Prayer that may be used on occasion of the Close of a Year, or the Commencement of a New Year.

ALMIGHTY and immortal God, whose mercies are like thy years, unnumbered, we, thy dependent creatures, humbly adore thee for thy manifold goodness to us, and to all the children of men. Awaken in our hearts a thankful sense of thy forbearing mercy in preserving our lives through the dangers, and all the changes and trials of another year of fleeting time. We acknowledge thee as the Lord of our life, by whom we escape death, and that it is of thy mercy that we are not consumed. As the years of our life are passing away, help us, we beseech thee, so to number our days, so to estimate the shortness and uncertainty of life, that we may apply our hearts to the wisdom which is from above; that we may know thy truth, and do thy will. Pardon, O Lord, our many sins and transgressions, during the time which is passed and gone. Who can tell how oft he offendeth: cleanse us, we beseech thee, from all our secret faults, and preserve us from presumptuous sins; let them not have dominion over us. Lead us not into temptation; but deliver us from evil. Thou hast made our days but as a span, and our age is as nothing in respect of thee. A thousand years in thy sight are but as yesterday. The heavens, which are the works of thy hands, shall perish; but thou remainest ever the same, and thy years fail not. Give us grace to redeem the time; to use the world as not abusing it, and to be always ready to leave this world at any day or hour in which the Lord our God shall call us. Make us more sensible that in the midst of life we are in death; that we have no Savior in heaven but thee, and that there is none on earth that we can reasonably desire in comparison of thee. May we not be so careful and troubled about the things of this world, as to forget or neglect that which is most needful. May we choose that good part which shall not be taken from us. Make us, O our God, duly thankful for all the favors bestowed upon us from our earliest infancy to this present hour, and especially for the many and great blessings which are still continued to us. Make us sensible how often and how much we have abused thy favors, and how unfruitful of good works our lives have been. O may we not be cut down as cumberers of the ground; but, for the sake of our blessed Savior, Jesus Christ, be spared another year, and have grace to show our thankfulness with our lips and in our lives, by a holy and obedient walking before thee. Support us, O our heavenly Father, in all the trials of life which await us. In seasons of prosperity may we be thankful and humble; in adversity, patient and resigned. As times and seasons to us are renewed, may our hearts be also renewed and created again unto good works.

And wilt thou, O Lord, revive thy work in the midst of the years. Extend, we beseech thee, the light of thy truth to those who are sitting in spiritual darkness and in the shadow of death. Be merciful to those who are living without God in the world, or any sure hope of immortal blessedness, spending their days and their years in vanity and sin. Bless thy word wherever it is spoken, and send it to those places where it is not heard.

Assist us mercifully, O Lord, in these our supplications and prayers, and dispose our ways towards the attainment of everlasting salvation, that, among all the changes and perils of this mortal state, we may ever be defended by thy most gracious and ready help. May we labor faithfully in doing those good works which thou hast ordained for us to walk in, before that night cometh in which no man can work. We ask these things in the name and through the mediation of Jesus Christ, our blessed Lord and Savior. *Amen.*

For a New Year.

O HOLY, just, and almighty God, whose days are without end, and whose mercies cannot be numbered, we bless thee for thy patient goodness to us, thy unworthy creatures. We adore thee for thy creating power which called us from dust and darkness into life and being. Awaken in our hearts a still more thankful sense of thy forbearing mercy, in prolonging our lives from day to day, and from year to year; and especially for thy preservation, and blessings bestowed upon us during the perils and changes of the last year, now passed and gone; and that thou art still giving us time and opportunity to amend our lives, and prepare for our eternal state. Teach us, we beseech thee, so to number our days and estimate thy goodness, that we may apply our hearts unto true wisdom; that we may better know thy truth, and more faithfully do thy will. Should it be, O gracious Father, thy good pleasure that our days may still be prolonged on the earth, and thou shalt let us continue this year also, may our hearts and lives be devoted to thee, in a sober, righteous and godly living. While days, and weeks, and years are so continued to us, may our love to thee increase, and may we manifest our thankfulness by doing all those good works which thou hast ordained for us to walk in. May it be our endeavor and delight to do good unto all men, especially unto them who are of the household of faith. May we remember the words of the Lord Jesus, how he said, It is more blessed to give than to receive; and rejoice to follow the steps of him who went about doing good. Enlarge our hearts with compassion for the sons and daughters of sorrow; and, according as we have opportunity and power, may we be ready to give, and glad to distribute, and to offer that sacrifice with which thou art well pleased. Assist us mercifully, O Lord, in all we do, with thy most gracious favor, and dispose our hearts and our ways towards the attainment of everlasting salvation, that among all the changes and trials of this mortal life, we may ever be defended by thy most gracious and ready help; and when days and years with us shall end, and time shall be no longer, may we be received into those realms of life eternal, where sorrows shall cease, and prayer shall be changed to endless praise. Grant this, O merciful God, through Him, who is the resurrection and the life, thy Son, our Savior, Jesus Christ. *Amen.*

Prayers that may be used at the Closing of a Convention.

O God, whose never-failing providence ordereth all things in heaven and on earth, and who dost ever help and govern those whom thou dost bring up in thy steadfast fear and love, keep us, we beseech thee, under thy holy care and protection, and make us to have a perpetual fear and love of thy holy name. Grant us the help of thy grace, that, in keeping thy commandments, we may please thee in will and deed. May we love the things which thou commandest, and desire those which thou dost promise; and among the sundry and manifold changes of this world, may our hearts be surely fixed where true joys are to be found, through Jesus Christ our Lord. *Amen.*

Almighty and everlasting God, by whose Spirit the whole body of the church is governed and sanctified, receive our supplications and prayers for all estates of men in thy holy church, that every member of it, in his vocation and ministry, may truly and godly serve thee. Send down upon our bishops and other clergy, and upon the congregations committed to their charge, the healthful spirit of thy grace; and, that they may truly please thee, pour upon them the continual dew of thy blessing. We beseech thee to inspire continually the universal church with the spirit of truth, unity, and concord;

and grant that all they who do confess thy holy name may agree in the truth of thy holy word, and live in unity and godly love. And grant, O Lord, we beseech thee, that the course of this world may be so peaceably ordered by thy governance, that thy church may joyfully serve thee in all godly quietness, through Jesus Christ, our Lord. *Amen.*

We yield thee humble and hearty thanks, O heavenly Father, for thy merciful goodness to us and to all men. We bless thee for thine inestimable love in the redemption of the world by our Lord Jesus Christ; for the preaching of his gospel; the establishment of his church; the means of grace, and the hope of glory. We render thee our thanks and adoration for thy blessings bestowed upon the churches and congregations of thy people with whom we are more particularly connected. We bless thee that we have been permitted, as the council of those churches, to assemble here in thy name and presence; we give thee thanks for the harmony that has prevailed during our deliberations, and the brotherly intercourse which we have enjoyed. Give us, we beseech thee, that due sense of these and all thy mercies, that our hearts may be duly thankful, and that we may show forth thy praise, by a holy obedience to thy holy will, through Jesus Christ our Lord; to whom, with thee and the Holy Ghost, be all honor and glory, world without end. *Amen.*

The peace of God, which passeth all understanding, keep your hearts and minds in the knowledge and love of God, and of his Son, Jesus Christ our Lord; and the blessing of God Almighty, the Father, the Son, and the Holy Ghost, be amongst you, and remain with you always. *Amen.*

A Prayer that may be used after an Evening Lecture.

Almighty and everliving God, who art the Author and Giver of all good, we humbly and thankfully acknowledge thy manifold mercies to thy sinful creatures. We bless thee for the benefits which we have received during the day past, and for the favor of this opportunity of worshipping in thy house. Pardon, we beseech thee, the sins that we may have committed in thy presence. Accept the prayers and thanksgivings which we have offered before thee. Forgive us wherein we have asked amiss. Grant that what has been faithfully asked, according to thy will, may effectually be obtained, to the supplying of what we need, and to the promotion of thy glory and praise. Grant, O Lord, that what has been read this evening from thy word, and what has been spoken according to thy will, may be to all who have heard it a savor of life unto life; may it be so impressed upon our hearts as to establish, strengthen, and settle us in the faith of Jesus Christ, and bring forth in us the fruit of righteousness and peace. We pray that thy good Spirit may go with us to our respective dwellings; may thy kind, protecting Providence watch over us whilst we sleep; preserve us through the silent watches of the night, and fit us for the duties of the following day. And whilst our lives are prolonged upon the earth, take us, we beseech thee, O heavenly Father, and all that is near and dear to us, under thy holy care and keeping. Direct our steps in the paths of righteousness and peace, and dispose all our ways towards the attainment of everlasting salvation, that we may live to thy glory in this world, and in the world to come enjoy eternal life, through Jesus Christ our Lord. *Amen.*

Another Prayer which may be used after a Lecture.

GRANT, we beseech thee, Almighty God, that what has now been spoken according to thy word and will, may be grafted in our hearts, and fruitful in our lives. Pardon us wherein we have spoken or heard amiss, and direct our desires and dispose our ways towards the attainment of everlasting salvation. And grant, O Lord, that by the operation of the Holy Ghost, all Christians may be so joined together in unity of spirit, and in the bond of peace, that they may be a holy temple acceptable unto thee. And especially to this congregation, and to those who worship thee in this house, give the abundance of thy grace, that with one heart they may desire the prosperity of thy holy apostolic church, and strive together for the faith of the gospel which was once delivered to the saints. O thou blessed Spirit of the living God, Sanctifier of the faithful, dwell in their hearts with thy love and favor. Defend them from error, heresy, and pride. Enlighten their minds with the truth of thy word; graft in their hearts the love of thy name; increase in them true religion; nourish them with all goodness; and of thy great mercy keep them steadfast in the ways of thy laws, and in the works of thy commandments. And grant, we beseech thee, that the course of this world may be so peaceably ordered by thy governance that we, and all thy people, may serve thee in godly quietness; that we may walk in the ways of truth and peace, and at last be numbered with thy saints in glory, through the merits of Jesus Christ, our blessed Lord and Savior. *Amen.*

A general Prayer for Mariners and People at Sea.

O ETERNAL God, the Creator and Preserver of all mankind, who art glorious in power, and of majesty incomprehensible, we adore thee as the King of kings and the Lord of lords. By thy word were the heavens made, and all their host by the breath of thy mouth. Thou gavest to the sea thy decree, that the waters should obey thy commandment. Thou, O God, art the confidence of all the ends of the earth, and of them who are afar off upon the sea. We humbly ask for thy blessing upon ourselves, and upon all for whom we ought to pray, and especially upon them who go down to the sea in ships, and do business upon the great waters of the ocean. They see thy works and thy wonders in the deep. At thy command the stormy winds arise, and the floods lift up their voice. The waves of the sea are mighty; they rage and swell; but thou, Lord, who dwellest on high, art mightier. Thou rulest the raging of the deep, and when its waves arise thou stillest them. We humbly implore thy blessing and providential care for all who are exposed to the perils of the ocean, and are borne upon its mighty waves. Give them, we beseech thee, a lively sense of thy providential care, and of the wonders which thou dost for the children of men. Help them to know thy unspeakable love in the redemption of mankind by Jesus Christ. At all times, and in every peril and distress, may they look unto thee, as the Lord God of their salvation, who spreadest out the heavens, and rulest the raging of the sea, and art a present help in every time of need.

Grant them a pious trust in thy kind protecting providence. While we in greater safety enjoy thy blessings on these peaceful shores, may we feel for those who are deprived of the privileges of thy house and sanctuary. O hear our prayers for them, who for the mutual benefit of distant climes, and to multiply the blessings of life, encounter the perils of the sea. In storms and tempests; in every danger and all distress, be thou their help and comfort. Preserve them from sickness; from shipwreck; from the violence of enemies, and from every evil to which they be exposed. Prosper them in the business and the occupation in which they may be engaged. Conduct them in safety to the countries and havens where they desire to be; and in thy good time conduct them to their homes, their families and friends, in prosperity and peace; and dispose them, we beseech thee, to be thankful for thy goodness, and to live to thy praise. These things, O heavenly Father, and whatever thou shalt see to be necessary or convenient for their present happiness and their eternal good, we humbly ask in the name and through the mediation of Jesus Christ, our blessed Lord and Savior. *Amen.*

A Thanksgiving for Escape from great Danger at Sea.

Adorable and everliving God, whose mercy is over all thy works, we adore thee for thy manifold goodness to the sons of men. Thou holdest our soul in life, and sufferest not our feet to slip. Thou hast shut up the sea within its bounds, and said, Hitherto shalt thou come, but no farther, and here shall thy proud waves be staid. They who sail upon the waters of the ocean see thy glorious works, and thy wonders in the deep. At thy command the stormy winds arise, which lift up mighty waves, and fill the hearts of men with fear. But when they cry unto thee in their trouble, thou bringest them out of their distress: thou makest the storm to cease so that the waves of the sea are still. Then are they glad, because they are at rest, and thou, in the plenitude of thy mercy, bringest them unto the haven where they would be. Help us, O Lord, to praise thee for thy goodness, and for all the wonders thou dost for the children of men.

We desire, O Lord, especially to render thee our humble thanks and praise for conducting in safety through the perils of the sea thy *servant*, who desires now in the presence of thy people to adore thee for thy merciful goodness in preserving *him* from perishing. When surrounded with terrors, dangers, and death, thou didst deliver *him* from a watery grave: thou didst say to the winds, Peace; be still, and there was a great calm. Many have perished in the ocean, and sunk amidst the waters of the deep, while, through thy great goodness, *this* thy *servant* has been rescued from impending death; preserved through the toils and dangers of the sea, and restored to safety and peace. Accept, O merciful God, *his* humble offering of thankfulness and praise; and give *him* grace to manifest *his* sense of thy goodness, by a steadfast reliance upon thy providential care, and by devoting *himself* to thy service in a holy obedience to thy laws, through Jesus Christ, our Lord and Savior. *Amen.*

Prayers which may be used at Sea when the regular public service is not performed.

A Prayer for God's Grace and Protection, that may be used daily.

ADORABLE and everliving God, who art always more ready to hear than we to pray, we look unto thee as the hope of all the ends of the earth, and of them who remain upon the broad sea. Thou in thy strength settest fast the mountains; thou stillest the raging of the sea, and the noise of his waves, and the madness of the people; by thy righteous providence thou dost govern all things in heaven and on earth. We beseech thee, O Lord, to behold with thy favor and blessing thy dependent, unworthy creatures; to forgive our sins, and blot out our transgressions. Remember not, Lord, our offences; but thy mercy in Jesus Christ. For his sake hear our prayers, sanctify our affections, and renew a right spirit within us. O thou Father of our spirits, take us, we entreat thee, under the protection of thy almighty arm. Preserve us from the dangers of the sea, and from every evil to which we are, or may be, exposed. While we are wafted by mighty winds amidst the waves of the ocean, be thou our Ruler and Guide. In every danger, and difficulty, and distress, help us to look unto thee for succor, and to put our trust in thy providential care. May we be ever mindful of thy presence; that thou art about our path, and about our bed, and spiest out all our ways. There is not a word in our tongue, nor a thought in our heart, but thou, O Lord, knowest it altogether. Whither can we go from thy Spirit! If we take the wings of the morning and dwell in the uttermost parts of the sea, even there shalt thou lead us, and thy right hand shall hold us. O be thou our safeguard and defence. Preserve us from all undue reliance on human skill or the help of man. Without thee nothing is strong, and without thy blessing the labor of man is vain.

We desire, O God, with thankful hearts to bless thy holy name for thy daily goodness and providential care from the commencement of our lives to this present time. To thy watchful care we owe it, that we are preserved from day to day, and borne in safety upon the mighty waters of the deep. Give us hearts to be thankful for thy great goodness, and give us grace to show forth thy praise by living according to thy word and will. Help us to perform every duty which we owe to thee, and to our fellow-men. May we reverence thy holy name, and have that fear of the Lord which is the beginning of wisdom. Preserve us from all presumptuous sins, and vouchsafe, we beseech thee, to direct, sanctify and govern our hearts and our bodies in the ways of thy laws, and in the works of thy commandments, that through thy most mighty protection, both in this our present voyage, and through all the course of our future life, we may be preserved from sin, and from all manner of evil. We beseech thee, O Lord, to give such prosperity and success to the business and occupation in which we are interested or engaged, as shall promote thy glory, and our own best good. Give us grace to be prudent and upright in all our dealings, and to be faithful to all in whose business we are trusted or employed. To thy gracious protection, O heavenly Father, we commit ourselves and all our concerns. Direct and defend us in all we do, and in every danger. Prepare us for every event of thy providence. As our days so may our strength be. We pray thee to turn from us the evils which our sins have deserved, and grant that in all our troubles and difficulties we may put our whole trust and confidence in thy mercy, and evermore serve thee in holiness and pureness of living, to thy honor and glory, through Jesus Christ, our Lord and Savior. *Amen.*

Another, for a prosperous Voyage, and for Friends on Shore.

ADORABLE and everliving God, who alone spreadest out the heavens, and rulest the raging of the sea, in humble adoration we look unto thee as the Author of our being, the Giver of all good, and the hope of all the ends of the earth. Unto thee all hearts are open, all desires known, and from thee no secrets are hid. We, thy sinful creatures, beseech thee to behold us in mercy; to forgive our sins, to sanctify our hearts, and to hear with favor these our supplications and prayers. Enter not into judgment with thy servants, O Lord; for in thy sight shall no man living, in his own righteousness, be justified. We look unto thee in the name and through the merits of thy Son, our Savior Jesus Christ, by whom thou hast graciously taught us to ask, that we may receive; to seek, that we may find. We pray thee to give unto us, who humbly ask of thee, O heavenly Father, thy blessing upon us and ours. We pray thee to take us, and all that appertains to us, under thy merciful care and protection. Preserve us, we beseech thee, in every danger: conduct us in safety over the mighty waters of the deep; give us prosperity in our present voyage, and enable us to arrive at the haven where we would be, with a thankful sense of thy providential care.

And wilt thou, O Lord, in thy merciful goodness, accept our prayers for our families and friends, from whom we now are absent. Preserve them, we beseech thee, from sickness and sorrow, and from every evil; and graciously watch over them for good. Grant that in thy good time we may meet them in prosperity and peace, and with them unite in thankful acknowledgments of thy great goodness.

And to our prayers we desire, O blessed Lord, to give thee humble and hearty thanks for all thy goodness and loving kindness to us, and to all men. We bless thee for all the favors and benefits which we have received from the commencement of our lives to the present hour. We thank thee especially for the mercies vouchsafed to us during the present voyage. And we beseech thee to give us that due sense of all thy mercies, that our hearts may be unfeignedly thankful, and that we may show forth thy praise, not only with our lips but in our lives, by giving up ourselves to thy service, and by walking before thee in holiness and righteousness all our days, through Jesus Christ, our blessed Lord and Savior. *Amen.*

A Prayer which may be used in Storms, and other Dangers at Sea.

Almighty and everliving God, who art the hope of all the earth, and our only refuge in danger and distress, behold us, we beseech thee, in mercy, and save us, Lord, or we perish. Remember not, Lord, our offences, nor take thou vengeance of our sins. O be merciful unto us, and save us for the sake of thy Son, our Savior Jesus Christ.

O thou blessed Jesus, who didst save thy disciples when ready to perish, deliver us from peril and destruction. The winds and the sea obey thee. If thou speak the word, we shall be delivered from fear, and restored to safety and peace. Spare us, good Lord, spare thy people whom thou didst die to save. O thou Father of our spirits, and Giver of our lives, forsake us not in this perilous hour, nor leave us to perish. We commit ourselves, and all that is ours, to thy almighty protection. Thy mercy, O Lord, reacheth unto the heavens, and thy faithfulness unto the clouds. Be merciful unto us, O God, be merciful unto us, for our soul trusteth in thee; in the shadow of thy wings we make our refuge, until this calamity be overpast. O be not thou far from us when trouble and distress are near. Spare us a little, before we go hence and be no more seen. Let our prayer come before thee, and incline thine ear unto our cry; for our soul is full of trouble, and our life draweth nigh unto the grave. Thou, O God, art to be feared, and who can stand when thou art angry? Nothing is too hard for thee, nor is there any one who can deliver out of thy hands. Thou art a strong-hold in the day of trouble, and with thee all things are possible. Thou hast taught us to call upon thee in the day of trouble. O deliver us, that we may glorify thee, and declare the wonders which thou dost for the children of men. Help, O Lord, we beseech thee, and deliver us for thy mercy's sake: hear our prayers, and save us for the infinite merits of thy Son, our Savior Jesus Christ. *Amen.*

A Form of Thanksgiving at Sea for Escape from Danger.

ALMIGHTY and most merciful God, who art the Giver and Preserver of our lives, wonderful are the works which thou hast done: unnumbered are thy mercies vouchsafed to the sons of men. Thou art patient and long-suffering, and in the midst of judgment rememberest mercy. It is of thy mercy that we are not consumed, and because thy compassions fail not. Thou killest and makest alive, and there is none who can deliver out of thy hand. Thy name, O Lord, is excellent in all the earth, and thy glory is above the heavens: according to thy name, so is thy praise. Great art thou in wonders; there is no end of thy greatness, and greatly art thou to be praised. Thou art the God of whom cometh salvation; thou art the Lord by whom we escape death. Thou stillest the raging of the sea, and the noise of its waves. Thou measurest the waters in the hollow of thy hand, and hast meted out heaven with a span. Thou sittest upon the circle of the earth, and the inhabitants thereof are reputed as nothing in comparison of thee. Heaven is thy throne, and the earth thy footstool. Thy kingdom is an everlasting kingdom, and thy dominion endureth throughout all generations. At thy word the stormy winds arise, which lift up the waves of the sea, filling the hearts of men with fear. When they cry unto thee in their trouble, thou bringest them out of their distress: thou makest the storm to cease, so that the waves of the sea are still. Then are they glad because they are at rest, and thou bringest them in safety to the haven where they would be. Then do they praise thee for thy goodness: and we, O God, would praise thee for that thou hast heard us in the hour of distress, and art become our salvation. Thou art a God full of compassion, and plenteous in mercy. When we called upon thee in our trouble and distress thou wast nigh to help, and attentive to our cry. Not for our worthiness, but from thy mercy are we now alive to render thee our humble thanks and praise. When we were in misery, thou didst help us; when trouble was hard upon us, and all hope that we should be saved was taken away, we found that thy almighty arm is a ready help in time of need. Thou hast chastened us, but not given us over unto death. Nothing is too hard for thee to effect, nor is any thing too great or too good for thee to bestow. Thou hast made us glad through thy work, and we will rejoice in the operation of thy hand. We bless thee, O God, that thou didst not give us over unto death. Many have perished in the ocean, and sunk amidst the waters of the deep, while we remain among the living, to praise thee for thy goodness, and to declare the wonders that thou dost for the children of men. Help us, O Lord, to show forth thy praise by obedience to thy laws; may we ever be mindful of thy goodness, and devote to thee, and to thy service, the lives which thou in mercy hast preserved. Hear our prayers, O Lord, and bless us for the sake of thy Son, our Savior, Jesus Christ, in whose name we offer all our prayers and praise. *Amen.*

The following, through inadvertency, was omitted in its proper place.

A general Prayer for the Sick, with Collects adapted to some particular Occasions.

Almighty and immortal God, who art the Giver of life and health, and in whom we live, and move, and have our being, we look unto thee as the God of mercy, and our only help in the hour of distress. We acknowledge that sickness, and pains, and sorrows are the dispensations of thy righteous hand, and are less than our sins deserve. Remember not, Lord, our offences, neither take thou vengeance of our sins; but spare in mercy, those whom thou hast in love redeemed. Look with compassion upon our infirmities, and for the glory of thy name turn from us those evils which our sins have deserved. In all our troubles, and all the trials of life, may we put our whole trust and confidence in thy mercy.

Thou hast taught us in thy word, that all things and all events are under the power and the direction of thy wise and good providence; that not a sparrow falls without thy permission, and that all things work together for good to those who love thee, and are called according to thy purpose. If thou be for us, nothing can be effectually against us. Give us grace, we beseech thee, in all things to submit to thy righteousness, and to be conformed to thy will. If the cup of affliction may not, consistently with thy wisdom, pass from us, be it not as we will, O God, but as thou wilt. Grant that we, who have received so much good at thy hand, may never murmur, nor charge thee foolishly when we receive evil. Help us to take the cross and follow Him who patiently endured the pains of mortality, to purchase for us eternal life. Preserve us from all faithless desire that things should be according to our mind. May we rejoice and bless thy holy name, that our afflictions, which comparatively are light, and but for a moment, will, if we are patiently exercised by them, and submissive to thy will, work in us a far more exceeding and eternal weight of glory. May we learn obedience by the things which we suffer, and know that it is good for us to be sometimes afflicted.

In the midst of life we are in death, continually liable to calamitous accidents and various diseases. May such visitations be sanctified to our spiritual and eternal good. May seasons of sickness, when we are retired from our worldly occupations, remind us that we are mortal, and be wisely viewed as gracious opportunities of raising our thoughts from the world to thee; of attending to the concerns of our immortal souls, and laying up treasures which neither moth nor rust can corrupt.

We bless thee, O God, that in the midst of judgment thou rememberest mercy, giving ease to pains, and mingling many comforts with the evils of life; that thou dost not deal with us according to our sins, nor reward us according to our iniquities. Justly mightest thou reject our prayer, and take thy Holy Spirit from us. But thou art God, and not as man; thou art a refuge to the needy: a present help in time of trouble.

In this confidence, we entreat thee, O Father of mercies, to accept our prayer and intercessions in behalf of this our *sick brother*, whom we humbly desire to commend to thy compassionate goodness. *His* case, O Lord, and *his* wants are all before thee; help, we beseech thee, and bless *him* according as *he* has need.

Here may be used any of the following Collects which shall be appropriate to the occasion.

For Sleep, and Rest, and temporal Comforts.

Grant *him*, O Lord, if it be consistent with thy wisdom, such sleep and quiet rest as may, through thy blessing, refresh *his* spirits, and recruit *his* strength. Compose and tranquillize *his* mind; may *he* be freed from bodily pains and distress, and from all doubts, needless fears, and faithless apprehensions. May *his* reason be clear, and *his* mind be in a suitable state for religious thoughts and meditations. Grant *him* such temporal comforts as shall help *him* to make the right improvement from the present visitation. And give *him* grace to be duly thankful for thy goodness vouchsafed to *him* at all times, and especially during *his* present sickness.

For Patience and Resignation.

Whatever may be the pains, and the weakness, and other sufferings, which thou, in thy unerring wisdom, shalt call *him* to endure, give *him* grace, we entreat thee, to bear the affliction with patience and resignation to thy holy will, saying, with thy servants of old, It is the Lord: let him do what seemeth to him good; though he slay me, yet will I trust in him. May *he* remember the patience of Job, and the end of the Lord, who, for us men, and for our salvation, endured the cross, despising the shame. May *he* remember the days that are past, and thy mercies which have ever been of old; that the Lord is pitiful and long-suffering, and that his mercy endureth forever. May a sense of thy daily goodness, and of thy promises in Jesus Christ, help *him* in patience to possess *his* soul. According to *his* days so may *his* strength be. Knowing that the Lord is just in all his dealings, and righteous in all his ways, give *him* grace in every trial, and in all things to be resigned to thy holy will.

For Grace to make Improvement.

We beseech thee, O Lord, in thy merciful goodness, to give *him* grace to make due improvement under thy chastising hand. Awaken in *his* mind a just and lively sense of thy power and authority over all thy creatures and all thy works, and cause *him* to have a greater desire that this affliction should be sanctified to his spiritual benefit, than that it should be removed. May it work in *him* repentance not to be repented of, and awaken in *his* mind a serious consideration of the shortness and uncertainty of *his* continuance in this present world. May *he* call to remembrance the sins of *his* life past, and plead, in a holy faith, for pardon and forgiveness through Jesus Christ. O hide thy face from *his* sins, and blot out all *his* iniquities. May a sense of *his* weakness add strength to *his* faith, and seriousness to *his* repentance, and earnestness to *his* prayers for pardon and acceptance; and may *he* so rely upon thy gracious promises, that the language of *his* soul may be, For me to live is Christ, and to die is gain.

For a new Heart and a lively Faith.

Thou hast taught us in thy word, that except a man be born again he cannot see the kingdom of God; and that without faith we live in sin. We beseech thee to enlighten the understanding of this thy *servant*, that *he* may see the wonderful things of thy law; and being convinced of sin, of righteousness, and of judgment, may look unto Jesus Christ as the way, and the truth, and the life; and as the only name given under heaven by which men can be saved. Make *him* sensible of the sinfulness of *his* nature, and cause *him* to see the wonders of thy love in sending thy Son into this world, that they who believe in him should not perish, but have eternal life. Awaken in *his* soul an earnest desire to flee from the wrath to come, and to lay hold on eternal life. Grant *him* that holy faith in Jesus Christ which renews the heart, and brings forth fruit meet for repentance. Reveal thyself to *him* as thou dost not to the world; sanctify all *his* affections, and renew a right spirit within *him*. May thy promises of pardon, and acceptance in Jesus Christ, be *his* comfort in life, and *his* hope in a dying hour, when *he* shall resign *his* spirit to thee, as into the hands of a faithful Creator. Remove all doubt and darkness from *his* mind, and give *him* a clear understanding of what *he* must do to be saved. Not trusting in *his* own righteousness, may *he* look unto Him who alone has the words of eternal life, and is the end of the law for righteousness to those who believe. Being justified by faith, may *he* have peace with God through Jesus Christ.

For a sick Penitent.

To thee, O righteous God, belong mercy and forgiveness, though we have rebelled against thee. A humble spirit, a broken and contrite heart, thou wilt not despise. Behold, O Lord, in mercy, this thy *servant*, who acknowledges *his* transgression, and whose sin is now before *him*. The remembrance of it is grievous unto *him*; the burthen is more than *he* can bear. Have mercy upon *him*, O God, according to thy loving kindness: according to the multitude of thy tender mercies, blot out *his* transgressions. Enter not into judgment with thy *servant*, O Lord, for in thy sight shall no man living, for his own merits, be justified. A broken and a contrite heart thou wilt not despise. O wash *him* thoroughly from *his* iniquity, and cleanse *him* from *his* sin. Cause *him* to hear with joy and gladness of thy mercy revealed in Jesus Christ. Create in *him* a clean heart, and renew a right spirit within *him*, that *his* soul may adore thee for thy goodness, and all that is in *him* may praise thy holy name. Strengthen *his* resolution to walk in the way of thy commandments; and while *his* days are prolonged upon the earth, to devote himself to thee in a sober, righteous and godly life.

For one troubled with Doubts or Despondence.

Just art thou, O Lord, and righteous in all thy dealings: if thou withholdest comfort from thy sinful creatures, the punishment is less than our sins deserve. If thou, Lord, shouldst strictly mark iniquities, who could stand? but there is forgiveness with thee, that thy people may not despond, nor faint when rebuked of thee. Look, we entreat thee, with compassion upon this thy afflicted *servant*, who suffers thy terrors with a troubled mind. Thou makest *him* to possess *his* former transgressions, and through apprehension of thy displeasure *his* soul is disquieted within *him*. Thou hast caused all holy Scriptures to be written for our learning, that we, through patience and comfort of thy word, might have hope, and hast promised that they who mourn for their sins shall be comforted; grant unto *him*, we beseech thee, a right understanding of *himself*, and of thy mercy in Jesus Christ, that *he* may neither cast away *his* confidence in thee, nor place it in any beside thee. Speak peace to *his* troubled mind, that *he* may rejoice in the comfort of thy pardoning love. Reveal to *him* clearly the way of *his* duty, and what *he* must do to be saved. Increase *his* faith; O help thou *his* unbelief. Break not the bruised reed, nor shut up thy mercy in displeasure. Preserve *him* from all faithless apprehensions and needless fears. In the multitude of the thoughts and the sorrows which *he* hath in *his* heart, may thy comforts refresh *his* soul. Speak peace to *his* troubled mind: lift up the light of thy countenance upon *him*, that *he* may rejoice in the hope of thy salvation.

For Recovery from Sickness.

To thee, O Lord, belong the issues of life and death: all medicines act by thy decree; all means will prevail if thou direct and bless them. We humbly ask for thy blessing upon the remedies which may be prescribed or used for restoring *him* to health and strength. Make *him* sensible that thou art the hope of all the ends of the earth,—that to thee only it appertaineth to give life and health, and all good things, and that without thy blessing vain is the help of man. Let no vain confidence in worldly means, or human skill, diminish *his* hope and trust in thee. If it shall be thy good pleasure to restore *him* to health, and prolong *his* days upon the earth, may *he* be duly thankful for thy great goodness, and devote them to thee in a sober, righteous, and Christian life.

And wilt thou, O Lord, teach us to pray, and accept our prayers for all who are any ways afflicted or distressed in mind, body, or estate; that it may please thee to comfort and relieve them according to their several necessities, giving them patience under their sufferings, and a happy issue out of all their afflictions. Extend, we beseech thee, to all those who are visited with sickness, such temporal comforts, and spiritual consolations, as to thy wisdom may seem fitting. May thy fatherly correction awaken them to righteousness, and raise their thoughts from the world to thee. Look upon them with the eyes of thy mercy; comfort them with a sense of thy goodness; preserve them from the temptations of the enemy; give them patience under their affliction, and in thy good time restore them to health, and enable them to lead the residue of their life in thy fear, and to thy glory; or else give them grace so to take thy visitation, that after this painful life is ended, they may dwell with thee in life everlasting, through Jesus Christ, our Lord. *Amen.*

www.ingramcontent.com/pod-product-compliance
Lightning Source LLC
LaVergne TN
LVHW010235110826
845151LV00004B/1302

* 9 7 8 1 4 2 5 5 2 4 9 9 9 *